JAINISM   A Pictorial Guide to the Religion of Non-Violence

*If anybody developed the doctrine of
non-violence, it was Lord Mahavira, think
over it and translate it into action.*

Mahatma Gandhi

Mirpur Jaina Temple, Rajasthan. All is set for the annual ceremony during which the Tirthankara images in the temple are re-consecrated.

JAINISM

A Pictorial Guide to the Religion
of Non-Violence

by
Kurt Titze
with contributions by
Klaus Bruhn
Jyoti Prasad Jain
Noel Q. King
Vilas A. Sangave
and others

MOTILAL BANARSIDASS PUBLISHERS
PRIVATE LIMITED • DELHI

First published 1998
by Motilal Banarsidass Publishers Private Limited, 41 U. A. Bungalow Road,
Jawahar Nagar, Delhi 110 007, India

ISBN: 81-208-1534-3

Design, layout, typeset and the photographs – taken with a Leica CL camera – are,
unless otherwise specified, by the author

For the symbol of *Ahimsa* on the title-page turn to page 234

MOTILAL BANARSIDASS
41 U.A. Bungalow Road, Jawahar Nagar, Delhi 110 007
8 Mahalaxmi Chamber, Warden Road, Mumbai 400 026
120 Royapettah High Road, Mylapore, Chennai 600 004
Sanas Plaza, Subhash Nagar, Pune 411 002
16 St. Mark's Road, Bangalore 560 001
8 Camac Street, Calcutta 700 017
Ashok Rajpath, Patna 800 004
Chowk, Varanasi 221 001

PRINTED IN INDIA
BY JAINENDRA PRAKASH JAIN AT SHRI JAINENDRA PRESS,
A-45 NARAINA INDUSTRIAL AREA, PHASE I, NEW DELHI 110 028
AND PUBLISHED BY NARENDRA PRAKASH JAIN FOR
MOTILAL BANARSIDASS PUBLISHERS PRIVATE LIMITED,
BUNGALOW ROAD, DELHI 110 007

To KAILASH CHAND JAIN of Safdarjang
Development Area, New Delhi, who made me write
this book by first befriending me and my wife Martha
at Parasnath Hill in Bihar in February 1989 and who
thereafter, by just being himself, opened our ears
and eyes to the moral and artistic beauty of Jainism

A Jaina saying of old: *The one who
writes or makes others write, the one
who hears, or makes others hear, the
one who gives or makes others give
is noble and a sharer of punya*

(*punya* = salutary karma)

CONTENTS

MAPS AND SITE PLANS: India 13 • Karnataka 28 • Aihole 30 • Hampi 38 • Moodabidri 46 • Chandragiri 54 • Shravanabelagola Town 55 • Tamilnadu 66 • NW Maharashtra 78 • Mangi-Tungi 82, 83 • Ellora Jaina Caves 87 • NE Maharashtra: Muktagiri / Karanja / Ramtek 91 • Deogarh / Chanderi / Tikamgarh / Papora / Ahar / Sonagiri / Sironji 100 • Deogarh Temples 117 • Mahavirji 129 • Chulagiri and Un 130 • Delhi Chandni Chowk 134 • Delhi and Hastinapur 138 • Central Rajasthan 140 • Jaipur 141 • Jaisalmer Fort 151 • Mt. Abu / Achalagadh / Kumbharia / Idar / Taranga 154 • Dilwara Temples 155 • Taranga Temple 168 • Rajasthan: Sirohi and Southern Aravalli Range 170 • Ranakpur 180 • Udaipur 182 • Chittorgarh Fort 186 • Gujarat (Hindi map) 187 • Gujarat 188 • Patan 191 • Shatrunjaya Temple City 197 • Girnar 198 • Kutch 200 • Bhadreshwar 201 • Central Bihar 202 • Rajgir 204 • Distribution of Jainas 255.

CONTRIBUTORS

Prof. Dr. KLAUS BRUHN was born in Hamburg, Germany, and pursued Indian Studies at the university of his hometown under Walther Schubring and Ludwig Alsdorf. Inspired by a suggestion made by Dr. U.P. Shah whom he visited in Baroda (now Vadodara) in 1954, he travelled to Deogarh and was at once convinced that a study of the Jaina temples there would be most rewarding. A two-and-half-year scholarship granted by the Government of India enabled him to stay at the site of his research during three consecutive seasons. In 1969 – by that time he was Professor of Indology in the Freie Universität Berlin – his monograph *The Jina-Images of Deogarh*, a large-size book with 297 photos, numerous drawings and maps, was published in the Netherlands by E.J. Brill, Leiden. Ever since Prof. Bruhn has specialised in Jaina literature, Jaina art and Indian iconography.

Dr. JYOTI PRASAD JAIN, who lived and worked in Lucknow (U.P.) but died before the plan of the present book materialised, is known for his lucid style of writing, a virtue greatly appreciated by new-comers to the religion and philosophy of Mahavira. His *Religion and Culture of the Jains*, to name just one of his publications, saw three editions within seven years (1975, 1977 and 1982); a rare occurrence in the field of Jaina book publishing.

Prof. Dr. NOEL Q. KING was born at Taxila in what is now Pakistan. He was familiar with Jainism as a young child but only got to know some of the deeper teachings from the Army Mess Caterer at Chittagong and Mingaladon (now Bangladesh and Myanmar) towards the end of World War II. He studied at Oxford and Nothingham and has served in Universities in England, Ghana, Uganda, the Indian Punjab and the South Pacific. Presently Professor Emeritus of History and Comparative Religion of University of California at Santa Cruz.

Prof. Dr. VILAS ADINATH SANGAVE, Honorary Director Shaha Research Institute, Shivaji University, Kolhapur, born in 1920 and educated at Poona and Bombay, was the first and so far the only sociologist who successfully undertook the task of writing a comprehensive social survey of the far and widely scattered Jaina community. The first edition of this work entitled *JAINA COMMUNITY A Social Study*, came out in 1959. The second revised edition bears the imprint of Popular Prakashan Private Ltd., Bombay, 1980. For other noteworthy publication of Prof. Sangave which should be of interest to readers of the present book *see* Bibliography.

As to the short quotations from writings of other authors, *see* the *Name Index* under: V. S. Agrawala; Gopilal Amar; Muni Gurudev Amar; King Ashoka (acc. 269 BC); Baron von Blomberg; John E. Cort; Helmuth Dietmar; Krishna Deva; Saryu Doshi; Paul Dundas; June Fog; Mahatma Gandhi; J. C. Harle; Hermann Jacobi; Helen M. Johnson; Count Hermann Keyserling; Acharya Sushil Kumar; Payal Kumar (in *The Hindustan Times*); Ravi Kumar; Padmanabh S. Jaini; Jodh Singh Mehta; José Pereira; Sister Nivedita; Fernaô Nuniz; S. Settar; U. P. Shah; L. M. Singhvi; R. Srinivasan; Ralph Strohl; Michael Tobias; Carlos G. Valles, S. J. – Texts not assigned to a particular author or translator are by Kurt Titze who also drew most of the maps.

ACKNOWLEDGEMENTS

For a free-lance writer of limited means like myself who has no connection to a university and therefore no chance of getting a scholarship or some kind of grant, it is no easy matter to study and do fieldwork, on and off for quite some years, with just one objective in mind – the writing and composing of a book the kind of which has not been attempted before and well knowing that the returns from it will by far not equal the expenses incurred. This being so, and there is no use lamenting over it, I am all the more indebted and grateful to the many individual Jainas who went out of their way to help us two strangers – that is my wife and me – to get on the right bus, to find a roof for the night, to reach a particular sacred Jaina site not marked on any tourists' map; and who invited us into their homes for a meal, offered us seats in their pilgrims' buses, took us – as it happened to us in Tamilnadu – on motor-bikes to places we would never have found by ourselves, and who never failed to draw our attention to particularly appealing objects of Jaina art. As to us, observing all the while the pleasure they found in showing us something of their cherished faith, heightened our determination to do our part in making this religion better known in the world. The following names may stand for those many helpers in time to whom we offer our thanks in vivid rememberance: Padmashri Sumatibai Shah, Sholapur; Smt. Surekha S. Shah, Raichur; Dipak Sutaria, Ahmedabad; Satish Sangai, Amaravati; Nirmalchand Soni, Ajmer and Madras; Mohan S. Jain, Bombay; Sanjay Jain, Calcutta; Veerendra Heggade, Dharmasthala; Ashok Kumar Jain, Delhi; Akshaya K. Jain and R.P. Jain (Co-ordinator for promotion of Jainism abroad) New Delhi; A. Shetthu and Pon Appandai Rajan, Gingee; Kothari Surendrakumar Popatal, Idar; Ajit Kumar Singh Kasliwal, Indore; Ajit Bharat Kumar, Palitana; A.K. Jain, Noida (U.P.); Mayur Vrajal Shah, Patan; Mahavir Minda, Udaipur.

As to whom we might express our gratitude for the good luck which was with us during our travels when it mattered to be at the right place on the right day must remain an open question. Without these unexpected encounters with religious events, and with acharyas, bhattarakas, monks, nuns and knowledgeable lay persons at places as far apart as Madhuban in Bihar, Idar in Gujarat and Gingee in Tamilnadu, this book would not have been written and illustrated the way it eventually has.

Luck further followed me when it came to asking scholars working in various fields of Jainology for contributions, and to selecting short quotations from other authors, the aim being to entice the prospective reader to ask himself questions about the fascinating body of Jaina teaching, art, history and cosmology, and to take up one or other of the books mentioned in the bibliography.

The chapter of *Jaina Art of Gwalior and Deogarh* by Prof. Klaus Bruhn, was specially written for this book, as was the one by Prof. Noel King of Corralitos, California, whom I happened to meet in New Delhi at the initiation ceremony of an elderly layman into monkhood (*see* page 95). The chapters by Dr. Vilas Sangave, whom I had the pleasure to meet twice at his home town of Kolhapur, and the ones by the late Dr. Jyoti Prasad Jain are slightly edited texts from earlier publications. To all these distinguished scholars named in my book I would like to express my gratitude.

To Prof. Willem Bollée of Heidelberg, Germany, I am indepted for valuable suggestions of how to improve the flow of the text and for his advice to go and meet – next time we visit Gujarat – Muni Jambuvijaya. This we did in due course and returned greatly enriched by the Muni's blessings. At Udaipur it was Shri Mahavir Minda who generously drove us about a hundred kilometres to the south where – on an open road – we met Acharya Kunthusagar and his group of munis. It is through encounters like these, to which I would like to add our meetings with Acharya Vimalsagar at Madhuban not long before his passing away, with Acharya Aryanandi at Ellora, with Acharya Sushil Kumar just one month before his death in Delhi, Acharya Vidhyasagar at Ramtek, Muni Gurudev Amar at Rajgir, Acharya Yashodev Suri at Palitana, and Archarya Gunratna Suri and the Terapanthi Acharyas Tulsi and Mahaprajna in Rajasthan, which leave a lasting impression on one's mind.

After my first pilgrimages to sacred Jaina sites, undertaken between 1969 and 1985, it was Karmayogi Charukeerty Bhattarak Swami of Shravanabelagola who invited and encouraged me to contribute to his monthly magazine *GOMMATAVANI* the reading of which (sadly now no longer published) taught me much about Jainism. For this I should like to extend my thanks to His Holiness.

I am specially grateful to Mr. Worgul of Bad Blankenburg, Germany, for devoting his masterly skill in preparing the monochrome enlargements. Finally, my sincere thanks go the Shri Kailash Chand Jain of New Delhi who instilled in me the idea of a Pictorial Guide to Jainism and to whom this book is dedicated. And, being myself a stranger to the way books on Jainism get published in India, it was his untiring efforts, in spite of his failing health, and the generous help of his sons Shri Subhash Chand Jain and Shri Magan Chand Jain as well as of Shri H.C. Jain, New Delhi, that my wife Martha and I have the great satisfaction of seeing this book published by the distinguished Delhi publishing firm of Motilal Banarsidass.

Books as a rule travel slowly, that this one will reach the Jaina diaspora in North Amerika and Europe right after publication we gratefully owe to Dr. Dhiraj Shah and Dr. Mahendra Pandya, leading members of the Federation of Jain Associations in North America; Dr. Jagat Jain, Niagara University New York; Nemu Chandaria, Co-ordinator of The Institute of Jainology, London, UK; Premchand Gada, Vice-President of Jain Academic Foundation of North America, Lubbock in Texas, and Ajit Benadi, Vice-President of Jain Association International (Germany).

PUBLISHER'S NOTE

We are glad to bring out this book on Jainism painstakingly prepared and profusely illustrated with exquisite photographs by Kurt Titze who along with his wife has shown exemplary courage, perseverance, devotion and adventurous spirit for a noble cause. He really deserves commendations of the readers and particularly of the Jaina community for having done his job most successfully in the face of adverse circumstances and paucity of funds.

At some remote period the Jainas turned their attention to sacred mountain tops and covered them with religious shrines forming temple-cities. These mountain sanctuaries represent some of the most wonderful monuments of architecture and sculpture ever raised by the aspiring spirit of man.

V. S. Agrawala (1954)

ABOUT THIS BOOK

Jainism is a religion which appeals to the eye at first sight. Visitors to places like Ranakpur or Shravanabelagola will verify this observation. Paradoxically, Jainism is at the same time one of the least known religions in the world.

The aim of this book is not to explain this regrettable fact, nor to name any culprits for it, but to entice the reader to ask his way to spots and sites that are not mentioned in tourist guide books. To the Digambara Meru temple in Old Delhi, for example, or to the Veerayatan Ashram on the outskirts of Rajgir run by Jaina nuns, or to the rock-cut twenty-four Tirthankaras near Gingee in Tamilnadu. That an increasing number of people who pick up this book may do so instead of climbing the ramparts of yet another fort or of gazing at yet another collection of horrifying weapons – this is the hope of the author.

As there is more to any given religion than its houses of worship, the user of this guide is asked not to bypass the less spectacular sights. This would mean, for one thing, approaching a sacred place on foot rather than by motorized transport. Anyhow, many Jaina sites of pilgrimage can only be reached by walking.

En route to a sanctuary like Sammeta Shikhara or Mangi-Tungi, a newcomer to Jainism will soon lose his feeling of being an outsider or even an intruder, pilgrims walking the same route beside him will see to this providing he looks upon himself as just being one of them and keeps to a few simple rules such as not smoking, not carrying articles made of fur or leather, and circumambulating the marked sacred spots clockwise.

Again and again, while frequenting those remote places of religious worship, the wanderer will be fascinated by the sight of turrets, cupolas and lofty spires crowning a mountain range or lying nestled in the lap of mother earth. Whether it is a large stone-image of a Jina on the wayside bearing the marks of many a century, or a row of Tirthankaras chiselled into a huge boulder which suddenly comes into view around a corner, the beholder will for longer than just a fleeting moment be in accordance with the Jaina saints of old who criss-crossed this vast subcontinent barefooted for the sole purpose of keeping a faith alive that teaches, more so than any other

1

religion, reverence to all that lives – humans, animals, plants. The Jaina saints of today are still following that path.

At other times, the eyes of our imaginary traveller may capture a picture which will give him an insight into the essence of the religion of which by then he will have seen many a famous temple, a picture that, being little suited to a shot with the camera, will engrave itself in his mind. An example:

It was in the small town of Shankesvara in Gujarat on a pleasant day in February. We (my wife and I) had come with the hope of meeting Muni Jambuvijaya, a senior Shvetambara monk. We were asked to sit down in front of a simple screen of cloth behind which the *muni* (monk) had retired. After a while he emerged, and as he exchanged words with us he kept glancing at his raised left hand. There, on the tip of his thumb, a fly was sitting. Without showing any apprehension, as flies otherwise do, it sat there, and it was still resting there as the muni took his leave; later he would meet us again.

I have forgotten the words which I have exchanged with Muni Jambuvijaya on that first encounter, but his loving glances at the fly on the tip of his thumb have remained in my memory; they taught me as much, perhaps even more, about the foremost message of Jainism than many a learned essay I had read on this subject until then, the message that all creatures are equally precious.

May, then, this book be a first guide to regarding an undeservedly overlooked religion with open eyes and a loving heart.

Kurt Titze

The Arhats and Bhagavats (the worthy and venerable ones) *of the past, present, and future, all say thus, speak thus, declare thus, explain thus: all breathing, existing, living, sentient creatures should not be slain, nor treated with violence, nor abused, nor tormented, nor driven away.*

Mahavira
Acaranga Sutra (book 1, lect. 4, lesson 1), trans. Jacobi

MEANING OF JAINISM

Vilas A. Sangave

Jainism is a religion propounded by a Jina. Principles enunciated by a Jina, constitute Jainism, and the follower of Jainism is known as a Jaina (or Jain, *the editor*). Further, a Jina is neither a supernatural being nor an incarnation of an all-powerful God. The word Jina means the conqueror or the victorious, that is, one who has conquered the worldly passions by one's own strenuous efforts. Human beings are entitled to become Jinas and as such Jinas are persons of this world who have attained supreme knowledge, subjugated their passions and are free from any sort of attachments. Jainism is nothing but a set of principles preached by such persons known as Jinas. Hence Jainism is not an *apaurusheya* religion, that is, a religion propounded by a non-human being or based on a sacred book of non-human origin. On the contrary, Jainism is a religion of purely human origin and it has emanated from the mouth of a dignitary, a Jina, who has secured the omniscience and self-control by his own personal efforts.

Thus, the people who worship the Jina or the Tirthankara and who follow the religious tenets proclaimed by the Jina are called the Jainas and their religion is Jainism.

As the Jinas possessed the supreme knowledge, they are called the *Kevali-Jinas*, that is, the Jinas who attained infinite knowledge. These *Kevali-Jinas* are also of two kinds, viz., *samanya-kevali* and *tirthankara-kevali*. While the *samanya-kevalis* are those Jinas who are mainly concerned with their own salvation, the *tirthankara-kevalis* are the Jinas who after the attainment of infinite knowledge are not only concerned with their own salvation but are also concerned with showing the path of liberation to all. These *tirthankara-kevalis* are generally known as Tirthankaras ('fordmakers'), because they are the builders of the ford (*tirtha*) which leads human beings across the great ocean of existence

Emphasis on non-violence

The most distinctive contribution of Tirthankara Mahavira and Jaina *acharyas* (heads of mendicant groups) consists in their great emphasis on the observance of *ahimsa*, that is, non-injury to living beings, by all persons to the maximum extent possible. *Ahimsa* in full significance was realised and preached by twenty-three Tirthankaras preceding Tirthankara Mahavira who lived 2500 years ago in North India. In fact, the philosophy and rules of conduct laid down in Jaina religion have been based on the solid foundation of *ahimsa* which has throughout and consistently been followed to its logical conclusion. That is why the Jaina religion is considered as

3

the religion of *ahimsa*. The significance of this principle of *ahimsa* was very power-fully reiterated by Tirthankara Mahavira as the practices of committing violence on different pretexts had become rampant at that time.

During the later Vedic period utmost importance was attached to the performance of sacrifices with a view to secure the favours of God and to avert His anger. The sacrifices were very elaborate, complicated and hedged with various restrictions. The peculiar characteristic of these offerings to a deity was that they were usually accompanied by the slaughter of animals. Along with this practice, the flesh-eating or non-vegetarian diet was extremely popular among the different sections of the people.

Tirthankara Mahavira launched a vigorous attack against meat-eating and the performance of sacrificial rites by propagating the principle of *ahimsa*. He therefore asserted that as no one likes pain, one should not do unto others what one does not want others to do unto oneself. Since all living beings possessed a soul the principle of non-injury was obviously extended to cover all living beings. He considered injury or violence of three kinds: firstly, physical violence, which covered killing, wounding and causing any physical pain, secondly, violence in words which consisted in using harsh words, and, thirdly, mental violence, that implied bearing ill-feeling to-wards others. Further, he made it clear that violence or injury should be avoided in three ways, that is, it should not be committed, commissioned or consented to.

All these teachings of Jaina religion regarding the strict observance of the principle of *ahimsa* to the maximum extent possible by every individual in society produced far-reaching effects in social fields. The practice of performing sacrificial rites and especially the slaughter of animals at the time of making offerings to a god considerably fell into disuse. Similarly killing of animals for hunting, sports and decoration purposes was greatly reduced. Further, the slaughter of animals and birds with a view to use their flesh as a form of diet slowly became unpopular. In this way injury to living beings was greatly reduced and the practice of vegetarian diet was adopted by large sections of population in different regions of the country.

Thus Tirthankara Mahavira emphasised the basic fact that every living being has a sanctity and a dignity of its own and therefore one must respect it as one expects one's dignity to be respected by others. He also firmly insisted that life is sacred irrespective of species, caste, colour, creed and nationality. In this way Tirthankara Mahavira convinced the people that the practice of *ahimsa* is both an individual and a collective virtue and showed that *ahimsa* has a positive force and a universal appeal.

<<<<<◇>>>>>

4

THE JINAS: THEIR NAMES AND SYMBOLS

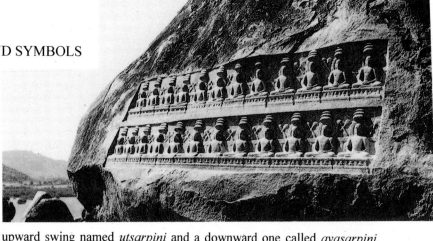

1. Twenty-four Tirthankaras cut into a boulder in two rows. Near Gingee, South Arcot, Tamilnadu. Fifth/sixth century.

The universe, according to Jaina teaching, has no beginning and no end. Time is an unbroken and never-ending succession of cosmic cycles, each of which consists of an upward swing named *utsarpini* and a downward one called *avasarpini*. During the last phase of each downward swing as well as during the final stage of each upward half-cycle the religion of the Tirthankaras gradually loses its influence upon the people to the extent of total oblivion. The reason given for this state of change is the progressing deterioration of living conditions during the latter part of the downward half-cycle and the ease with which one can satisfy all one's desires in the last phase of the upward swing. Then, during the middle phases of every succeeding half-cycle, again twenty-four Tirthankaras are born who once more revive the religion of *ahimsa*. In the current downward swing, Rishabhanatha was the first and Mahavira the last Tirthankara.

Illustration **2** (*below*) gives the names and cognizances of the twenty-four Jinas of our era. The drawings follow the Shvetambara tradition as represented in the left column of the text. The method of marking the image of a Jina by a symbol carved below the figure was developed in the fifth/sixth centuries. In the beginning, it was almost exclusively practised by the Digambaras (and even there not regularly), but since the eleventh/twelfth centuries the device is also found in the art of the Shvetambaras.

Shvetambara:	Early Digambara tradition:
1. Rishabhanatha or Adinatha (bull)	(bull)
2. Ajitanatha (elephant)	(elephant)
3. Sambhavanatha (horse)	(horse)
4. Abhinandana (monkey)	(monkey)
5. Sumatinatha (**Krauncha bird**)	(Koka bird)
6. Padmaprabha (red lotus)	(red lotus)
7. Suparshvanatha (**swastika**)	(nandyavarta symbol)
8. Chandraprabha (crescent)	(crescent)
9. Pushpadanta or Suvidhinatha (crocodile)	(crocodile)
10. Shitalanatha (**shrivatsa symbol**)	(swastika)
11. Shreyamsanatha (rhinoceros)	(rhinoceros)
12. Vasupujya (buffalo)	(buffalo)
13. Vimalanatha (boar)	(boar)
14. Anantanatha (**falcon**)	(porcupine)
15. Dharmanatha (vajra symbol)	(vajra symbol)
16. Shantinatha (antelope)	(antelope)
17. Kunthunatha (goat)	(goat)
18. Aranatha (**nandyavarta symbol**)	(Tagara blossom)
19. Mallinatha (water-jar)	(water-jar)
20. Munisuvrata (tortoise)	(tortoise)
21. Naminatha (blue lotus)	(blue lotus)
22. Neminatha or Aristanemi (conch)	(conch)
23. Parshvanatha (serpent)	(serpent)
24. Mahavira (lion)	(lion)

5

THE FACE OF THE JINA
IN JAINA ART

3 Colossal head of a Jina. 5th century. Mathura Museum • 4 Bronze
head of Adinatha. Found at Akota, Gujarat. 5th century. (Courtesy Baroda
Museum) • 5 Head of a standing Parshvanatha. Humcha, Karnataka. Late ninth century • 6 Head of
a seated Adinatha. Khajuraho Museum • 7 Head of a standing Mahavira. Bronze. 12th/13th century.
Tamilnadu, South Arcot district. (Courtesy Govt. Museum, Madras).

THE STORY OF A FATHER AND HIS TWO SONS

Man's craving for power has been the cause of much suffering in this world – and still is. Thus, understandably, mythologies, that is, accounts of how it may have begun with mankind, usually begin with the description of a merciless fight between good and evil. The need to kill and to be killed is thereby not questioned and consequently rejected but accepted as an unavoidable fact of life.

The mythology of the Jainas takes off on a different note. Here, man is neither pictured as a helpless victim of sinister forces nor as a slave to his bodily needs and whims. Right from the beginning – vividly told in a story of a father and two of his sons – emphasis is laid on man's innate ability to master his own destiny. No one and nothing but our mental blindness is to be blamed for our faults and misfortunes. Not by chance, we may assume, has the open eye become a characteristic sign in Jaina art. The 'keep-your-eyes-open-to-the-world' is to the Jaina the first step towards understanding the world.

In the annals of history few instances are recorded of ruling monarchs who at the height of their success voluntarily relinquished their powers and privileges. Jaina literature, in contrast, abounds in stories of princes and kings who gladly exchanged their pursuit of might and riches for the pursuit of knowledge. To forgo one's power is not interpreted as a sign of weakness but of moral strength. A striking testimonial of this ethical ideal is the colossal image of Bahubali (also known as Gommata or Gommateshvara) at Shravanabelagola. With its height of almost eighteen metres it is the world's tallest and in the view of many far-travelled men and women the most impressive monolithic statue. To merely name it an image of a Jaina saint, as writers of guide books tend to do, ignores the lofty message this monument stands for – man's definite NO to violence in thought, speech and deed.

A war is averted

Some millions of years ago, at a time when human beings used to grow to a height of five hundred bows, there lived in the city of Ayodhya a wise ruler named Rishabha. He had two wives, the first was to be the mother of his first-born son Bharata as well as of ninety-eight further male offsprings; his second wife bore him a son who came to be called Bahubali, the 'Strong-Armed'.

King Rishabha saw to it that his sons and with them the men of his kingdom were instructed in the various trades and handicrafts and in cultivating the land; to his daughters he imparted the arts such as writing, dancing, making music and many more such skills (old Jaina manuscripts list sixty-four ladies' arts).

One day, whilst watching a dance performance, as he liked to do, Rishabha

7

witnessed the sudden death of Nilanjana, his favourite female dancer. Feeling deeply shaken by this unexplainable event, it dawned upon him that the day had come to abandon his hitherto carefree mode of living and turn his mind to that which is of a more lasting nature than one's mortal body. In fact – but this he did not know – it was Indra, the king of the gods and also known as Shakra, who had staged the dancer's sudden death; by doing this he meant to open Rishabha's eyes, not primarily to the ever present threat of death, but to the need of reviving the religion of the Jinas and to accepting the task of becoming the first Tirthankara in the second half of the current cosmic cycle.

Awakened to the heavenly call, Rishabha renounced his kingly rights and went on to divide his empire into two: the northern half with Ayodhya as capital he gave to his eldest son Bharata, the southern half with the royal city Podanapura was given to Bahubali. This settled, he disposed of all his belongings, including his clothing, and took to the life of an ascetic in search of enlightenment.

At first all went well in the divided empire. But then a discus of the kind used in warfare was detected in Bharata's armoury, a disc of stone which possessed the quality of never missing a target. Bharata was delighted with the pundits' explanation that this occurrence must surely be interpreted as a sign from heaven that he, Bharata, had been chosen by the gods to be the universal monarch (*chakravartin*) over all the known kingdoms.

The news of his having an invincible weapon spared Bharata the trouble of waging long wars. One prince after another saw no choice but to beg for submission under his supremacy. But then one day, having just returned from another victorious display of military power, the magic discus stopped short at the city's gate. All attempts to move it failed. The king's astrologers who were summoned to the scene saw in it a sign that there was work left to be done by the discus, for none of his many younger brothers had as yet acknowledged his authority over them, nor had his half-brother Bahubali. Thus being reminded of this omission, Bharata, the proud and young *chakravartin*, had ambassadors sent to all his brothers with the message that they had no choice but either to kneel down to him or to join their father in the forest. All of them, except Bahubali, chose to follow the example of their father Rishabha. "O Lord," these were the words they spoke to him in the forest, "O Lord, let us attain to a path like yours by which we may overcome the fear of loss of honour caused by subjection in existence after existence. For ascetics thrive happily in the forest along with lions, and have overcome the fear of humiliation which arises in the loss of honour." *

Bahubali, however, was not to yield to Bharata's boisterous demand. When the

* This and the following quotation I owe to Dr. Ralph Strohl's translation of The Story of Bharata and Bahubali in *The Clever Adulteress*, edited by Phyllis Granhoff, Delhi 1993.

8

ambassador to Podanapura arrived back in Ayodhya with Bahubali's sharply phrased reply, Bharata fell into a fit of anger and hastily he ordered his army to march towards the capital of his brother.

When Bahubali was informed of the approaching forces, he reacted by putting his army on the alert. A fierce battle seemed inevitable, a battle in which many lives would be sacrificed for the selfish ends of a mere few. But then, as the soldiers of the two brothers were about to attack each other, the ministers of both parties joined hands and voices in a last attempt to stop the two pig-headed youngsters of royal descent. "Leave off this fighting," they called out after they had been given permission to speak, "leave off this fighting, for it is without cause, yet causes the destruction of human life. In a battle like this there is much unrighteousness and a great loss of fame. A test of supremacy is possible in a completely different way. And in that contest between you, you must both bear defeat without anger or victory without pride. This is the correct way between brothers."

Bharata and Bahubali, thus being spoken to in the presence of their respective vassals, saw the point and accepted the proposal by their ministers to settle their dispute by a triple combat between themselves: (1) a battle of glances (the first to blink would be the loser); (2) a water-fight (the first to duck away from the splashes of the other lost), and, thirdly, a 'fight of the arm' (wrestling). Blood was not meant to be shed, this would have been against the religion which was about to be revived once again.

With a show of great pomp the two kingly combatants entered the cleared arena between the confronting armies. The sign to fight was given; whereupon combat followed combat. In all three Bahubali was declared the winner. With a mighty shout he proclaimed victory. For the humiliated Bharata this was too much to bear; over-taken by the urge of revenge he aimed his magic discus at his brother, but instead of hitting him it flew thrice round his head, as if to honour the victor of the triple combat.

Feeling ashamed of his ill-tempered outburst, Bharata knelt down to Bahubali and offered him his kingdom. At this very moment, Bahubali became aware of his own self-centred behaviour; he reposed and clearly in his mind he saw the futility of man's craving for power and fame. No more of this for him! "Keep your kingdom," he told Bharata, "and take mine as well."

For one full year, the narrator of the legend continues, Bahubali remained standing, naked and without food and drink. Creepers wound their way up his limbs. His eyes are opened to the north from where the Himalayan peaks beckoned the awakened pilgrim. Outwardly he appeared calm, but inwardly he was fighting a battle with his proud ego. Only after another visit by Bharata and his two sisters in the course of which the former assured him once more of his devotion, whereas his

*   *   *

This humane message of Shravanabelagola, the teaching of non-violence and universal peace, should be spread all over the globe, because the world today still requires education and training in Ahimsa. It is absolutely necessary to bring home to the people of the world that non-violence is not merely a theoretical principle but also a practical way of life which can solve various problems clamouring for solution in the world and thus help in establishing universal peace and goodwill among the nations.

Vilas A. Sangave

10

two sisters dared to hint that it was about time for him to 'dismount his elephant', an Indian way of saying 'discard your pride', he shed the last fetters of self-love and attained enlightenment.

Bharata, who had turned into a just and peaceable monarch, was one of Bahubali's many admirers. To honour him, he had a golden statue built at Podanapura which portrayed Bahubali in all his glory and in full size, that is, 525 bow-length tall.

9. The treble contest between Bharata and Bahubali as depicted on a small-scale panel kept in the Chaturmukha Temple at Karkala, Karnataka.

A dream shows the way

What has been described this far took place during the third phase of the descending half of the present cosmic cycle of time. Some millions of years later – the natural size of man had by then shrunk to six feet and his allotted span of life to eighty years – there lived under king Rajmalla of Talakad (a district near today's Mysore) an able and rich minister by the name of Chamundaraya. The time was nearing the end of the first Christian millennium.

Chamundaraya and his family, especially his adored mother Kalaladevi, followed the religion of the Jinas. Then one day a Jaina monk by the name of Jinasena related

8 (*opposite*). Lord Bahubali of Shravanbelagola, also known as Gommata or Gommateshvara. At a height of almost eighteen metres it is the tallest free-standing monolithic image in the world. It symbolises the Jaina ideal of detachment and non-violence. Tenth century, last quarter.

11

to the minister's mother the tale of the two half-brothers Bharata and Bahubali whereby he mentioned the golden statue at Podanapura which no living human had ever been allowed to behold. Greatly moved by the story, Kalaladevi beseeched her son to outfit a caravan and accompany her and Muni Jinasena to Podanapura so that she could pay homage at the feet of the golden statue. Chamundaraya consented, and soon they were on the way in search of the fabulous image of Bahubali of which no one knew where it might be found.

After some days' travelling, they reached Shravanabelagola, which at that time was already a holy place for Jaina pilgrims. On Chandragiri, the smaller of the town's two hills, they put up camp. During the night, Chamundaraya had a dream in which goddess Padmavati told him that it was not possible for mortal humans to go and see the statue as it was guarded by winged monsters, but he could rest assured that Bahubali would reveal himself in due course. The minister's mother dreamed a similar dream.

Next morning, having observed the various religious rites, Chamundaraya took his bow, as he was told to do in his dream, and dispatched an arrow in the direction of Indragiri, the bigger of the two hills. At the very moment the arrow struck the tall upright rock on the summit of Indragiri, Chamundaraya had a vision: he saw, hidden in the protruding crag, the exquisitely sculptured image of Bahubali. He was overwhelmed by its beauty, and realised that they had reached the destination of their pilgrimage.

Chamundaraya succeeded – and this is no longer the account of a mythical legend but recorded history as found engraved on a stele of granite – in conveying his vision to a master sculptor who in turn knew how to guide and oversee his team of stone-masons in their allotted task of transforming the visualised picture of a saintly hero into a work of sculptural art.

When at last the stone-masons put aside their hammers and chisels – it was the year 980 or thereabouts – the tale of a prince who conquered his ego and valued the pursuit of knowledge higher than swaying the sceptre of worldly power was successfully transplanted from the storehouse of the storytellers to the treasure-house of sacred art. Once more man has convinced himself of the truth he has known all along but which he desires and needs to be reminded of again and again, of the truth that man does not live on bread alone but that there are resources within him that make him create works of art of which he is unable to say if he himself or some supernatural power guided his hands and imagination.

12

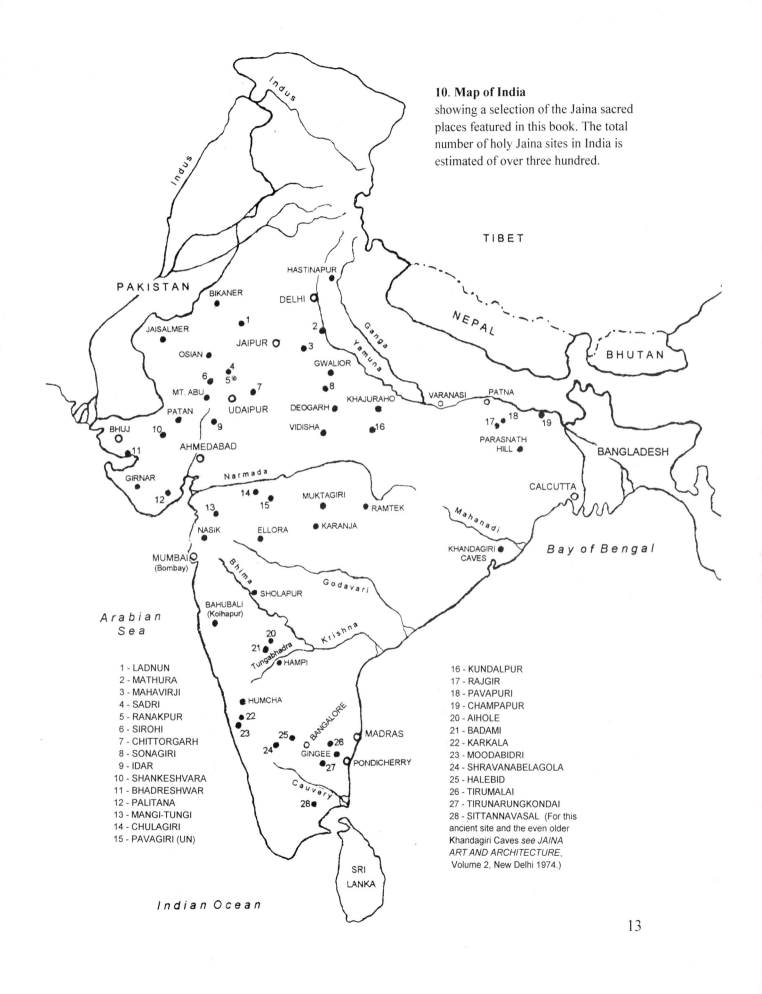

10. Map of India

showing a selection of the Jaina sacred places featured in this book. The total number of holy Jaina sites in India is estimated of over three hundred.

TIBET

PAKISTAN

NEPAL

BHUTAN

HASTINAPUR
BIKANER
DELHI
JAISALMER
JAIPUR
1
2
OSIAN
3
GWALIOR
6
4
5
MT. ABU
7
8
PATAN
UDAIPUR
DEOGARH
KHAJURAHO
VARANASI
PATNA
BHUJ
10
9
VIDISHA
16
17
18
19
PARASNATH
HILL
GIRNAR
AHMEDABAD
Narmada
BANGLADESH
11
12
CALCUTTA
14
MUKTAGIRI
13
15
RAMTEK
NASIK
ELLORA
KARANJA
Mahanadi
MUMBAI
(Bombay)
Bhima
Godavari
KHANDAGIRI
CAVES
Bay of Bengal
Arabian
Sea
SHOLAPUR
BAHUBALI
(Kolhapur)
Krishna
20
21
Tungabhadra
HAMPI

Ganga
Yamuna

HUMCHA
22
23
25
26
BANGALORE
MADRAS
24
GINGEE
27
PONDICHERRY
Cauvery
28

1 - LADNUN
2 - MATHURA
3 - MAHAVIRJI
4 - SADRI
5 - RANAKPUR
6 - SIROHI
7 - CHITTORGARH
8 - SONAGIRI
9 - IDAR
10 - SHANKESHVARA
11 - BHADRESHWAR
12 - PALITANA
13 - MANGI-TUNGI
14 - CHULAGIRI
15 - PAVAGIRI (UN)

16 - KUNDALPUR
17 - RAJGIR
18 - PAVAPURI
19 - CHAMPAPUR
20 - AIHOLE
21 - BADAMI
22 - KARKALA
23 - MOODABIDRI
24 - SHRAVANABELAGOLA
25 - HALEBID
26 - TIRUMALAI
27 - TIRUNARUNGKONDAI
28 - SITTANNAVASAL (For this ancient site and the even older Khandagiri Caves *see JAINA ART AND ARCHITECTURE*, Volume 2, New Delhi 1974.)

SRI
LANKA

Indian Ocean

13

A monk or a nun, seeing big trees
in parks, on hills, or in woods, might
speak about them in this way: "These trees
are fit for palaces, gates, houses, boats,
beds, buckets, ploughs, sheds;" considering
well, they should not use such
sinful language.

A monk or a nun, seeing big trees in
parks, on hills or in woods, should speak
about them in this way: "These trees are
noble, high and round, big; they have
many branches, they are magnificent;"
considering well, they should use such
sinless language.

Mahavira
Acaranga-Sutra (book 2 lect. 4)

MONKS AND NUNS. It makes no difference, whether you adhere to the orthodox belief that Jainism is a periodically reoccurring religion or to the view, expounded in most books on Jainism by western authors, that it began with Mahavira (599–527 BC) or possibly with Parshva or Parshvanatha (the Sanskrit word *natha*, meaning 'Lord', is a 'honorific' implying respect) about 250 years earlier – the answer to the query as to how it began remains the same. It began – or began anew – with the appearance of a *shramana* (ascetic) of outstanding intellectual and moral status. The building of temples and the codification of the doctrines into symbols and written words came later. Even those Jainas, the Shvetambara Sthanakavasi and Terapanthi, who renounced the building of temples and the worship of idols have to this day retained their order of monks and nuns.

In India, one must distinguish between two main streams of religious thought. One tradition, usually called Vedic (a name derived from the oldest books in Hinduism), has its origin in early man's tendency to associate the forces of nature with gods and goddesses.

Gods are, in the belief of humans, somehow resembling themselves. So, when it came to pacifying an angry god, making offerings was considered an effective device for obtaining results. The priest was born, arising from the experience that the preparation and presentation of offerings as well as the wording and enunciation of the accompanying prayers required personalities of a special disposition. They were soon forthcoming; and as the practice of making offerings occasionally does show the desired effect – the law of probability sees to that – the priest was on the way to becoming an honoured and indispensable member of the Vedic community.

The other line of thought, known as the Shramana tradition, has its basis in the perception, arrived at by ascetic individuals after intense concentration and self-observation, that man is by no means that helpless and hapless animal-like creature he is commonly thought to be. On the contrary, he possesses within himself all the resources necessary for leading a life free of fear and mental suffering. All that is required of him is to acknowledge and to develop his mental and spiritual capabilities.

Jainism and Buddhism are both Shramana religions. Both have managed reasonably well without a priestly caste. Both traditions, the Vedic and the Shramana, seem to have existed side by side for thousands of years. Not always peacefully. From the eighth century AD on-wards, in the south of India even earlier, Buddhists and Jainas suffered persecution at the hands of local Hindu and, somewhat later, Muslim zealots. That the Jaina religion – in contrast to Buddhism – survived the calamity of the at times relentless suppression is remarkable.

Wanting to understand Jainism calls for making oneself acquainted with its ascetic tradition. Reading about it is helpful, but this can be rather tedious and

16

might easily lead to misconceptions. Imagine someone who has never met a monk or nun happening to open the Jaina-*Sutras* at the chapter in which the Jaina mendicants are advised not to brush their teeth. What will he make of that? He will, undoubtedly, acquire a false picture of the mendicants' attitude to cleanliness. The reason not mentioned for this extraordinary rule in the Sutras makes sense if one is acquainted with the Indian custom, still in use today, of chewing one end of a freshly cut twig till it resembles a brush suitable for brushing one's teeth. For a Jaina monk or nun to go about it in this way would be a violation of the vow not to harm living beings, plants included: "As our body is born, plants are born. As we grow, so plants grow. As we have consciousness, so plants have consciousness. As our body is damaged when cut, so a plant is damaged when cut." Heeding this statement in the *Sutrakritanga* (book 1, lect.9, vs. 13), Jaina monks and nuns use their fingers for cleaning their teeth after every meal; and as for them there is no nibbling at sweets between meals their sense of cleanliness is enhanced rather than impaired.

In books on the world's religions one frequently comes across incorrect statements about matters concerning Jainism. The reason for this may to a great extent be due to the circumstance that their authors never had or never tried to find the opportunity of meeting Jaina monks and nuns in person. Those who subscribe to a merely mental picture of monkhood – this would apply to most Westerners – usually have a rather distorted view of religious asceticism.

Only after one has actually met Jaina mendicants, listened and talked to them and observed the matter-of-fact respect and devotion they receive from the laity, only then does one begin to see and comprehend the strong bonds which hold together this ancient but widely scattered community of individualists. There seems to be something of a monk in about every Jaina. To stand apart – a typical ascetic virtue – and be able to circumscribe one's place in the world is more to the liking of a believer in Jainism than to be submerged in a faceless mass of people. The Jaina ideal, moreover, is not the merging of one's soul in a universal 'world'-soul where all individuality ceases, but the unattached singular soul. The *Acaranga Sutra*, translated by Hermann Jacobi clearly states: "When the thought occurs to a mendicant: 'I am myself, alone; I have nobody belonging to me, nor do I belong to anybody', then he should thoroughly know himself as standing alone – aspiring to freedom from bonds" (book 1, lect. 7, lesson 6).

There are many books in which Westerners relate their life with Buddhist monks; most of them make good reading. There is as yet (1998), to my knowledge, no book about a Westerner's prolonged association with Jaina ascetics.* Regrettably, for

* One exception is a book in French called *La voie jaina* by N. Shanta, Paris 1985. For the English translation, entitled *The Unknown Pilgrims: History, Spirituality, life of the Jaina Women Ascetics*, see bibliography.

whenever we chance upon a remark by non-Indians about their encounter with Jaina monks and nuns we would like to learn more about it. The following extract has been taken from a published letter by Miss June Fog of New York who spent a month as a disciple of the late Jaina head-nun Sadhvi Mrigavati at the Shvetambara Vallabh Smarak in Delhi. She writes: "I first met Sadhvi Shri Mrigavati Ji in 1976 on a spiritual pilgrimage to India.(...)

What endeared me to her so thoroughly was that on my second fortuitous meeting in 1982, as I entered into her presence, she looked at me in the eyes clearly and lovingly and said, 'I am not perfect!' That's all. I realised she admitted her humanness and her humbleness and her honesty touched me deeply. She saw beyond the persona – the mask. She helped to see me, to love myself as I am, thereby enabling me to love all.(...). She helped me and, I am sure, many by her unparalleled exemplary behaviour. Her selfless, benevolent, inspiring life stands as a beacon for all to follow."

12. Sadhvi Shri Mrigavati (1926–1986).*

As the monastic orders constitute the backbone of the Jaina religion, it is but logical that its two major sects have been named after the outward appearance of their respective monks. That community whose monks wear white garments is thus known by the name Shvetambara, meaning 'white (cotton)-robed', the other group whose monks go about naked is called Digambara, meaning 'sky-robed'. The division into these two sects happened a few hundred years after Mahavira's nirvana (death) in the year 527 BC according to tradition. What really caused the split remains an open question. It was, it seems, more a drifting apart due to the vastness of the Indian subcontinent than grave differences in questions of faith.

Monks and nuns of the Sthanakavasi and Terapanth sects keep their mouth covered by a so-called *muhpatti*, not as a precautionary measure against accidentally swallowing or inhaling insects, as many Westerners tend to think, but in order to protect the invisible 'air-bodies'. These minute single-sense creatures, it is believed, are liable to get hurt and even killed by the moist stream of air we cannot help emitting whilst speaking. Shvetambara monks and nuns, who wear no *muhpattis*, keep a white cloth at hand with which to cover their mouth while speaking.

* Courtesy Atma Vallabh Sanskriti Mandir.

18

The rite of ordination called *diksha*

It was through acts of renunciations, undertaken by outstanding ascetics at a time long past, that the Jaina religion took its roots and began to grow and blossom. This in turn provides today's followers of the twenty-four Tirthankaras with ample reason for looking upon every new act of renunciation as an event worthy of rejoicing and celebration, regardless of whether the aspirant is a minor or an adult of either sex and any age. Among the Shvetambara the novice must not be younger than eight or nine years. The Digambara aspirant to monkhood has to serve a lengthy period of probation, so he will as a rule have reached adulthood by the time the question of ordination arises. (For illustrations *see* pages 96, 97.)

The initiation ceremony, called *diksha*, varies little from one sect to another. In its centre stands the candidate's oath of allegiance to the Five Great Vows (*maha-vratas*), their wording, in the translation of Hermann Jacobi, reads as follows (for the twenty clauses omitted here *see, Acaranga Sutra*, book 2, lect. 15):

The first great vow, Sir, runs thus:
I renounce all killing of living beings, whether subtile or gross,
whether movable or immovable. Nor shall I myself kill living beings,
nor cause others to do it, nor consent to it. As long as I live, I confess
and blame, repent and exempt myself of these sins in the thrice threefold way, in mind, speech, and body. This is, Sir, the first great vow:
Abstinence from killing any living beings.

The second great vow runs thus:
I renounce all vices of lying speech arising from anger or greed or fear
or mirth. I shall neither myself speak lies, nor cause others to speak lies,
nor consent to the speaking of lies by others. I confess and blame, repent
and exempt myself of these sins in the thrice threefold way, in mind,
speech and body. This is, Sir, the second great vow.

The third great vow runs thus:
I renounce all taking of anything not given, either in a village or a
town or a wood, either of little or much, of small or great, of living
or lifeless things. I shall neither take myself what is not given, nor
cause others to take it, nor consent to their taking it. As long as I live,
I confess and blame, repent and exempt myself of these sins in
the thrice threefold way, in mind, speech, and body.
This is, Sir, the third great vow.

The fourth great vow runs thus:
I renounce all sexual pleasures, either with gods or men or animals.
I shall not give way to sensuality, nor cause others to do so, nor
consent to their doing so. As long as I live, I confess and blame,
repent and exempt myself of these sins in the thrice threefold way,
in mind, speech, and body. This is, Sir, the forth great vow.

The fifth great vow runs thus:
I renounce all attachments, whether little or much, small or great,
living or lifeless; neither shall I myself form such attachments, nor
cause others to do so, nor consent to their doing so. As long as I live,
I confess and blame, repent and exempt myself of these sins
in the thrice threefold way, in mind, speech, and body.
This is, Sir, the fifth great vow.

These five vows are meant to be observed by laymen and laywomen as well, but in a less strict way. Among them they are known as *anuvratas*, meaning small vows. If, let us say, a Jaina layman is asked by a hunter the way a fleeing animal has taken, he should lie to him and send him off in the opposite direction. Monks and nuns are not supposed to respond in this way, they are bound to keep silence.

According to Jaina teaching it is more the actual process of one's actions than the underlying good or bad will which determines the kind and amount of karmic matter being drawn onto the soul by the respective deed.

Jaina monks and nuns will never use force, not even in self-defence. Laymen however are no pacifists; if they themselves or their family or country are threatened they are free to fight the attacker and even to kill him, but they should know – and they do know – that by acting in this way their road to salvation is considerably lengthened. This explains why in the Jaina version of the Ramayana epic it is not Rama who finally kills the evil-doer Ravana, as it is the case in the Hindu story of Rama and Sita, but his brother Lakshmana. Herein we may detect one of the major differences between Hindu and Jaina ethics. Traditional Hindu law distinguishes between the killing of a Brahmin – about the most detestable crime – and the murder of a casteless person which is considered much less blameworthy. As to animals, in the view of Hindus some may never be killed, cows for example, others may. To a Jaina this means bad logic, to him all acts of killings are sinful.

Meeting Jaina monks and nuns

Jaina ascetics will never either lock or unlock a door. Their detachment from every-day life as we know it does not make them recluses in the literary meaning of the

20

word. On the contrary. The further they progress on the 'path of purification' (*see* P. S. Jaini's *The Jaina Path of Purification*) the more they are in demand by the laity. Jainas think of themselves as belonging to a 'fourfold community' (*chaturvidha-sangha*) consisting of monks, nuns, laymen (*shravakas*) and laywomen (*shravikas*).

Westerners are welcome to both the laity and the ascetics. To comply with the basic rules of conduct when calling on a member of a monastic order is not outrightly expected from a non-Indian, but gladly appreciated. These rules are, to name a few, removing one's footwear as well as any apparel made of leather or fur, not to wear shorts or sleeveless frocks or blouses, not to hand over any object from hand to hand but to place it on the ground in front of the seated monk or nun. Reciprocally, when being given something, one should not grasp at it but hold out both one's hands palms up. Kneeling down to a monk with folded hands and asking for blessings, a common gesture for Jainas at which no words need be spoken, does at first not come naturally to a Westerner, but will after a while be looked upon and practised as a graceful way of expressing one's esteem.

Occasionally a monk will decline to answer one's questions or suddenly fall silent; his motive for acting that way is not a whim of his but the vow, taken for that day, not to speak for a set lapse of time. Foreign students of Jainism, no matter of which age or sex, will have little difficulties in finding a group of monks or nuns with whom they will be permitted to travel – on foot.

TWO TRIBUTES OF RESPECT

"Once I was giving a lecture to about a hundred Jain nuns, that is, to a hundred half faces and a hundred white veils neatly arranged in rows before me. Now, when I talk I like to see my listeners, and it helps me to watch the effect of my words as reflected on their faces; but here I had only the broken mirrors of the half faces to watch. I said: 'I am determined to have a good time with you, and I am not going to be satisfied until I get your smiles to show beyond your little white rags.' They laughed so heartily that I realised how when a person really smiles it is not only her lips that smile, but her whole face, as the eyes, brows, foreheads and cheeks of those loveable Sisters burst into sincere joy in person-to-person communication. I had a great time with those splendid Sisters. None of them, however, unlocked the veil from even one ear, and the true ascetical tradition was upheld." *

In her *In Memorium* to Muni Jayantavijaya, author of the book *Holy Abu*, Dr. Helen M. Johnson, an American scholar of Jainology, wrote, in 1949, about her encounter with Shvetambara monks (*sadhus*) the following: "In the spring of 1922, Shri Vijaya Dharma Suri and his group of disciples were in Indore and there I met Jain sadhus for the first time. I had the two handicaps of being a woman and a foreigner in addition to lack of experience with sadhus, but from the first I was impressed by the thoughtfulness and consideration as well as the scholarly assistance of these monks.(...) From the time that the Jains, sadhus and laymen, knew that I was a student of Jainism, I have had most generous assistance (...)."

* From *Sketches of God* by Carlos G. Valles, S.J., Anand, Gujarat, 1987: 123–141. Carlos G. Valles is a Spanish Jesuit who was sent to India in 1949 to start a university college in the city of Ahmedabad, where he still resides. He has published many books and writes in English, Spanish and Gujarati.

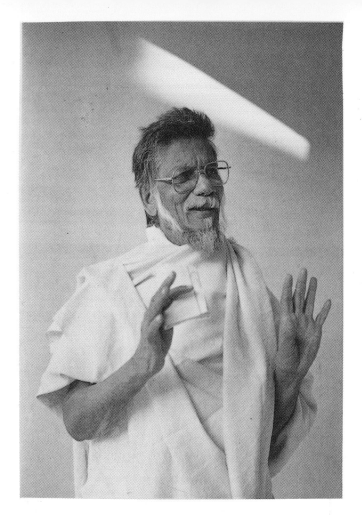

Walking, listening, teaching, avoiding actions harmful to living beings, bestowing blessings, these are, in addition to studying the scriptures, begging for food and meditating, the main duties of the Jaina monks and nuns, commonly known as sadhus and sadhvis. Muni is an older and more appropriate designation for a male ascetic. *Aryika*

13 (*left*). Acharya Yashodevsuri, known for having revived the Jaina art of miniature painting. He has the visions – the actual painting is done by Hindu artists.

14 (*above*). Acharya Kunthusagar. At the request of passers-by he has interrupted his walk so that he may answer questions and bestow blessings.

15. Digambara muni on his walk to another temporary abode. He carries a whisk-broom of a kind typical for ascetics of this sect, and a water-gourd, the content of which is meant for toilet purposes only, not for drinking. The broom, made from feathers shed by peacocks (not from killed birds) is used for gently removing insects.

stands for the Digambara nun. Jaina monks can easily be distinguished from Hindu sadhus by their not marking their bodies with paint or ash, and not wearing adornments. Twice or three times a year they remove their hair from the scalp and face by pulling them out with their own hands (not the eyebrows). This rite of hair-plucking is obligatory for the nuns as well.

16 (*right*). Muni Jambuvijaya, an internationally renowned scholar of Sanskrit. He would have the oft-cited saying 'Live and let live!' altered into 'Let live and live!' (*See* also *About this Book*, page 2.)

17. Shvetambara nuns and monks carry long wooden sticks, the upper end of which show a stylistically carved temple. Their fly-whisks are made, unlike the ones of the Digambaras, of woollen tufts. When taking them apart for inspecting them for insects, which they frequently do, an embroidery of coloured symbols, normally covered by an outer cloth, becomes visible.

18. Muni Guptisagar, giving a lecture at a function at Indore. To his right Muni Nijanandsagar, one of the few Digambara monks who are fluent in English. Jaina monks and nuns preach and lecture by request only; they have no need of manuscripts.

19 (*right*). Detail of a wall-painting depicting the ritual of giving food to a Digambara monk. A ritual which has changed little, as can be observed from the following two photographs. Eighteenth century. Matha Temple, Shravanabelagola.

20. To serve food to monks and nuns is regarded to be meritorious. The monk is welcomed by walking round him three times and uttering the words, "Come and enter; the the food here is pure." 'Pure' is meant to say that the food does not contain meat, eggs, honey and other ingredients unacceptable for mendicants.

21 (*below*). Shvetambara nuns and monks collect their food in bowls by going from house to house, usually twice a day. Digambara ascetics visit only one house and take food and drink but once a day, that is, at the place where the alms are offered. They do not use a receptacle and eat while standing. Each morsel is examined for impurities and no word is

spoken. The entire procedure is accompanied by an air of solemnity.

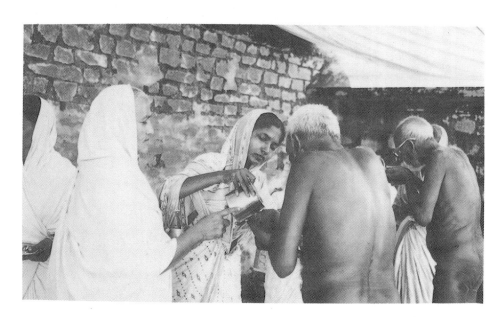

24

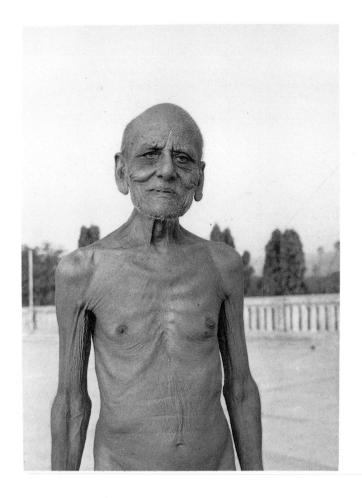

22 (*left*). Acharya Muni Aryanandi, founder of several Jaina schools in the State of Maharashtra. His exemplary life is mirrored in his face. It is men like him who are most esteemed in Jainism.

23 (*below*). To thoroughly wash oneself before going for alms is a daily routine of the Jaina monk. He cannot take a bath. However, statements like 'Jain ascetics are to this day enjoined not to wash themselves' (Dundas 1992: 1, 134) do not tally with what one sees when meeting Jaina monks.

24 (*above*). A Jaina temple at Tikamgarh. Acharya Nimalsagar on the way to nearby Papora with his group of munis and *ailakas* (probationary monks allowed to wear one piece of clothing), is given a festive welcome by the Digambara congregation of the town. A laywoman (sitting opposite the Acharya) has the privilege of celebrating the rite in which a Jina statuette is anointed and worshipped in honour of the esteemed Acharya who died three years later, in 1995.

25 (*left*). 'Sheer elegance and purity of a Jaina nun as captured in a painting of a European artist of the past era of the East India Company', *c*. 1855. (Courtesy M. K. Singhi, Calcutta.)

26 (*above*). Digambara head nun overseeing the study of her junior nuns. Shantinatha Temple, Ramtek.

27. After the day's only meal, taken in seated posture but without using a plate, the Digambara nun has her peacock-feather fly-whisk – a kind of status symbol – ceremonially handed back to her. Participating in the rite of giving food to a nun or monk affords no segregation of the sexes.

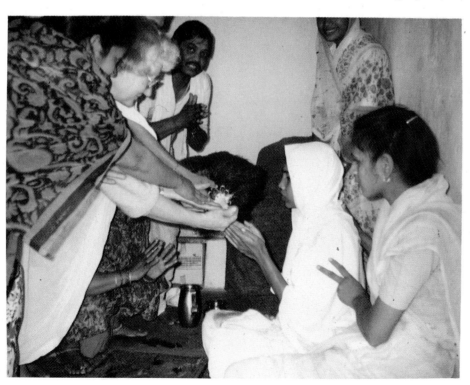

28. Having walked all the way from Rajasthan, a group of Sthanakavasi nuns has reached the outskirts of Shravanabela-gola in the far south. Sthanakavasis do not approve of idols and temples; still they like to follow the tradition of going on pilgrimages to sacred Jaina places.

29 (*below*)**.** A *samani* nun explains to the wife of the author the ceremonial inauguration of the tenth Acharya of the Terapanth sect in February 1994 (*see* chapter on Ladnun, p.144). Determined to spread the Jaina message of *ahimsa* world-wide, Acharya Tulsi, the then ninth Acharya, established a lower order of male and female ascetics called *samanas* and *samanis* who are permitted, after six years of schooling at Ladnun, to travel abroad, to use footwear and to do away with the *muhpatti* (mouth cover) – to name just some of the concessions granted.

30 (*above*)**.** Aryika Jnanamati who, in 1972, inspired the foundation of the Digambara Jaina Institute of Cosmographic Research and, a decade later, the building of the huge model of Jumbu-dvipa at Hastinapur (*see* pages 138/39).

27

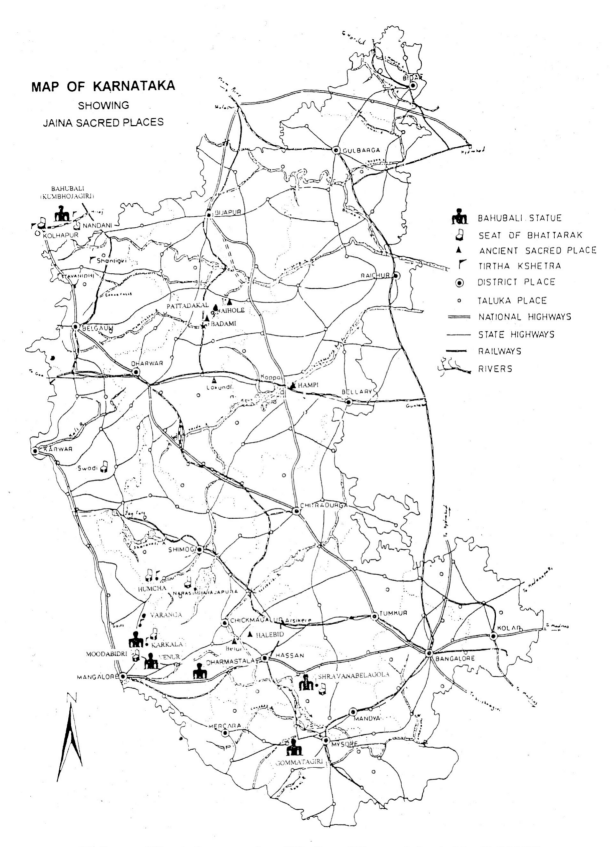

MAP OF KARNATAKA
SHOWING
JAINA SACRED PLACES

BAHUBALI STATUE

SEAT OF BHATTARAK

ANCIENT SACRED PLACE

TIRTHA KSHETRA

DISTRICT PLACE

TALUKA PLACE

NATIONAL HIGHWAYS

STATE HIGHWAYS

RAILWAYS

RIVERS

31. Courtesy Vilas A. Sangave, author of *The Sacred Shravanabelagola,* New Delhi 1981.

28

KARNATAKA

Present-day Karnataka, that southern highland in which India's first free-standing monolithic statue of colossal size was envisaged and hewn out of an upright boulder of granite, is a pleasant state to travel in. The landscape is varied and seldom dreary, the climate healthy, the people one meets lovable and hospitable.

We do not know for certain when Jainism entered Karnataka and the other regions in the south; yet having encountered Gujarati Jaina monks and nuns at places like Kolhapur and Bangalore in the far south and southern monks from Belgaum in far-away Bihar, one is inclined to favour the view of those scholars who consider it likely that Jaina ascetics must have walked southward soon after Mahavira's death, learned the language of the people they met and started to spread Jaina culture. Documented Jaina history in Karnataka, however, begins with the conversion of the first Ganga king to the teaching of Mahavira by the Jaina monk Acharya Simhanandi. That may have taken place some time in the third century AD. In the course of time other royal families, notably those of Badami and Halebid, followed suit. It was a time of amity between Hindus, Jainas and Buddhists which lasted for many centuries, with occasional and temporary lapses into persecution of Jainas and Buddhists by Hindus.

By and by, when it became opportune for kings and princes to shift their main allegiance from Jainism to either Vedanta or Bhakti Hinduism, the movements initiated by the great Hindu teachers Shankara and Ramanuja respectively, instances were not wanting of royal families in which the kings declared themselves followers of Shiva or Vishnu whereas their wives remained faithful to the Jaina Tirthankaras. According to old dedicatory inscriptions a great number of Jaina temples and sculptures were commissioned by queens and the mothers and sisters of kings.

Our survey of Jaina sites in Karnataka, necessarily limited, begins with Aihole in the north and ends with the Bahubali at Gommatagiri in the south.

32. Landscape near Moodabidri with tombs of Jaina Bhattarakas. Monuments of this kind are not found elsewhere.

AIHOLE

Aihole, once a mercantile metropolis with a flourishing Jaina community, but today little more than a hamlet, is well worth a visit though it is not a Jaina *tirtha* (holy place of pilgrimage) in the true sense of the word. None of the about a dozen Jaina sacred buildings is in active worship. Some of them have been converted into Hindu shrines while others were used until recent times by local farmers as stables for cattle and as human dwellings.

Among the inhabitants of Aihole there are at present no Jaina families. But "only here," writes J.C. Harle in his 1986 Pelican *History of Indian Art and Architecture* (p. 166), "is it possible to see side by side, and already fully developed, temples of the 'northern' Nagara type and others in the Dravida mode of South India." This applies to both Hindu and Jaina shrines, the oldest of which date back to the sixth/seventh century.

Aihola has a small museum, a tourist bungalow but no *dharmashala* (lockable rooms for pilgrims). The buses to and from Badami halt at Pattadakal (*see* ill.**39**).

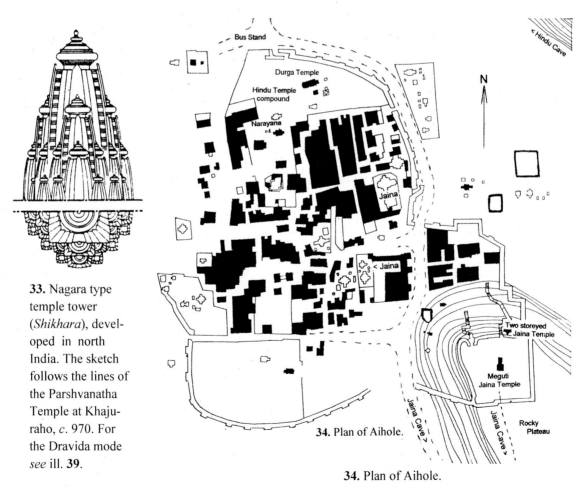

33. Nagara type temple tower (*Shikhara*), developed in north India. The sketch follows the lines of the Parshvanatha Temple at Khajuraho, *c.* 970. For the Dravida mode *see* ill. **39**.

34. Plan of Aihole.

34. Plan of Aihole.

30

35. Aihole. Meguti Jaina Temple, prominently placed on top of the highest hill of the village, was built in 634, as recorded in the famous Sanskrit verse-inscription embedded in the eastern outer wall (note the black plaque in the photo above). Only two of the original sculptures have survived: a large, seated Mahavira and a partly mutilated but still convincingly beautiful goddess Ambika.

36. Torso of a perfectly proportioned Jina. The tresses of locks on the shoulders indicate that it was a representation of Adinatha. Aihole Museum.

31

37, 38. Details from ceiling in the Menabasti Jaina Cave at Aihole showing (*above*) an amorous couple (*mithuna*) and (*left*) the motif of the disgorging warrior *Timingila*. The disgorged figure of a human symbolizes the coming and going of time. Seventh century.

39 (*opposite*). Pattadakal. Disused Jaina Temple, 1.6 km to the north-west of the village. An outstanding monument built in Dravida style. Eighth/ninth century. The pillars "though of sandstone, are partially 'lathe-turned', anticipating the more completely 'lathe-turned' pillars of schist and soapstone seen at Halebid and other places" (K.R. Srinivasan in *Jaina Art and Architecture*, Vol. I: 201). The standing Jina found in this temple has been removed to the local museum situated near the Hindu temple-enclave.

39. Pattadakal Jaina Temple (*see* opposite page).

BADAMI

The Badami Jaina cave, situated at the top-most end of four rock-cut shrines of which the first three are Hindu, is by its location, interior embellishment and layout a jewel of a sacred retreat. Noticeable at first sight, the warm, reddish-brown hue of the grained sandstone bestows upon the lovingly carved statues of Bahubali and his two sisters at one end of the outer *mandapa* (hall), as well as upon the equally impressive Parshvanatha on the opposite side, a pleasing life-like appearance. A seated Mahavira presides in the inner cell. Adinatha, the first Tirthankara, flanked by twenty standing and four seated Jinas demonstrates aloofness from the humdrum of the world. The dividing pillars, the remaining walls and the ceilings of the outer and inner *mandapa*, have all been subjected to the creative vision of the cave's builder and his sculptors. To work a rock which was not of the usually monotonous grey must have inspired them into giving the best of their skill.

Three Hindu caves are situated some flights of steps down the vertical cliff, in which Shiva wields his weapons of war and in which Vishnu is represented as a fierce fighter against all sorts of danger (J.C.Harle, the above mentioned author,

33

40. Badami,
Jaina Cave.
Bahubali
flanked by his
sisters and
worshipped by
two attendants.
Carved in the
7th century,
it is one of
the earliest
sculptures
representing
Bahubali.

denotes the figurative sculptures in these temples as 'self-assertive, almost brutal'.)
Unlike these caves, dedicated to Shiva and Vishnu, this somewhat removed Jaina
cave-temple emits a aura of serenity and self-reliance. For the Jaina, the first step
towards subduing evil is not the handing out of weapons for every available hand but

41. Badami, Jaina Cave. Parshvanatha with protective snakehoods over his head and adored by Padmavati (holding the umbrella). At his left foot his *Yaksha* (demigod) Dharanendra.

the presence of a steadfast and fearless mind. If it was a message the builders of this cave-temple wanted to convey to the pilgrims, it would be the assurance, as taught by the Jinas, that the powers of the mind are superior to the use of physical strength.

35

42. Hampi. Jaina temple popularly known as the Ganigitti (oil woman's) Temple. Built in 1385.

HAMPI

In the early nineteen-eighties, Hampi (alias Vijayanagar) was adopted by young travellers from abroad as an alternative hide-out next to Goa which at that time began to be overrun by tourists. It was a sensible choice to make.

The first Portuguese of Goa were quick in establishing trade links with the rulers of Hampi. At that time – Goa was taken by the Portuguese in 1510 – Hampi, the capital of the mighty Vijayanagar empire, was a fabulous rich city, and since it was known that the kings of Hampi, who originally hailed from Rajasthan, had grown fond of horses, enterprising Goan traders tried their luck in buying thorough-bred Arab horses and taking them to Hampi.

The Hindu empire of Vijayanagar, founded in 1336 as a reaction to the attempt of the Great Mughal's forces to capture still more Hindu strongholds in the south, succeeded for over two centuries to prevent the expansion of Muslim rule into South India. Bijapur, 250 kilometres to the north of Hampi, was at that time already a Muslim sultanate (in 1320, dismantled parts of Hindu and Jaina temples were used for building one of the first mosques of Bijapur).

In 1564, mainly due to the relapse of the Hindu feudatories into their old rivalry, and a deterioration of morale among the soldiers and the general population,

36

Hampi was overrun and ruthlessly looted by a Muslim army from the north, and subsequently deserted by its inhabitants.

The temples, sculptures, and civil buildings which withstood the fury of war and the iconoclastic fanaticism of the time are glorious reminders of Indian art and architecture at their best, though hardly any remained unscathed.

The most valuable Jaina building among the ruins of Hampi is the Ganigitti temple built in 1385 by Iruga, a Jaina minister of king Bukka II. It is a solid, unpretentious structure, devoid of Hindu sculpture and placed rather far apart from the next group of temples, but this conforms to Jaina tradition. Annoyingly, the door of this temple is usually kept locked.

A number of other Jaina temples are situated on the barren slope of Hemakutam hill (ill. **44**), conveniently close to the Hampi Bazaar which used to be the 'sacred area' of the royal city, the stately street where the temple cars were pulled along on festival days to the sounds of music and the chants of priests.

No Jina statues have been found in these temples. Thus, the most laudable Jaina 'monument' of Hampi which has come to us may well be the words noted down in or about 1536 by the Portuguese trader Fernaô Nuniz barely thirty years before the destruction of this fabulous city: "And in this kingdom," he recorded, "there is a class of men, native of the country, namely Brahmans*, who for the most part of them never kill or eat any live thing, and these are the best that there are among them. They are honest men, given to merchandise, very acute and of much talent, very good at accounts, lean men and well-formed, but little fit for hard work. By these and by the duties they undertake the kingdom is carried on" (Filliozat 1980: 165). Some members of that 'class of men' – men, women and children – must have survived the slaughter of 1564/65, which means that their descendants are still with us.

43. Crossing the Tunga-bhadra River in a round basket-boat at Talarigattu village east of Hampi, takes one to the ruined city of Anegundi. There, among its remains, are a Jaina temple and a group of standing Jinas carved on a vertical rock surface.

* Among Digambaras in the south, it is quite common to think of oneself of being a Jaina by religion and a Brahman by class, if this happens to be the case..

37

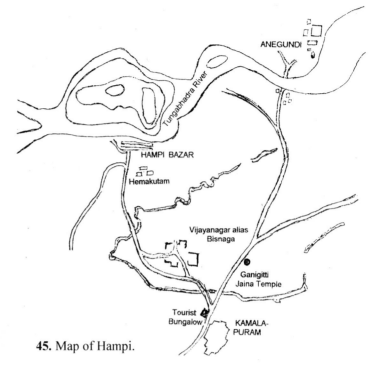

45. Map of Hampi.

44. Hampi. Tower of a Jaina temple
on the Hemakutam Hill.

46. Main Jaina temple at Humcha. On the left the residence of the Bhattaraka. Two further buildings
on the left (not shown here) contain a library and rooms for pilgrims and visitors.

HUMCHA

The history of Humcha (also Hombuja), a quiet, unobtrusive township and seat of a Jaina Bhattaraka (*see* next page), began about 1300 years ago with the arrival of Jinadatta, a royal prince of Mathura in the north, who had to flee his home city for family reasons.

Karnataka is known as the home of great story-tellers, and thus, in the course of the centuries, the account of prince Jinadatta's flight southward at the counsel of his guru Muni Siddhanta, a Jaina Digambara monk, grew into an embellished but rather long and complicated tale of adventure in which Padmavati, that popular goddess who likes to employ ways and means not easily understood by humans, plays the mayor part.

Heeding further advice from his guru, Jinadatta took a statue of Padmavati, strapped to his back, with him on his long journey south; she would protect him against dangers, the muni had told him. One day, on his long flight on horseback, at a place where Humcha's famous Lakki tree still grows from under the feet of the Padmavati image, the story continues, Jinadatta, while resting in the shade of a tree, had a dream in which he was told "to establish his capital at this place with the help of the people living round in the jungle."

Jinadatta did what he was asked to do: he founded a city, built two temples in honour of the Tirthankaras, spread peace and amity among the local people and made Padmavati the presiding deity of what soon became – and is to the present day – a *kshetra* or *tirtha*, a sacred pilgrims' place. The settlement prospered, and the princes in the line of Jinadatta continued to rule over this tiny kingdom for centuries. At some stage, however, the capital was transferred from Humcha to a place called Kalasa

None of the small southern kingdoms withstood the political upheavals brought about by the invasion of Muslim forces from the north, but at Humcha

47. Humcha. An elegant *manastambha* in front of an old temple of modest size. The sculpture on the top represents Brahma. More often these pillars are crowned by a Jina.

and some other places the Digambara Bhattaraka tradition has been kept alive till now (*see* map, page 28).

The present Bhattaraka of Humcha who bears the title Devendrakirthi Swamigal was traditionally chosen by his predecessor and installed in 1971 at the age of twenty-two. He is both an able conservator of Jaina traditions and values as well as an enterprising innovator in fields such as education and social welfare, and he is one of the as yet small number of Jainas who take an active interest in making Jainism better known in the world. Foreign visitors to Humcha who would like to stay for some time and learn the basic tenets of the Jaina religion and philosophy are welcome. The peaceful environment, the five temples with their sculptural treasures, and a library make Humcha an ideal retreat for study and meditation. Though situated at a rather far distance from the nearest interstate highway, this small town is well served with state and private busses (for address *see* appendix).

The Bhattaraka tradition

In the fourfold division of the Jaina society consisting of *shravakas* (male laity), *shravikas* (female laity), *sadhus* (monks) and *sadhvis* (nuns), the Bhattaraka, a specific Digambara institution, is placed above the laity but below the ascetics. He resides in a permanent domicile called *matha*, a term generally rendered 'monastery' (which is rather misleading), and is committed to living a celibate life. He uses, like a fully ordained monk, a fly-whisk made of peacock feathers but wears three pieces of clothing. However, he need not pluck his hair and may travel by any kind of transport. His main duties lie in the fields of education, social and medical welfare, in fostering amity among the members of the community, and in keeping religious rites and traditions alive. Further, he is expected to be well versed in matters of doctrines and sacred law as well as being an able administrator and negotiator when it comes to settling disputes with local or state governments.

Traditionally, a Bhattaraka nominates his successor, almost always from among his disciples. If for any reason he fails to do that, a committee of lay-people will select a new Bhattaraka. When death approaches, the custom prevails that a Bhattaraka will discard his three pieces of clothing, so that he may die the death of an ordained monk, that is, naked.

The Bhattaraka tradition is believed to have originated during the eighth century; however, of the once thirty-six seats of Bhattarakas only eleven still exist: one each in Rajasthan and Tamilnadu, three in Maharashtra and six in Karnataka.

Paying one's respects to a Bhattaraka when visiting a respective place of pilgrimage, is a well received gesture. There are strong minded and colourful men among these religious leaders.

A selection of Humcha's art treasures:

48 (*above left*). Ambika, with child and a bunch of mangoes. A boldly but none-theless masterly carved image of this popular goddess. It shares the wide open eyes with the Bahubali below (ill. **50**).

49 (*above*). Parshvanatha, guarded against the attack by Kamatha and his horde of ferocious animals by the snake-god whom he once saved from being burned. A fine piece of sacred art (for a close-up *see* page 6). Late ninth century.

50 (*left*). Detail of an early statue of Bahubali. Ninth/tenth century. The debris of the temple in which it once stood are being stored for future rebuilding.

51. Lake Temple at Varanga; a unique shrine in a picturesque surrounding.

VARANGA

The little known Jaina temples of Varanga are within easy reach if one asks the driver of the morning bus from Humcha to Karkala to drop one at the appropriate halt at the northern entrance of Varanga village.

From the bus-stop, having left one's luggage with the owner of the nearest tea-stall, it is but a straight walk of about a hundred metres to the east before a tall *manastambha* (free-standing pillar crowned by either a Jina or Brahmadeva image) and the first temple come into view, sign-posts pointing the way to the main shrine hidden behind trees at the bank of a lake. On request, the keeper of the temple will call a *pujari* (temple attendant authorized to conduct *pujas* – rites of worship) who will take one to the unique shrine in the middle of the lake. There, on that tiny islet, heavenly quietude awaits the visitor, and once more he will be taken in by that indescribable aura so typical of many Jaina holy places.

We had the good luck to meet a Jaina from Shravanabelagola who had come with his wife to his home village Varanga to see his mother and ask her to celebrate

42

with them the name-giving ceremony of their first-born son in that homely temple in the lake. On seeing us Westerners, they spontaneously asked us to join them, which we gratefully did.

Being taken across the water in a narrow boat built from a single log and two boards, and then watching the *pujari* opening the doors of the four-faced inner sanctum whereby, one after the other, the contours of four standing Jinas of exquisite beauty emerged, was a fitting prelude to the following ceremony which culminated in the light-waving and mantra-chanting rites called *arati* and *mangaldeep*. A memorable day.

52, 53. Ringing the bells with one's eyes fixed on the Jina in the holiest of holies (*above*) concludes the child's name-giving ceremony.

54. Jaina children are taught early in life to care for animals and never to kill a living thing. Varanga Lake Temple after the ceremony.

55. Varanga. Neminatha Temple, built of stone early in the fifteeenth century, in the thatched-roof style. The *torana* (ornamental entrance) shows a seated Jina. The best known Jaina temple of this type is found at Karkala, 12 km to the south. The one at Varanga is the more ancient one.

KARKALA

56. Twelve and a half metre high statue of Bahubali. Erected in 1431–32 on a slope of naked rock at the southern outskirts of Karkala, a township famous for its stonemasons. The Chaturmukha ('four-faced') *basti* or *basadi* (both terms mean temple), built in 1586–87, stands on the same slope. This architecturally important temple is sacred to the Tirthankaras Aranatha, Mallinatha and Munisuvrata who are represented by twelve black-stone images in standing pose and of identical shape and size facing, in four rows of three, the four cardinal points. Six more Jaina temples are found in the Karkala suburb of Hiriyangadi.

A three-kilometre walk through a lush landscape takes one to Karkala's historic Mangalpada quarry where the craft of giving shape to grey, black and reddish coloured blocks of gneis and granite is still carried on. In the nineteen-eighties the stonemasons of Karkala were given the task of dressing and sculpturing the statues and masonary parts for a new Buddhist temple in Japan. Before that they sculptured the huge Bahubali now standing on a hill at Dharmasthala (*see* ill. **317**).

57. Moodabidri's Thribhuvana Tilaka Chundamani Basadi, meaning 'The Crest Jewel of the Three Worlds', but better known as Hosa (new) Basadi. A temple which was built in stages between 1430 and 1516, being the last of the town's eighteen Jaina temples. The presiding Jina in the sanctum is a nine foot (2.74 m) high bronze statue of Chandranatha, it bears an inscription dated March 27, 1430. Two Jaina queens, Chitradevi and Bhairadevi by name, are credited with the construction of the two pillared front halls (*opposite*).

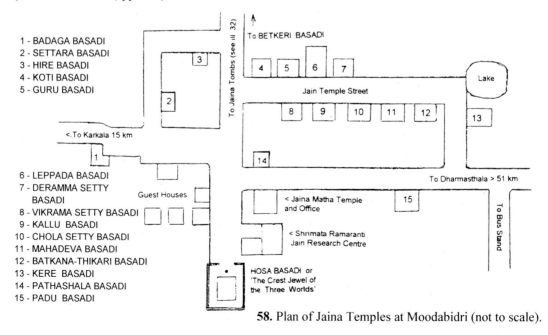

1 - BADAGA BASADI
2 - SETTARA BASADI
3 - HIRE BASADI
4 - KOTI BASADI
5 - GURU BASADI

6 - LEPPADA BASADI
7 - DERAMMA SETTY BASADI
8 - VIKRAMA SETTY BASADI
9 - KALLU BASADI
10 - CHOLA SETTY BASADI
11 - MAHADEVA BASADI
12 - BATKANA-THIKARI BASADI
13 - KERE BASADI
14 - PATHASHALA BASADI
15 - PADU BASADI

To BETKERI BASADI

To Jaina Tombs (see ill 32)

<.To Karkala 15 km

Jain Temple Street

Lake

To Dharmasthala > 51 km

To Bus Stand

Guest Houses

< Jaina Matha Temple and Office

< Shrimata Ramaranti Jain Research Centre

HOSA BASADI or 'The Crest Jewel of the Three Worlds'

58. Plan of Jaina Temples at Moodabidri (not to scale).

46

MOODABIDRI

Moodabidri (also Mudbidri), set amidst a countryside of hills, woods, lakes and fertile fields, and occasionally referred to as the Jaina Kashi (Varanasi or Benares) of South India, has been blessed with outstanding individuals among its Jaina community since early times, both men and women. They were the ones who had temples build, who collected and preserved valuable manuscripts, and who withstood, feerlessly and wisely, the not always peaceful attempts of kings and feudatories to eradicate Jainism altogether. At times, the temptation was great to yield to such pressures and change one's religious conviction for reasons of material gain or physical survival. Many succumbed, for Jainism does not subscribe to a doctrine of justifiable 'holy wars'. The religion of *ahimsa* must not be built on *himsa* (violence). There is a story of a south Indian Jaina monk of high standing who refused to flee from a burning temple, but his martyrdom, though admired, was never advocated as an example to be followed.

Surprisingly, though the Jaina population of Moodabidri town has dwindled to about sixtiy-five and in the surrouning villages to approximately three hundred families, there are as many Jaina as Hindu temples in Moodabidri, namely eighteen each. Of the Jaina temples, most of them are located on both sides of a so-called Temple Street which places them within walking distance from the Digambara Jaina Matha in the town's main thoroughfare. This *matha*, seat of the Bhattaraka Shri Charukirthi Swami, has an information office for pilgrims and tourists, a *dharma-shala* for about a hundred pilgrims and some guest-houses. Overseas visitors are welcome.

Moodabidri is famous for its many old manuscripts and treasures of Jaina sculptures. One outstanding piece is an almost three metre high Parshvanatha image made of black stone that was, according to tradition, discovered in a bamboo grove under a heap of debris at the beginning of the eighth century. The temple in which it was installed and in which it still stands, popularly called Guru Basadi, was built in 714.

59. Hosa Basadi. Pillars in the hall built by queen Bhairadevi. Though of stone, a strong influence of wooden architecture is evident.

47

VENUR

60. Due to some rivalry between the northern and southern Bhattarakas of this area at the beginning of the seventeenth century, a third Bahubali of colossal size came to be erected at Venur, a then and still small village twenty-five kilometres east of Moodabidri. According to inscriptions, the ten and a half metre high statue was consecrated in March 1604. By that time Indian sculptural art had lost much of its vigour and grandeur. Still, the Bahubali of Venur has the distinction of having dimpled cheeks and a hooked nose, facial marks which are not unknown among the inhabitants of this region. Close to the low hill with the tall statue on the top there is a temple dedicated to Shantinatha. – Not all the buses that take the route through Venur stop at this sacred site; however, if requested the drivers will oblige with a halt.

HALEBID

The capital of the Hoysala kings who ruled for nearly three centuries, from 1047 to 1343, was, for most of the time, what today is the vilage of Halebid(u) – *hale* = old, *bidu* = capital. There is evidence to presume that the Hoysala dynasty came to power with the help of a Jaina ascetic by the name of Shantideva. Bittiga, the considered greatest king of the Hoysalas, began his reign, that lasted from 1106 to 1141, as a Jaina. Later, having come under the sway of the erudite Hindu teacher Ramanuja, he converted to the Vishnuite branch of Hinduism and changed his name to Vishnu-vardhana. None the less, his queen, Shantidevi, remained an active follower of the Jaina religion. Her steadfastness, one may assume, will have facilitated the continuous building of Jaina temples at Halebid and other places in the Hoysala kingdom which included present-day Karnataka. Nowadays, the term 'Hoysala' stands for a distinctively South Indian style of temple architecture and sculptural art that developed under the rulers of Halebid. A characteristic component of Hoysala art is the use of black schist, a stone suitable for fine carving.

61. About four hundred metres south of the enclosure with the famous Hoysala Hindu temple of Halebid and the museum, there stand, arranged in line and within a well-kept compound, three Jaina temples. All of which face north, making them difficult to photograph, specially during the winter months, the best time to visit them. The temple at the westernmost end is dedicated to Parshvanatha, the next in line, which has no pillared hall in front, to Adinatha and the third one to Shantinatha. All three are in active worship for the benefit of the pilgrims. The other Jaina temples of Halebid are in a lesser state of preservation.

62, 63. The interior of the three temples depicted in illustration **61** could be interpreted as a grandiose manifestation of perseverance. The massive pillars, placed so close to each other, give the impression that there is more for them to support than the roof alone. Are they meant to remind us of the accumulated weight of the many layers of karma that presses down on us? At the same time, they – the polished black pillars – seem to convey the message that this is no place to lament the passing of time. Timelessness seems to be their message. Thus, logically, the builders of these temples contrasted the inertia of the perfectly balanced pillars not by seated Tirthankaras – that would have been too much of the same intention – but by a typically Jaina equivalence of 'time-does-not-matter', that is, the Jina in the 'abandonment of the body' (*kayotsarga*) posture. It is the three standing Thirtankaras, one in each temple and equal in height to the weighty pillars, that prevent the notion of heaviness from becoming oppressive. Time is ever-lasting and of little concern. To reach this blessed stage of awareness while still treading the roads and by-ways of this world is a major aim of the Jaina pilgrim who comes to this and many a similar place of worship. To symbolize the successful shedding of heaviness, the picture of a Hoysala Jina in *kayotsarga* pose, initially worshipped in a Halebidu temple and now displayed outside the local museum, has been chosen for the cover of this book (*see* following page).

50

64. Halebid. Museum compound. Statue of a Jina in *kayotsarga* pose.
Hoysala style. Black stone.

SHRAVANABELAGOLA

Shravanabelagola – so spelled by the Jaina authorities of this town but also known as Shravana Belgola and by other spellings – is in more than one respect a most remarkable place of pilgrimage. Its giant image of Bahubali has already been featured in chapter two. Another first held by Shravanabelagola is in the field of inscriptions. Nowhere else in India have a greater number been found in so limited an area, not to mention the long span of time covered by these rock-cut writings. About five hundred have been discovered; there would be even more but some have been erased in the course of time while others have been covered by erected temples. The oldest record dates from the sixth century, the last bears the date 1889. Most of them have been found on Chandragiri, the lower of the two historic hills (*giri* = hill).

Another noteworthy peculiarity is the fact that the history of Shravanabelagola knows of no wars having been waged for gaining possession of it and that very little damage was done to the local temples and sculptures by iconoclastic zealots. It was the awe radiating from the face of the huge statue of Bahubali, it is believed, that turned would-be vandals into admirers of timeless art.

A further first mention would go to Shravanabelagola if a list were to be compiled of sites which have become favourite places for men and women resolved to end their life by observing *sallekhana*, the Jaina rite of letting one's old or sick body die peacefully by slowly reducing one's intake of food and liquid. This way of dying, which is no suicide and as a rule needs the permission of a superior monk, goes back to Mahavira and even further; it is uniquely Jaina and must not be confused with the Hindu practice of offering one's life to a god or, as in the case of *sati*, to the burning of wives on the stake of their husbands.

The study and translation of the inscriptions, that began in 1889 with the publication of a book by the Englishman B. Lewis Rice entitled *Inscriptions of Shravanabelagola*, yielded substantial support to the literary tradition that some time in the third century BC the great Jaina saint Bhadrabahu decided to leave North India with his *sangha* of monks and head south for fear of a forecast long famine. With him on his walk south was his close disciple Chandragupta, India's first Maurya emperor who had his empire made over to his son Bindusara while choosing for himself the life of a naked Jaina monk. On reaching Shravanabelagola, Bhadrabahu, sensing his approaching death, advised his monks to proceed south under a new leader appointed by him, while he would retire to a cave on the hill, now known as Chandragiri, to prepare himself for death by the rite of *sallekhana* attended to by Chandragupta, the emperor-turned-monk. A pair of rock-cut feet mark the spot where Bhadrabahu is believed to have died. Chandragupta lived on for another twelve years, to *c.* 297 BC, before parting from his body the way his teacher had.

The memory of these two spiritual heroes, kept alive by story-tellers, resulted in Chandragiri becoming a sought-after site for ending one's life the way they did. "This process of death," writes S. Settar in his *Guide to Sravana Belgola* of 1981, "was more popular among saints and nuns during early stages (AD 800), and it gradually became popular among lay-disciples in the subsequent period. Of an estimated 106 such deaths in this centre, (between 6th and 19th cent.), 64 are of monks, 11 of nuns, 23 of male lay-disciples, and eight of female lay-disciples.(...). Among notable lay-disciples there are three kings, about ten ministers and generals, two merchants, two local officials, and two warriors."

Today, Chandragiri, thus sanctified in the course of centuries, offers the pilgrim ideal spots for quiet meditation whereas Shravanabelagola town has of late become a centre of many activities. Here the Jaina virtue of knowing how to give one's life direction and purpose is at work. A water supply system, a hospital, schools, guest-houses and the like have been built; and trees are being planted. A class of about thirty *brahmacharis* (celibate students of religion), attached to the *matha* temple, adds a touch of youthfulness to the historical centre of the town. New-comers to Jainism should not miss being present when these dedicated students celebrate their morning and evening *puja* in the courtyard of the Matha Temple.

The above mentioned innovations – not all have been named – are to a great extent the work of the present Bhattaraka of Shravanabelagola who early in his life received the honorary title of Karmayogi, a distinction reserved for religious leaders who, as the word *karma* (action) denotes, make it their duty to improve the living condition of their flock in matters of health, education and livelihood without neglecting the spiritual duties of their office.

65. Before entering the first gate of the temple complex on top of Shravanabelagola's Indragiri, the pilgrim's attention is caught by a boulder showing rock-carved monks and Jinas.

CHANDRAGIRI

66. Site plan of temples.

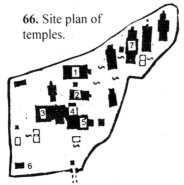

1 - CHAMUNDARAYA BASTI
2 - SHASANA BASTI
3 - KATTALE BASTI
4 - CHANDRAGUPTA BASTI
5 - PARSHVANATHA BASTI
6 - SHANTINATHA BASTI
7 - SAVATI GANDHAVARANA BASTI,
    BUILT IN 1123 BY QUEEN SHANTAL
    DEVI, WIFE OF A HOYSALA KING.
    INSCRIPTIONS

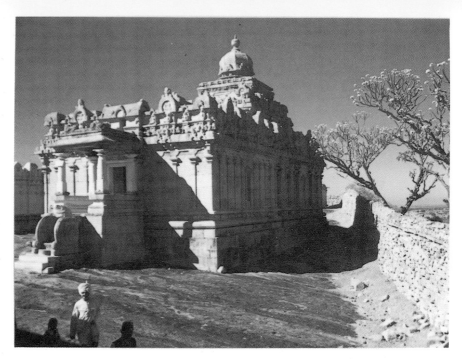

67. Chamundaraya Basti. Late tenth century. "This granite structure is a perfect specimen of Ganga workmanship and of Dravidian architectural features.(...) We find here some of the finest creations of the Indian artist. A maiden brimming with adolescence, beauty and innocence is one amog them" (Settar).

68 (*below*). One of the *nishidi* pillars on Chandragiri commemorating men and women who died a voluntary death on this hill by the rite of *sallekhana*.

69. Yakshi Kushmandini, the patron goddess of Shravanabelagola. Later in date than Chamundaraya Basti in which she flanks a Jina.

54

70. Bhandari Basti with Indragiri in the background, *c* 1159; dedicated to the twenty-four Tirthankaras and accordingly also known as '*Chaturvimshati* Tirthankara Basti'. It is the largest temple at Shravanabelagola. The about one metre high figures of the 24 Jinas stand in line on a raised pedestal at the far end of the inner temple hall.

71. The last three Jinas in the row of twenty-four: Neminatha, Parshvanatha and Mahavira.

72. Plan of Shravanabelagola Town.

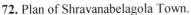

1 - AKKANA BASTI
2 - SIDHANATA BASTI
3 - DANASHALA BASTI

Tank

Jinanathapura
700 m

Matha Temple and Office

4 - MANGAYI BASTI
5 - BHANDARI BASTI
6 - GURUKULA

73. Shravanabelagola main square. In the rear the Matha Temple, annexed to it the residence of the Bhattaraka. The *manastambha* faces the Bhandari Basti. On certain holy days a small gilded statue of Bahubali is carried through the town accompanied by players of wind instruments.

55

74. View from Chandragiri towards Indragiri with the beacon-like statue of Bahubali on top.

75. Detail of a mural in the Digambara Matha Temple at Shravanabelagola depicting scenes from the life of Parshvanatha.

78. Plan of the above temple

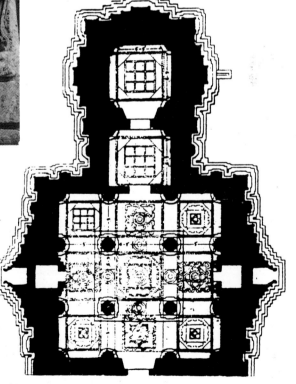

76 (*top*). Shantishvara Basti at the village of Jinanathapura, about 400 m north of Chandragiri temple-complex. End of twelfth century. This Basti "is one of the great glories of Jaina art in the area, and is the only temple built in the ornate Hoysala manner" (Suryu Doshi *Homage to Shravana Belgola*, 1981: 93).

77 (*above*). Shantishvara Basti, detail of external wall.

GOMMATAGIRI

79, 80. Close-up of the five and a half metre high Bahubali at Gommatagiri. Hewn from black granite, the statue (*right*) stands on a solitary hillock about twenty-five kilometres north-west of Mysore city on the road to Hunsur. The inhabitants of the sparsely populated area call the colossus 'Shramana Gudda'. For an unknown span of time it was inaccessible because of a split in the rock and the dense growth of vegetation. It received public attention from 1950 onwards when, thanks to the *Gommatagiri Tirthakshetra Committee* in Mysore, the thick growth was cleared and the cleft in the rock breached. Since then this little-known and in some ways unique Bahubali statue is freely accessible by way of ascending a steep flight of steps cut into the rock. Once a year, in September/Oktober, the annual head-anointing ceremony (*mastakabhisheka*) is attended by hundreds of devotees.

58

THE GENESIS AND SPIRIT OF JAINA ART

Jyoti Prasad Jain

The avowed aim of the Jaina religion is the perfection of man, or the transformation of the individual mundane soul (*atman*) into the very state of Godhood (*paramatman*). It exhorts and helps to bring out the divinity inherent in a person through the realization of the spiritual Self. The path generally is one of severe discipline, self-control, renunciation and austerity. But art, too, may be said to be, in a way, 'one of the purest means to attain, and become one with, the Divine', and it would perhaps not be an exaggeration to say that 'nothing more nearly approaches the spirit of true religion than the spirit of true art'. The emotional, devotional and popular aspects of the creed as well necessitated the creation of various works of art and architecture, and in making them really beautiful no pains or money were spared. Nevertheless, the spirit of the Jaina religion is clearly reflected in its art, which, though very varied and luxuriant, is characterized by a marked absence of the erotic, vulgar or common. It is rather sober, sublime and uplifting, inspiring feelings of self-abnegation, peace and equanimity, besides giving aesthetic pleasure. A sort of unworldliness that is attached to it is conducive to the attainment of spiritual contemplation and the upper reaches of self-realization.

Pieces of Jaina art and architecture belonging to different types and ages are scattered all over the country, but the places of Jaina pilgrimage are in particular veritable store-houses. And the ideal of a religious aspirant in Jainism is exactly what the term 'pilgrim' implies, namely, 'one journeying through life as a stranger in the world'. He lives his life in the world and scrupulously performs his duties and discharges his obligations; yet his attitude is that of a stranger, an onlooker or an observer. He does not identify himself with the show, does not let himself be engrossed in worldly relations and objects. He is a pilgrim who journeys through the world, taking the triple path, made up of Right Faith, Right Knowledge and Right Conduct, and pursues his spiritual pilgrimage till he attains the goal, nirvana. As a matter of fact, in Jainism a place of pilgrimage is called a *tirtha* (literally, a ford), because it helps the aspirant in crossing over the ocean of *samsara* which is full of pain and misery, and in attaining liberation from the otherwise unending round of births and deaths. The primary aim of Jaina pilgrimage is, therefore, spiritual edification.

Pilgrimage to holy places is a coveted undertaking in a devotee's life. These places, with their artistic monuments, images, etc., are the living reminders of deities, personages, events and happenings held sacred and memorable, and a visit to them is considered meritorious and spiritually purifying, which fact is substantiated by the life led by the pilgrims there. Almost the entire time is spent in different religious activities – continence, abstinence, fasting, worship, meditation, study of scriptures, listening to religious discourses, chanting and recitation of hymns or devotional songs, charity and alms-giving. People, young and old, men and women, from different walks of life and from different parts of the country live together in perfect peace and amity, and full of pious thoughts.

It is a fact that the Jainas have been amongst the foremost in contributing to the cultural heritage of India. They have enriched the country's art-treasure with numerous and diverse specimens of art and architecture, not a few of which are unique and vie with the best in their grandeur and artistic merit.

It is also true that Jaina art has been essentially religious, and as with everything else in life, it would appear that the Jainas have carried their spirit of acute analysis, and even asceticism, into the sphere of art and architecture, so much so that in conventional Jaina art the ethical object seems to predominate, and one may sometimes find in it a lack of the purely aesthetic element conducive to its growth. There are minute details, for instance, in texts like the *Manasara*, which show that there was a regular system of sculpture and architecture to which the workers in these arts were expected to conform strictly.* But the same thing holds true in the case of the Buddhist and the Brahmanical religious art; if there was any difference, it was only one of degree.

In the representation of the many lesser deities or godlings of the Jaina pantheon, such as Indra and his spouse, the *Yaksha* and *Yakshi* attendants of the Tirthankaras, the goddess Sarasvati, the *Kshetrapalas* ('guardians of the region') or the lay-worshippers, men and women, in the depiction of scenes from the life-stories of the Tirthankaras and other celebrities of yore, and in the use of various decorative motifs, however, the artist was not restrained by any rigidly prescribed formulae and had greater freedom. He could also give full play to his genius in carving or painting natural objects and secular scenes from contemporary life, which are sometimes marvellous, very informative and full of aesthetic beauty. But here too he had to keep in mind the puritanical character of the creed and avoid eroticism, obscenity or unethical subjects.

As regards architecture, the early Jaina monks being mostly forest recluses and wandering ascetics, natural caves on the sides or top of hills, situated away from human habitation, served as temporary refuges and places of stay for them. Even the early artificial caves were simple and often contained polished stone beds for those who performed *sallekhana*. From the third-fourth century AD the practice of living

* Those 'workers in the arts' were then – as they are to this day – no Jainas. Dr. John E. Cort, on the occasion of the exhibition *The Peaceful Liberators: Jain Art from India* at the Victoria and Albert Museum, London (Nov. 1995 to Feb. 1996), put it in the following words, "Jaina art is art for the Jains by non-Jains." Naturally, the visions used to come and still come from members of the Jaina religion. (*The editor*)

more or less permanently in out-of-the-way temples or establishments gradually began to gain ground with a large section of Jaina ascetics, and it gave encouragement to the making of rock-hewn cave-temples.

In their temple-architecture the Jainas, while adopting the styles prevalent in the places and times where and when they built their temples, also introduced certain characteristic features in keeping with their own culture and ideology, which tended to make it almost a distinct Jaina art. In certain localities, they created whole 'cities of temples'.

The Jainas also distinguished themselves by their decorative sculpture, as distinct from individual statuary, and attained a considerable degree of excellence in the perfection of pillared chambers, one of their favourite forms of architecture. Some of these richly-wrought chambers have been declared by reputed art-critics to be the finest specimens of the ancient and early medieval Indian architecture. Many a time the carvings and bas-reliefs are so full of human interest that it looks as if the austere asceticism symbolized in the huge, stoic and nude Jina images was more than counterbalanced by the abundance and variety of these sculptures.

No gainsaying that the ideology and spirit of the Jaina religion and culture are very much reflected, as they ought to be, in Jaina art and architecture.

<<<<<◇>>>>>

81. A master stonemason of Jaipur, a Hindu by faith, has been assigned to do the sculptures for a new Jaina temple at Palitana. Now he has come to this famous town with one of his sons to complete the job away from home. He will be paid by the inch, that is, the height of each finished statue determines its price. Not the kind of arrangement that produces great art.

61

82, 83. Twenty-four Tirthankaras in bas-relief. Fifth/sixth century. The place is known, according to *Jaina Art and Architecture* (New Delhi l974), under Siruka-dambur or Tirunatharkunru. There is a rock-cut inscription mentioning the *nishidhi* (death by the rite of *sallekhana*) of two Jaina monks. One of them, an acharya by the name of Chandra-nandi, died by fasting for fifty-seven days. – An ancient flight of stairs made of rock leads up to the historic site. Facing the east, this impressive monument near Gingee ought to be visited during the early hours of the day.

62

TAMILNADU

Since Gingee, a minor town in Tamilnadu easily accessible by bus from Madras, Pondicherry and Bangalore, has got a new hotel, conveniently situated opposite the bus stand, it offers itself as an ideal station for users of this guide.*

The two districts of North and South Arcot, with Gingee in the centre, constitute a vast expanse of fertile land, here and there dotted with abruptly rising mountains of moderate heights, that has acquired and retained a charm of its own, a charm further enhanced by the good-looking and very hospitable inhabitants.

There is no need to travel great distances to still another village with an old Jaina temple kept in active worship and usually located at the end of a so-called 'Jain Street'. When viewed from the exterior, these temples may look poor, but most of them contain precious images of Tirthankaras and attendant figures in both stone and metal, in some cases in such great number that there is hardly room to display them all. Here lies ample scope for students of Jaina art, since as yet very few of these objects have been documented.

Being taken care of by two Jaina families from Gingee, as it happens to us, means more than just being guided to places of worship, it also means meeting the people who do the worshipping. These worshippers are the descendants of Tamilnadu's once predominant Jaina population. Not long after the nirvana of Mahavira, it is believed, Jaina monks reached the land of the Tamils, learned their language and began to spread the message of non-violence. Being shown the dressed stone-beds of those early missionaries (ill. **86**) leaves one in awe of what human beings, calling nothing their own, are capable of accomplishing. In their case they succeeded to give an old culture a new direction.

From these early beginning to about the ninth/tenth century, great sages such

84. Take a guide or look for this sign on the right-hand side of a dirt track, about two kilometres north of Gingee. Cross the track and follow the bridlepath westward. The hill of the twenty-four Tirthankaras lies to the left of the path.

* *See* map, page 66, and appendix.

63

as Acharya Kundakunda kept the teaching of the twenty-four Tirthankaras alive in the land of the Tamils. Wise kings saw to it that tolerance was observed between Hindus, Jainas and Buddhists. It was a vigorous age: temples were built, statues sculptured, metal icons fashioned and literary masterpieces composed. But then, in the aftermath of a religious Hindu resurgence, a period of persecution of Buddhists and Jainas by fanatical Hindu leaders and rulers took its course. These ugly events in which many Jainas were put to death, tapered off in the thirteenth century, thanks to a few enlightened kings; however, because many Jainas had succumbed to the proselytising pressure and accepted conversion, the glory of the once lively Jaina culture in this part of India never returned. Still, not all was lost and at present there are signs of Jainism becoming once more a driving force in Tamilnadu. According to census figures, the Jaina population in Tamilnadu has increased from 41,097 in 1971 to 66,900 in 1991.

The village of Melsittamur, eleven kilometres east of Gingee (take a bus to Velam, then walk two kilometres), is the religious centre for the Jainas living in North and South Arcot. Here the only Bhattaraka of Tamilnadu resides in a spacious building next to a walled temple of enormous size. There exist close links between the Bhattarakas of Melsittamur and Humcha in Karnataka, their common bond being the adoration of Padmavati Devi.

Because of lack of space only a limited number of Jaina places in Tamilnadu can be featured in this chapter, so there are great sights left to be looked for by the adventurous traveller. A comprehensive survey of Jaina temples and holy sites in Tamilnadu needs still to be undertaken. Their number, according to a leaflet circulated in 1981 by the *Digambara Jaina Youth Forum* in Madras, 'may be in the order of 500 to 600'; the number of worthy objects of art should be several times this figure.

85. Detail of an inscription at Ennayiramalai. The letters are Brahmi, the language is Tamil. *See* next page.

64

ENNAYIRAMALAI

A fascinating place of great antiquity, but little-known and difficult to locate. At some remote period it was the centre of a famous order of Digambara monks where hundreds of naked ascetics – popular belief speaks of eight thousand – used to gather. Its locality – a hill of boulders of enormous size – lies about thirty kilometres to the south-east of Gingee. Illustration **86** (*above*) shows one of six rock- sheltered 'rooms' which provide a total of thirty-five such polished beds with raised pillow-like mouldings. The uppermost bed of each 'compartment' was reserved for the leader of the respective group of monks. More such shelters are known in other regions of Tamilnadu. The inscriptions found at these ascetics' abodes date from the third century BC to the early centuries AD. In the rock-cut inscription (detail *see* ill. **85**) at the lower end of the above pictured row of beds, a donor pays homage to the Jinas and commits himself to materially supporting the *sangha* (order of monks).

87. Tamilnadu, North and South Arcot Districts.

1 - Tirumalai
2 - Thatchur
3 - Odalavadi
4 - Ponnur Hill
5 - Ponnur
6 - Kil-Sathamangalam
7 - Venkundram
8 - Tirakkol
9 - Valathy
10 - Thorapady
11 - Thondur
12 - Viranamur
13 - Melsittamur
14 - 24 Tirthankaras
15 - Ennayiramalai
16 - Tirunarungkondai

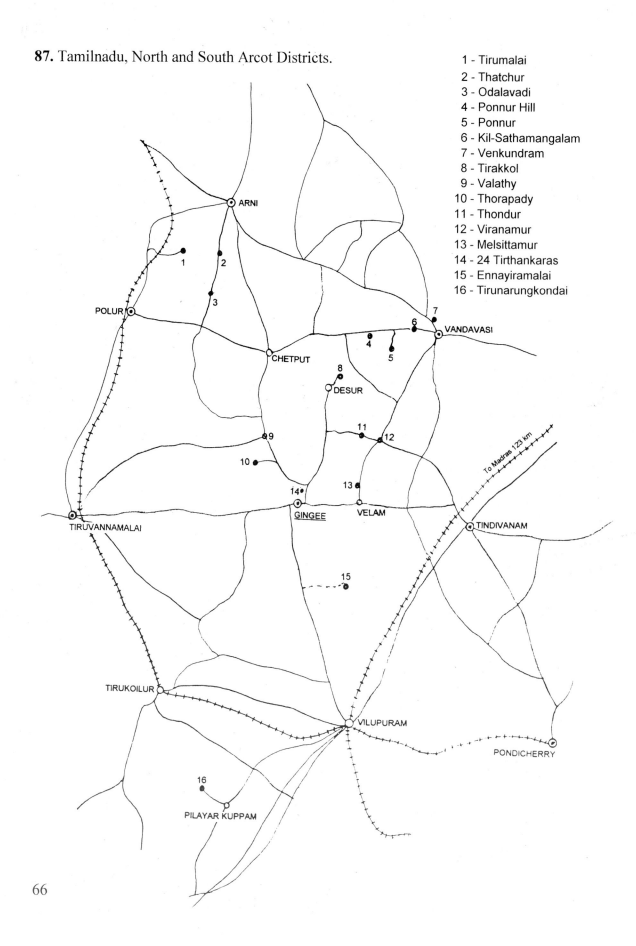

TIRAKKOL

The Jaina sights of Tirakkol – a remote hamlet about 25 km north of Gingee – deserve to be seen twice: once well before noon, and another time in the afternoon. To get there, take a bus at Gingee bound for the market town of Desur. On arrival ask your way to the Jaina temple where anyone present will be eager to tell you the way to Tirakkol. Insist that you prefer to walk; it is a short hour's hike through appealing countryside.

88 (*above*). Seated Tirthankara with *chauri*-bearers, facing east. Seventh century. Cut in the same boulder, there are two more panels, but they must be seen and photographed in the afternoon. On the left, in the rear, a front pillar of the village Jaina temple. On the right a small ruined shrine. Illustration **89** (*right*) shows a closer view of this old building as seen from the south. Next to nothing is known about this still picturesque piece of architecture.

90. This large Parshvanatha Temple at Thirunarungkondai, with its two towers of uniquely Tamil architecture, was built above and around a cave-like cleft between two boulders. During the month of May each year a festival, lasting for ten days, attracts thousands of pilgrims.

91 (*right*). Detail of the above tower showing a seated Jina with *chauri*-bearers (*chauri* = fly-whisk) and two *Yakshis,* one riding an elephant the other a lion.

68

92. Seated Jina, bathed in a beam of light deep down in the temple, radiates serene peace.

THIRUNARUNGKONDAI

The name of Thirunarungkondai applies to both the village – situated some sixty kilometres south of Gingee – and the nearby hill with a Jaina temple at the top. One of the legends, collected from rural folk by Colonel Mackenzie between 1810 and 1815

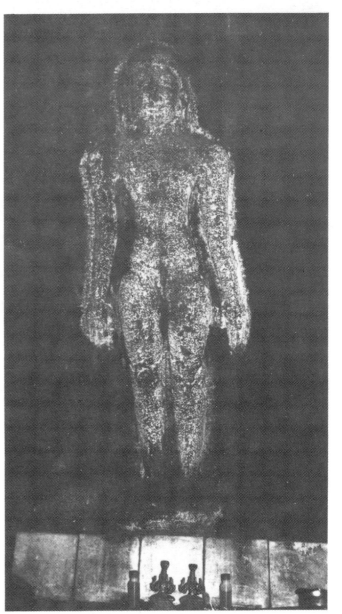

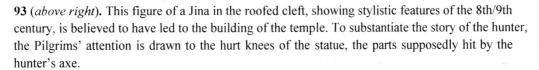

and preserved in form of manuscripts, reports of a hunter and his wife who once upon a time went to Thirunarungkondai in search of edible roots. While digging the ground, his axe struck on an image of Parshvanatha carved in high relief. There was a flash of light, emitted from the figure, that made him blind in both eyes. The hunter lamented his mistake and prayed to the Lord to restore his sight. Parshvanatha conceded to his prayer and made him see again. The tribesmen, learning of the miracle, cleared the image of the accumulated earth and built a temple around it.*

93 (*above right*). This figure of a Jina in the roofed cleft, showing stylistic features of the 8th/9th century, is believed to have led to the building of the temple. To substantiate the story of the hunter, the Pilgrims' attention is drawn to the hurt knees of the statue, the parts supposedly hit by the hunter's axe.

* These legends were edited by T.V. Mahalingam, University of Madras, and published in 1972.

94.

95.

96.

94 (*left*). General view of the towers of the 'new' (16th cent.) temple of Melsittamur as seen from the roof of a nearby building. The two old templs (9th cent.), housing several impressive sculptures, lie a short way beyond the blackened tower.

95 (*far left below*). Sculpture on a pillar facing from within the main entrance of the 'new' temple. It represents Bhairava with the dog functioning as the *kshetrapala* of the place. *Kshetrapalas* are guardian spirits protecting a temple or village compound.

96 (*left below*). Goddess Ganga on a doorway jamb of the main temple.

97 (*right*). The massive tower of Melsittamur's main temple, adorned with Jinas. In front of it a flagstaff and a *mana-stambha*.

MELSITTAMUR

To reach the village of Melsittamur, board any morning bus at Gingee bound for Tindi-vanam and alight at the eastern end of Vellam village; a ride of just ten kilometres. From there it is a delightful half-an-hour's walk northwards past rice-fields at different stages of cultivation. At one point, however, it means wet feet as a shallow brook needs to be waded through. The temples and the Jaina Matha, a stately building, are located at the further end of the village. It is advisable to pay one's respects to the Bhattaraka, Shri Swamigal Lakshmisena, and ask for permission to take photographs. Once a year, in the month of April, Melsittamur has a Jaina temple-car festival, lasting for ten days.

98, 99. The Bhattaraka of Melsittamur with two visitors from Gingee. Note the items displayed on the table before him – some books, a fly-whisk made of peacock feathers, a metal water-jug – and compare them with those depicted on the pedestal of the

image of a Bhattaraka (*above*). The book-stand symbolises the scriptures which a Bhattaraka is expected to study. Images of these Digambara pontiffs are very rare. This one is kept by Bhattaraka Laxmisena in his room.

100 (*left*)**.** Ponnur Hill. Once a year the rock-carved footprints of Acharya Kundakunda at the top of the hill are ceremoniously worshipped. There is a Jaina school at the foot of the hill; and recently a printing and mechanical training centre has been built and named after Acharya Kundakunda. This great Jaina monk and author, who is accepted by both the Digambaras and Shvetambaras, was born in this area some time in the second or third century AD.

101. Every day anew, the Jina images in temples or private *puja*-rooms must be lustrated*, otherwise they lose their spiritual value. Here, in a Tamilnadu Jaina temple, the musical accompaniment to this sacred rite is provided by the attentive children of the *pujari* (Tamil = *vathar*).

102. Viranamur; a village with some forty Jaina families. The picture was taken on a day late in December when traditionally 365 oil-lamps are lighted in the local temple to the singing of hymns by the assembled congregation. The lights are kept burning till about January the 15th. A custom peculiar to the Tamil Jainas.

* **Lustrate**, v.t. Purify by expiatory sacrifice, ceremonial washing, or other such rite (The Concise Oxford Dictionary).

103. Tirumalai. Bahubali visited by his two sisters. Eleventh century.

104. A seated Mahavira flanked by two large lions grace this disused temple on top of the hill. Under the tree in the rear there are rock-cut footprints (*padukas*) commemorating the *nirvana* (death) of some renowned ascetics.

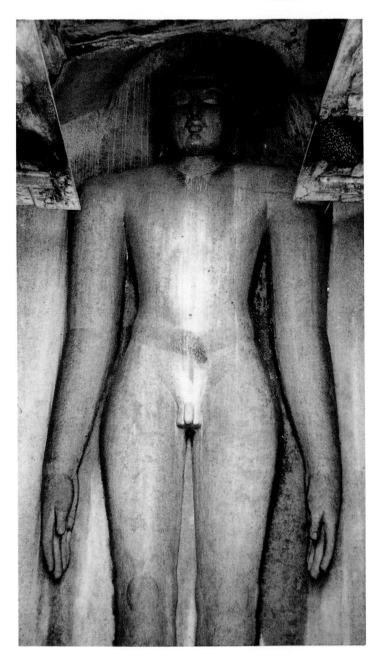

TIRUMALAI

The temple-hill at Tirumalai (*malai* = hill) is another ancient Jaina site in Tamilnadu which touches a string in the mind and heart of the not so frequent visitor to this remote place about half-way between Arni and Polur. The work of the builders, excavators and sculptors commenced in the tenth century and continued, joined in the course of time by mural painters, for some hundreds of years. The main temple, dedicated to Neminatha, is known as Kundavai Jinalayam, so named after the wife of a Chola king (*Jinalayam* denotes a Jaina shrine). A small, solid temple crowns the top of the hill (*above*). The temples further down, partly excavated and partly built in tiers within cavernous recessions of the rock, contain sculptures in high and base relief (*opposite*). Still further down, the rock-cut figure of a 4.8 metre high Neminatha. Illustration **105** (*left*).

75

VALATHY

107 (*above*). Natural cave near the western outskirts of Valathy, a village with a 400-year-old temple and a Jaina congregation of about thirty families. Illustration **106** (*above left*) shows a close-up of the cave's undated sculpture. Time, it seems, was of little concern then – and still is when judged by the potter (ill. **108**) seen at work in the yard of his reed-thatched dwelling halfway between the cave and the village.

JAINA CULTURE

The Jainas possess a distinct religion, a separate philosophy, a different ethical code, a set of peculiar beliefs, practices, customs and manners and a vast literature of their own. Though Jainas form a small minority at present, yet in the past they were not only numerous but also enjoyed royal patronage for a long time in various parts of the country. Consequently the Jaina rules of conduct are in observance throughout the last so many centuries. But as the Jainas were and are living in close contact with the Hindus, both influenced each other in several ways to such an extent that the Jainas, being in minority, came to be regarded as part of Hindus. Accordingly it was thought that the Jainas do no possess a way of life different from others, and especially from Hindus. Therefore with a view to know whether the Jainas think that there is anything like Jaina culture as distinct from other cultures in India, the question number 47 was asked.* From the replies it will be seen that out of 154 persons only fifteen think that the Jaina culture is not separate from other cultures of India, while there are 120 persons who forcefully assert that the Jaina culture is a separate entity altogether. The few persons belonging to the first school of thought consider that Jaina culture is a part of Hindu culture or they go a step further and say that Jaina culture is a part of Aryan culture which is built up by the Jainas, Buddhists and Hindus. But in saying so the persons of this category do admit that the Jaina culture is distinct to a certain extent, if not entirely distinct, from other cultures in India. On the contrary, the overwhelming majority of Jainas seem to side the second school of thought which categorically maintains that the finer thinking of Jaina philosophy of life differs greatly from others and therefore a truly Jaina conduct presents a different culture distinct in its outlook and far-reaching in its range. It cannot be denied, it is argued, that the features of Jaina culture are quite distinct from other cultures especially in matters like outlook towards life and world, insistence on spiritual progress, and observance of *Ahimsa* or creed of non-violence in all possible ways. The basic difference, it is stated, lies in the religious philosophy of the Jainas and as religion moulds the entire way of life, the Jaina way of life automatically becomes separate from other ways of life.

Vilas A. Sangave

* This is an extract from Prof. Sangave's *JAINA COMMUNITY A Social Survey*, 2nd edition, Bombay 1980: 349/50. A very recommendable book. On page 374 of this work Dr. Sangave writes:

"In philosophy the Jainas occupy a distinct position between the Brahmanic and Buddhist philosophical systems. Regarding the problem of Being the three hold different opinions. The Vedantins consider that underlying and upholding from within all things there is one absolute permanent Being, without change and with none other like it. On the contrary the Buddhists hold that all things are transitory. The Jainas, however, contend that Being is joined to production, continuation, destruction and they call their theory of multiple view points *anekantavada,* in contradistinction to the theory of permanency (*nityavada*) of the Vedantins, and of the theory of transitoriness (*vinashavada*) of the Buddhists. The Jainas think that the existing things are permanent only as regards their substance, but their accidents or qualities originate and perish.(...) As the Jainas have evolved a philosophy of their own, they follow a distinct ethical code based on their philosophy. Thus one of the significant contribution of the Jainas is the *Ahimsa* culture. If the Jainas are known for anything it is for the evolution of *Ahimsa* culture and it must be said to the credit of the Jainas that they practised and propagated that culture from ancient times."

≪≪≪◇≫≫≫

MAHARASHTRA

After little-known Tamilnadu – as far as holy Jaina places are concerned – Maharashtra also revealed itself as another state good for the unexpected. Even our first destination, the village of Anjaneri, just some hours drive north of Bombay, yielded a surprising find.

Anjaneri is a small village off a secondary road about twenty-four kilometres north-west of Nasik. Some books on Jaina art give it a mention for a number of ruined temples in its vicinity built in the eleventh/twelfth century. They are of interest to the student of architecture, yet for the unhurried but swift-footed pilgrim Anjaneri has a striking discovery in store. Availing himself of the help of a villager he will, after an hour's hike along a mountain range and a steep ascent up a narrow ridge, come to an easily overlooked entrance to a cave. No steps lead up to it, thus some more rock-climbing is needed, but having safely entered the cave he will be both exalted and saddened. Exalted by the sight of expertly carved Jinas and *Yakshis* in high relief, saddened by seeing how this hidden cave, an evident reminder of a once active centre of Jaina culture, has been converted into a Shiva shrine by the local inhabitants (ill. **110, 111**). This process could be reversed by appointing a villager to be the keeper of the cave and paying him a small monthly remuneration.

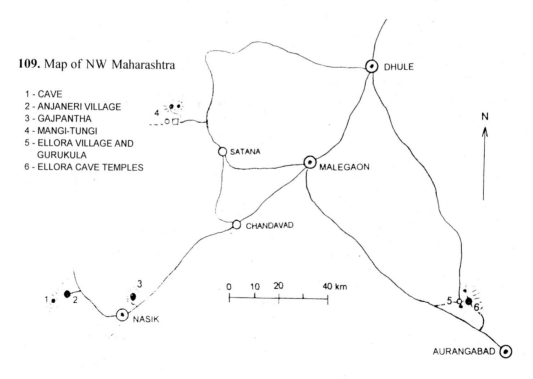

109. Map of NW Maharashtra

1 - CAVE
2 - ANJANERI VILLAGE
3 - GAJPANTHA
4 - MANGI-TUNGI
5 - ELLORA VILLAGE AND
    GURUKULA
6 - ELLORA CAVE TEMPLES

110, 111.
A hidden Jaina
cave-temple
(now a shrine of
the local Hindus)
near the village
of Anjaneri.
A two-roomed
cave, small in
size yet remark-
able for its
sculptures.
Height of the
images a little
over one metre.

ANJANERI

112. Meditating Jina at the entrance to Anjaneri village. In the direction the ox-cart is heading lie the extensive grounds of ruined temples, both Jaina and Hindu.

113 (*right*). Shows the partly restored Jaina temple. Eleventh/twelfth century. The cave (*see* page 79), which may be earlier than the temple, lies hidden in a ridge of the mountain range seen in the background.

GAJPANTHA

114. Pilgrims on their way up to Gajpantha: a small group of caves and temples sanctified by Jaina saints who chose this lonely – now regrettably denuded – hill for dying a religious death. The hill is visible from the highway, but it needs a motor-rickshaw or a taxi to cover the about nine kilometres from Nasik. There is, on the right of the highway, a Digambara temple with rooms for pilgrims. The buses stop here.

115 (*right*). A donor king or chieftain sitting on an elephant. Experts on historical Indian clothing should have little difficulty dating this panel of sculptures adorning a Gajpantha cave.

116. Gajpantha. Three Jinas carved out of black stone in high relief. The pillars are later additions.

MANGI-TUNGI

Sacred Mangi-Tungi – a sight to be seen! – is located at the end of a side-track in a thinly populated area of scenic grandeur. Rama and Sita on their flight from Ayodhya are said to have sojourned for a while at the foot of the Mangi, the western pinnacle of the twin-peaked holy mountain. Looking out from under the rock-sheltered spot where the princely couple is supposed to have meditated makes one believe in this ancient story (ill.**121**).

How and when it came to the excavation of the first caves at such a lofty height is not known. Work may have begun as early as on the Ellora caves which are not far distant, just about 250 kilometres to the south-east. Admittedly, the Mangi-Tungi sculptures lack the perfection and elegance of those found in the Jaina caves at Ellora, but this short-coming may be due to the understandable difficulty the builders must have faced in their search for master-sculptors willing to work at such a remote and dangerously high location (1306 m). Still, the feat of having accomplished the task of working the hard rock to such an extent deserves our admiration. It was no mean undertaking. Before the actual work could begin, round both the Mangi and the Tungi, a circumambulatory passage had first to be cut out of the vertical rock-face. This extra labour and expenditure was not required at Ellora.

Setting out to Mangi-Tungi, climbing the *c.*3500 steps, beholding from above the widely unspoiled country, and then encompassing the two mighty pinnacles and paying homage to the detached looking Jinas which are likely to outlast the gnawing teeth of time for another so many centuries, could well be an inducement to the pilgrim – as it was to us – to delve deeply into that spiritual side of human nature without which a fruitful coming together of visionary conception, determination, faith in oneself and others, artistic skill and work-manship, and *dana* (the giving of gifts) necessary to transform and sanctify a given piece of land into a *tirtha* would hardly materialize.

The three shrines and a large *dharmashala* at the foot of the mountain, surrounded by a wall, are of recent date. The oldest temple, dedicated to Parshvanatha, was build in 1915, the newest one was completed and inaugurated in 1996.

A convenient way of reaching Mangi-Tungi by public bus is from or via Satana or Malegaon. The gate to the temple compound is the final stop of the buses.

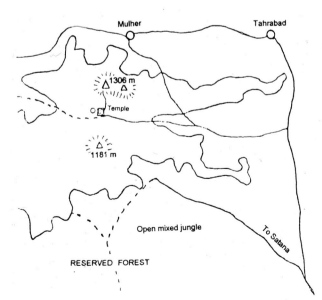

117. Mangi-Tungi and environs.

118. Part of the temple complex at the foot of Mangi-Tungi. There is, behind the Parshvanatha Temple in the background, a small hamlet of reed-thatched houses.

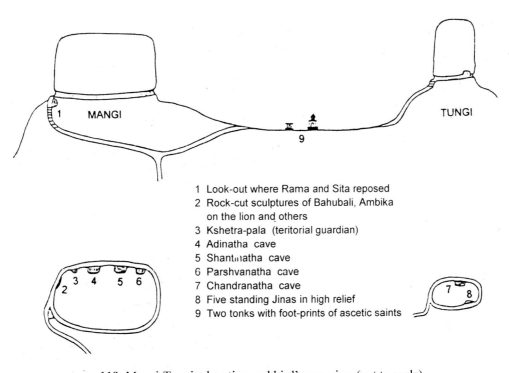

1 Look-out where Rama and Sita reposed
2 Rock-cut sculptures of Bahubali, Ambika on the lion and others
3 Kshetra-pala (teritorial guardian)
4 Adinatha cave
5 Shantmatha cave
6 Parshvanatha cave
7 Chandranatha cave
8 Five standing Jinas in high relief
9 Two tonks with foot-prints of ascetic saints

119. Mangi-Tungi: elevation and bird's-eye view (not to scale).

83

120. Tungi, the eastern pinnacle of the twin-peaked holy mountain; elevation 1306 m.
The man-made circumambulatory passage, meant to be walked clock-wise, starts at the top of
the stairway. Hardly a day passes without pilgrims making their way up and round the two
peaks – barefooted. The Mangi-Tungi cave-temples are about the highest
Jaina caves south of the Himalayan mountains.

121. The western panorama seen from the spot at the foot of the Mangi where Rama and Sita are thought to have meditated.

122. A grand view when seen from above, but from below it is an arduous climb up.

123 – 125. A limited selection of seated and standing Jinas in the Mangi-Tungi cave-temples. Apart from the Jinas there are rock-cut images representing *Yakshas* and *Yakshis* and a Bahubali.

86

ELLORA

"Visitors to Ellora see the Jaina temples only after they have looked at Buddhist and Brahmanical ones, that is, when exhausted after their mile-long walk, and with their visual memories loaded with powerful images. They can then be hardly expected to have any interest left for the Jaina sculptures, and their indifference not seldom turns to revulsion on their being confronted with the wild proliferation of images on the ill-lit cave walls, and which is so oppressive to the wearied sight and brain."*

This being often the case, I would advise my readers to begin their round of the caves with a pleasant early-morning walk to 'Parshvanatha-on-the-Hill', the furthermost of Ellora's famous sights. And as this shrine is the only one in active worship among the thirty-five Buddhist, Hindu and Jaina cave-temples, the pilgrim has the opportunity of beginning the day with a *puja* at the feet of this imposing statue before proceeding to the other caves along the bridlepath. This has the further advantage of not having to walk back in the hot midday hours. (When leaving 'Parshvanatha-on-the Hill' one had better not look back, for the concrete structure that has been put up in front of the shallow cave with the Parshvanatha statue is no delight to the eye.)

* José Pereira: *Monolithic Jinas,* Delhi 1977: xvii.

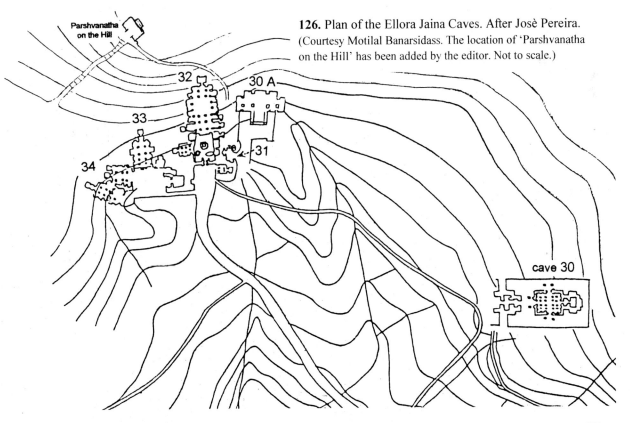

126. Plan of the Ellora Jaina Caves. After Josè Pereira. (Courtesy Motilal Banarsidass. The location of 'Parshvanatha on the Hill' has been added by the editor. Not to scale.)

127 (*oposite above*). View from the upper story of Cave 32 to-wards 'Parshvanatha-on-the-Hill' (ill.**131**), situated a short way beyond the bushes in the background.

128 (*opposite below*). Cave 32. Bahubali in penance flanked by his two sisters and adored by *vidyadharas* (divine messengers). Ninth century.

129 (*above*). Rock-cut friezes with a seated Parshvanatha. Ellora, Cave 32, known as Indra Sabha. Ninth century.

130 (*left*). Interior, Cave 32. "The most elegant temple in all Ellora" (Pereira 1977:26).

131. Ellora:'Parshvanatha on the Hill'. The inscription on the pedestal of the above 2.75 metre high statue bears the year 1156 of the Shaka era (AD 1234/35) and reads as follows: "Hail: in the year 1156 of the famous Shaka era, in the year called Jaya. In Shri Vardhanapura was born Rannugi (...) his son (*was*) Galugi (*whose*) wife (*was*) Svarna (...). From those two sprang four sons, Chakreshvara and the rest. Chakreshvara was chief among them excelling through the virtue of liberality. He gave, on the hill that is frequented by Charanas, a monument of Parshvanatha, and by (*this act of*) liberality (*he made*) an oblation of his *karma*! Many huge images of the lordly Jinas he made, and converted the Charanadri thereby into the holy *tirtha*, just as Bharata (*made*) Mount Kailasha (*a tirtha*). The unique image of faith, of firm and pure convictions, kind, constant to his faithful wife, resembling the tree of paradise (*in liberality*) Chakreshvara becomes a protector of the pure faith (...). Phalguna 3, Wednesday." (Pereira, 1977: 93)

90

MUKTAGIRI

The origin of Muktagiri as a centre of pilgrimage goes back to a memorable occurrence in which the leading part is played by a saintly monk. This is something characteristic of many places featured in this book and confirms the traditional conviction held by Jainas that their saints of old lived up to the code of conduct laid down by Mahavira. Being pioneers in the true meaning of the word, they were the ones who showed their followers, by their mode of living and their way of preaching, not only the revealed path to final salvation but also, and quite literally the ways to places of serene beauty which encompass within a limited space the requisites necessary to become fountain-heads of an ever-living faith. Muktagiri is such a fountain-head.

For he length of every rainy season, the vertically rising rock-formation, over-grown and with an ancient cave-temple in its eastern base, takes on the appearance of a green and reddish-brown back-cloth interwoven with gold, in front of which strings of glittering pearls purl down, seemingly descending from heaven, an awe-inspiring background for the second-last cluster of Muktagiri's forty-two temples.

Some day long ago, the story goes, a Jaina monk, sitting outside the cave, noticed how a frog was caught and deadly hurt by the gushing streams of water falling down the rocks. The monk knelt down to the dying creature and recited a *namokar-mantra* (the most holy hymn of the Jainas) whereby the frog was instantaneously reborn as a heavenly maiden who, out of gratitude, made a rain of pearls fall down on that spot of ground which has become known by the name of 'Muktagiri', meaning Hill of Pearls.

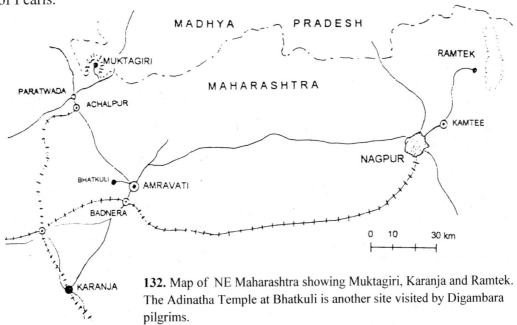

132. Map of NE Maharashtra showing Muktagiri, Karanja and Ramtek. The Adinatha Temple at Bhatkuli is another site visited by Digambara pilgrims.

133. Part view of Muktagiri, the 'Hill of Pearls'. A perfect blend of nature and architecture.
The entrance to the cave (ill. **134**) lies behind the trees on the left. On wet days in the rainy season
a stream of water falls down the vertical rock.

134, 135. Muktagiri. Jaina Cave.The vaulted façade and the interior (*below*) are reminiscent of wooden structures. The black patches across the eyes of the two seated Jinas are disfigurations caused by the moist conditions in the cave. Approximately late tenth century.

136. Karanja: Balatkara Gana Mandir. A sample of the superb wood-carvings
to be marvelled at in this seldom mentioned temple. Its other treasures – icons in both
stone and metal – are of an equally high standard.

KARANJA

Karanja, a town of around 51,000 inhabitants of which *c*.4500 are Jainas, is another place in Maharashtra State that leaves the visitor astounded at what he finds there in his pursuit of sacred art.

The Jainas of Karanja are descendants of Rajasthani families who left their home region of Kota and Bundi during Mughal times and eventually reached Karanja, some seven hundred kilometres south. The reason for their migration or flight is not known, yet, once settled in their new environment, they succeeded in establishing solid means of livelihood, in retaining their religion and in building temples. They also took to supporting the arts. Interestingly, experts on Jaina pictorial art had to amend some of their conclusions when a painting on cloth over twelve metres in length and about eighty centimetres in width was discovered in the Sena Gana Mandir at Karanja, for this find threw new light on how Jaina pictorial art expanded itself.

The painting is composed, as the name *pancha-kalyanaka pata* indicates, of a series of pictures (*pata*) which depict the five (*pancha*) benedictory events (*kalyanaka*) in the life of every new Tirthankara. In the present case it is Rishabha or Adinatha, the first of the last twenty-four. Unfortunately there is as yet no way of permanently exhibiting this rare piece of art within the Sena Gana Mandir, but sooner or later a generous patron of fine Jaina art should come forward and finance the building of an appropriately glazed encasement.

Whereas this painting – it may well be the longest of its kind in India – is for obvious reasons not freely accessible, the other art treasures in Karanja's three Jaina temples are there to be viewed and admired during the usual opening hours any day of the year. Of great attraction are the elaborately carved wooden pillars and architraves in the Balatkara Gana Mandir and a collection of miniature Jinas made of precious stones and metals in the same temple.

Another achievement of Karanja's Jaina community deserves the visitor's attention. It is the local Gurukula (residential school under the guidance of a spiritual teacher) located within a garden on the outskirts of the town. Founded in 1918, it is said to be the oldest of its kind as far as the Digambara sect is concerned.

137. At Karanja, as at other places, it happened to be a helpful rickshaw-driver who, one early morning after a night-long bus-ride from Indore, took us to the temples and the gurukula, the whereabouts of which we had no idea.

138. Detail from the twelve metre long painting on cloth kept in Karanja's Sena Gana Mandir. The scene symbolizes the third auspicious event in the life of Adinatha: his decision to renounce worldly life and become a mendicant. It depicts the abdicated emperor seated under a tree and pulling out his hair. To his left and right, members of the retinue who acclaimingly followed him on his way from the palace. The vertical panel on the right shows eight of the twenty-four emblems assigned to the Tirthankaras (*see* also page 5).

96

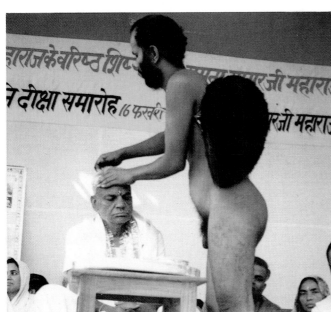

TODAY A KING TOMORROW AN ASCETIC

139 – 142. Scenes from a Digambara *diksha* (initiation) at a New Delhi suburb in February 1992. On the first day, the candidate to monkhood, a successful 60-year-old founder-owner of a construction enterprise, was led in a procession through the streets of his fashionable neighbourhood. For this occasion he was dressed like a king. The following day it was a white elephant on which, now clad in simple white, he was taken to the *diksha*-ground where about six thousand men and women waited to witness the ceremony that has become a favourite motive in Jaina art and that has changed little since Mahavira's time, or respectively since the unknown year in which the scene shown on the opposite page was painted. After plucking the hair, at which he was assisted by his mentor, Muni Amit Sagar, the initiation rite was performed using ancient texts. At the end he walked away naked. Never again would he sit on an elephant, or in a motor car, for that matter.

RAMTEK

143. Digambara Jaina nuns returning from their morning walk to the Ramtek Shantinatha Temple, their temporary abode (*see* pages 14, 15). The temple, situated at the western foot of a mountain range sacred to the Hindu god Rama, was built in the eleventh/twelfth century. (The fort and the Rama temples on top of the hill are of a much later date.) In the course of time more Jaina shrines were added to the Shantinatha temple-complex. Outside the wall there is a *dharmashala* that accepts foreign visitors who are prepared to follow the standard rules. During festive days, meals are available.

144. Shantinatha Temple, Ramtek. Pilgrims have come to have *dharshan* (to pay homage and receive blessings) at the feet of Acharya Vidhyasagar. A ritual much appreciated in Jainism, but the chances of performing it in the presence of a leading acharya are rare. A few days after this photo was taken, Acharya Vidhyasagar and his group of monks and nuns left Ramtek for another place of sojourn.

145. Tower of the Ramtek Shanti-natha Temple, a grand example of north Indian temple architecture before the rise of the Indo-Islamic style. Few temples built in this mode have survived.

146. Close-up of a figurative section of the frieze below the tower proper.

CENTRAL INDIA

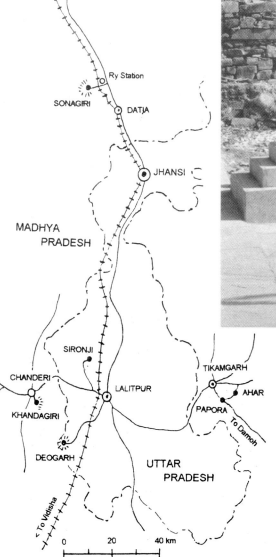

147. Deogarh: meticulously wrought pillars showing a multitude of seated Jinas. This sacred ground, served by buses from Lalitpur, lies on the site of an ancient fort at the southern end of a minor road. A *dharmashala*, secludedly situated at the foot of the hill, has a modern temple with an impressive old *manastambha* in front of it.

148. Map showing part of Central India that abounds in sites of Jaina art and worship. For lack of space only a selective few are featured in this chapter. The River Betwa follows the border to Madhya Pradesh west of Deogarh.

THE JAINA ART OF GWALIOR AND DEOGARH

Klaus Bruhn

Three seasons in a hospitable Indian village and the support of a co-operative Jaina community are remembered to this day, and I am grateful to KURT TITZE for an opportunity to return to a subject which I studied almost forty years ago as a young scholar. However, the present paper is not just an excursion into the past. No doubt the Jaina images and Jaina temples of Deogarh, as I saw them in the fifties, are still before my eyes, perhaps also an indication of the fact that in those days young scholars had more time at their disposal than today; rather than hurrying from place to place they could absorb the impressions of a single place or a limited area.

But in spite of vivid memories of past days, I have this time not only repeated results of earlier research in a condensed form, but also tried to show that Deogarh must be viewed in a wider regional context. This implies the inclusion of the Jaina sculptures of Gwalior, and it also implies occasional references to the whole of Central India – the art province to which Gwalior and Deogarh belong. The inclusion of Gwalior was possible thanks to the generosity of GÜNTER HEIL (Berlin) who provided the photo negatives for our illustrations.

Jaina art begins at Mathura shortly before and under the Kushana dynasty at *c.* 100–250. If we make some allowance for a period of limited activity, we can say that a new phase started under the imperial Gupta dynasty of Northern and Central India (320 to *c.* 500). The centre of Jaina art was still Mathura, but in the subsequent periods the activities of the Jainas spread to other places as well. In spite of continuing artistic activities, Jaina art in Central India regained its former importance only at a somewhat later date with Gwalior and Deogarh becoming centres of Jaina art (Gwalior: 700–800, Deogarh: 850–1150). The two places represent a new phase which is, on the whole, typical of Central India and which can be called a regional style. Before considering the sculptural art of Gwalior and Deogarh, we will say a few words about the general topographical and historical situation. Throughout the article, the reader will find references to the chronology of the monuments which are discussed or mentioned. Even a casual study of art objects cannot do without chronology.

The treeless Fort-rock of *GWALIOR* rises abruptly from the plain on all sides. It can boast of a number of exquisite Jaina sculptures. Some are rock-cut and facing narrow ledges in the vertical walls of the solid rock. Others are free standing (not rock-cut) and have survived on the plateau; they are now mostly kept in the newly built Archaeological Museum. Our chronological frame for the Jaina sculptures, which must have been executed by more than one generation of artists, is 700–800.

101

In spite of the iconoclasm of the Islamic invaders, the early Jaina sculptures of Gwalior have survived in fairly good condition so that their former splendour is not lost. The reliefs reproduced by us are cut into the cliff-wall below the Ek-khamba Tal (*tal* = tank) on the western side of the Fort-rock (*south-western group*), but there are early Jaina sculptures at other points as well. Naturally, Gwalior is above all a Hindu site. Two Hindu temples of the early period are still extant, the famous **Teli-ka-Mandir** (750–800) on the plateau and the small rock-hewn **Caturbhuja Temple** (876) a short way up on the left of the approach-road leading to the plateau.

A medium-sized Jaina temple, dated 1108, has survived in dilapidated condition. However, there was a revival of Jaina art at a much later date, viz. in the 15th century under the predecessors of Man Singh Tomar (1486–1516). Several groups of Jina figures have been excavated in the steep cliff immediately below the walls of the fortress. "The rock sculptures of Gwalior are unsurpassed in North India for their large number and colossal size but from the artistic view point they are degenerate and stereotyped." Well-known is the *Urvahi group* ("The western side of the hill is broken by the deep gash of the Urvahi ravine"). The largest Jina image of this group is a standing colossus measuring 57 feet (17.4 m) in height. However, the *south-eastern group*, half a mile in length and situated under the Gangola Tal is even more important than the Urvahi group. In 1527, the Urvahi Jinas were mutilated by the Mughal emperor Babar, a fact which he records in his memoirs. Babar wrested Gwalior gradually from the governor of the former Delhi Sultan who had taken possession of the Fort in the days of Man Singh's son. The rigorous iconoclasm of the Muslim invaders is well-known, but this is not to say that there was permanent hostility between Muhammedans on the one hand and Hindus and Jainas on the other. Often the contacts between the communities were so close that the orthodox members on both sides feared that their respective religions might lose their influence on the believers. Still, to this day the damage once caused by the invading armies can be seen in the whole of Northern India. *Hindu* art flourished at Gwalior in all periods. In 1093, Hindu architects completed the two **Sas Bahu temples**, both lavished with decoration, on the plateau of the Fort-rock of Gwalior. Much later, Gwalior came under the rule of the Tomara dynasty with Man Singh Tomar as the most prominent figure. This king built the magnificent **Man Mandir** and the **Gujari Mahal**, two palaces which are amongst the earliest specimens of Rajput architecture.

DEOGARH, situated further south, is a small village which can be reached by a metal-road from Lalitpur (*see* map, p.100). The village is situated in the low-lying lands ('Valley') at the foot of the Fort-hill on the right bank of the River Betwa. The ancient monuments are found partly on the Hill, within the circumference of the old Fort-wall, and partly in the Valley and near the village. Generally, the Hill does not stand out sharply from the surrounding area, but on its southern side it is cut by the River Betwa, a tributary to the Yamuna and the Vetravati of Sanskrit literature. "Flowing for the most part in a rocky bed, the Betwa forms a series of deep pools and picturesque cataracts. 'The narrow gorge where it forces its way through the Vindhyan hills and the magnificent sweep it makes below the steep sandstone cliff which is surmounted by the Fort of Deogarh is a scene of striking beauty'." Deogarh is known both for the **Gupta Temple** (500–550) near the village and for the group of Jaina temples in the eastern part of the Fort (850–1150). The Fort is over-grown with jungle which had not been completely removed from the Jaina monuments before the visit of D.R.SAHNI of the *Archaeological Survey of India* in 1917/1918. There are also various other monuments in the Deogarh area, most prominent being the dilapidated **Varaha Temple** on the Fort (700–800) and the sculptures (mother goddesses and other Hindu idols) cut into the cliff-wall (ill. **161**) along the **three ghatis** or flights of steps leading from the Fort down to the River Betwa (550–700). The Gupta Temple with its rich sculptural decoration is one of the great Hindu monuments of the Gupta period, and the sculptures (mostly images) of the Jaina compound (850–1150) are important on account of their stylistic and iconographic variety. The sheer number of images is impressive; not all of them, but more than four hundred can be labelled as 'deserving description' (*see* also References III). The material of the Deogarh monuments is sandstone, often of a warm brick-red colour.

The name 'Deogarh' is of little consequence. There are many places named 'Deogarh' ('fort of the gods'). Fortifications which encompass temples are certainly not rare, and 'Deogarh' may thus have become a popular designation for villages in the vicinity of temples within fort-walls. Furthermore, the present village is a settlement without history. In 1811, the Fort was wrested by a Colonel Baptiste from the Bundela Rajputs as we read in the *Imperial Gazetteer* of 1908. To date, nobody has tried to reconstruct the *local history* from the edited inscriptions recovered from the Hill or the Valley, and we do not know whether it will ever be possible to transform the scattered epigraphical evidence into a coherent account of the site. No doubt, we can date most of the remains on stylistic and palaeographical grounds, but these datings do not solve all the problems connected with the locality. We know the history of the dynasties ruling over this area, but we do not know what role the Fort-hill and the surrounding territory played in the wider political developments. We also do not know how far the ruling dynasties encouraged building activities in a particular area. The construction of the Jaina temples of Deogarh was at any rate an internal affair of the Jaina community as a merchant community.

The richness of the extant material and the clouded history of the locality call for an intensified evaluation of the available data and for the collection of new data. The debris of Hindu and Jaina monuments is promising material for the art historian, those Hindu and Jaina inscriptions which are still unpublished (some important and some not) can be properly edited, and trial trenches can be made, both on the hill and in the adjacent Valley. Such trenches might bring to light foundations of lost Hindu or Jaina temples to which a good number of the exposed sculptural fragments must be traced back. Further fragments below or even on the surface could be secured by adequate exploration of promising localities. Whether studies on these lines will produce a consolidated historical account we know not, but it is certain that they will give us a more complete and hence a more satisfactory idea of the site than we have today. 'Deogarh' is certainly more than the sum of its published monuments.

The Jaina temples (thirty-one according to D.R.SAHNI's counting) differ in character, size, and age (see ill. **158**, **159**, and **162**); some have considerable architectural merit, while others are basically shelters for the accommodation of images. The temples and images belong to two distinct periods, which we call 'early-medieval' (850–950) and 'medieval' (950–1150) respectively. The buildings and the images have suffered considerably under the devastation of the Islamic iconoclasts as well as under the effects of vegetation and temporary neglect, but there must also have been intervening schemes of reconstruction (*jirnoddhar* as the Jainas say). All the details are unknown. Moreover, the building of the Fort (in 1097, or earlier, under the name of *Kirtigiridurga*) must have been an event of considerable importance that affected the life of the Jaina community and the management of the temples to a large extent. The responsible Jaina community lived perhaps at some distance from the group of temples, as is the case today, but Hindu settlements must have been in the vicinity.

The *Imperial Gazetteer* records that 'Jains occasionally still worship there'. After 1930, when the Jaina temples were placed under the jurisdiction of the local Jaina committee, modern restoration work started. In the beginning, the emphasis was on preservation, circumspect reconstruction, and general maintenance of the temple group. There were hardly any changes made in the archaeological substance, although the construction of the Great Wall implied that the sculptures were set in mortar. This wall was built in those days in order to accommodate the majority of the vast number of sculptures lying in the Jaina compound in the open air. When all the absolutely necessary work had been completed, new activities started (in the sixties), and the idea of preservation ceased to be the sole consideration. The place had to be made attractive for pilgrims and other visitors alike. Besides, protective measurements became necessary. In 1959, art robbers had looted the temples, cutting off and pocketing the heads of many Jina figures. We are told that the miscreants were caught, but actually no accurate information is available about the culprits and the whereabouts of the booty. Subsequently the Temple Committee of the Jainas have taken various steps to ensure a better protection of the sculptures. They have also changed the general character of the site in so far as the Jaina temples are no longer lonely monuments in the jungle but rather elements of a comfortable park-like area which betrays a philosophy of improvement. However, in some cases, sculptures and minor structures have been treated in a way which makes the study of old photographs necessary for the art-historian. This would speak for future co-operation of the responsible bodies with experts whenever extensive work is undertaken in connection with religious sites. Likewise, the management guidelines for the UNESCO's World Cultural Heritage Sites might be taken into consideration.

The art province designated by us as *CENTRAL INDIA* is not well-defined, and yet some regional term cannot be dispensed with in a discussion of Deogarh and Gwalior. Ignoring the question of the southward extension and concentrating on Jaina remains, we will say that Central India includes Madhya Pradesh (with Gwalior) as well as adjacent parts of Bihar, of Uttar Pradesh (with Deogarh), and of Rajasthan. Outside Central India, the style of the Jaina monuments clearly changes. In Central India Jaina monuments outside Gwalior and Deogarh are rare in 550–950. Images have come to light, but not in great number, and noteworthy instances of Jaina architecture are hardly to be found. The only clear exception is the great Maladevi Temple near the village of Gyaraspur "perched picturesquely against a ledge of a hill supported on a high masonry platform" and built in 850–900. Gyaraspur belongs to Madhya Pradesh and is situated south of Bina Junction. About forty kilometres south-west of Gyaraspur is another important site, Bhilsa (now called Vidisha) with the nearby Udayagiri Hill. This locality was chiefly a Hindu centre but it has also produced a number of Jaina sculptures which date from the Gupta period to medieval times (400–1150). It is unnecessary to add that Mathura in the north has likewise yielded important Jaina sculptures in the period under review.

It is possible that the Jaina art of Deogarh was influenced by the Jaina art of Gwalior, but conclusive evidence for direct influence is lacking. Be that as it may, there are points of contact between Gwalior and Deogarh. A systematic survey of the Hindu and Jaina sculptures of Central India in the somewhat neglected period from 550 to 950 is at any rate a clear desideratum.

In the medieval period (950–1150), the realm of Jaina art expands, as a sequel of the expansion of the realm of Hindu art. There was an almost explosive development of Hindu and Jaina art which spread a carpet of fairly homogeneous monuments over the whole of Central India. Dozens of place-names could be mentioned for Jaina art, but we refer in this context only to Khajuraho. At Khajuraho (Madhya Pradesh) we find a group of medieval Jaina temples as well as exquisite medieval Jina images. A survey of Jaina art *after* 1150 – our lower boundary for 'medieval art' – will focus attention on isolated developments such as the uncomely (and insufficiently explored) later rock-cut sculptures at Gwalior which belong to the 15th century. Apart from this specific development, the Jaina art of Central India does not extend beyond the medieval period. Various Central-Indian Jaina temples, often built in groups, form a chapter in the history of *Jainism* rather than a chapter in the history of Jaina art. The dominant art region in post-medieval times – religious art, Jaina and non-Jaina – was *WESTERN INDIA* rather than Central India, but that is not part of the present report.

*   *   *

149. Jina composition with subsidiary Jina figures, Gwalior Fort. (Photo courtesy GÜNTER HEIL)

The descriptions which follow demonstrate the Jaina art of Gwalior and Deogarh and tell us at the same time what a Jina looks like or may look like. Let us mention in advance that the Jinas are normally shown stark naked. Jinas wearing a dhoti are only found in the Shvetambara art of Gujarat and South Rajasthan. The *naked* Jina is standard, and only the open split, some time in the first half of the first millennium AD, into 'Digambaras' and 'Shvetambaras' introduced the new element. 'Digambara' monks were then invariably naked while 'Shvetambara' monks always wore a dhoti, and this difference prompted the *Shvetambaras* to project their monastic dress on the Jina figures. Furthermore, Jinas are only shown in two postures: standing in meditation or seated in meditation, and hence they are always shown motionless. Jainism stands for external inactivity as the best protection against harmful actions, and this philosophy is possibly at the root of the choice of only two postures which both indicate meditation and deny external activity.

Jaina images at Gwalior

The extant Jaina images of Gwalior display a remarkable thematic variety. We find Jina images and panels, two Jina compositions, one representation of Bahubali, the meditating saint, who is well-known on account of the huge statue at Shravana Belgola, and two compositions which show the resting queen ('mother of the Jina') and Kubera-and-Ambika respectively. The Gwalior images are mostly rock-cut (cut into the cliff), and we will here concentrate on this part of the material.

Our ill.**149** (*above*) and **150** (*opposite*) show one of two big Jina compositions which take the form of niches in the steep rock. A tall Jina in the centre is flanked at waist-height by four additional Jinas, two on either side. The central Jina motif is enriched by the addition of further

106

Jina figures (1+4) and by the representation of numerous 'miracle motifs'. Most of these miracle motifs are contained in a list of eight as known from Jaina literature:

(1) An Ashoka tree   (5) a throne
(2) a shower of flowers   (6) a halo
(3) heavenly music   (7) heavenly drum(s)
(4) two fly-whisks   (8) parasol(s)

The expression 'miracle motif' refers to emblems of royalty which surround the Jina in a singular manner. The motifs mostly belong to the common stock of ancient Indian iconography – Hindu, Buddhist, Jaina – which developed during and after the Kushana period. They surround the figures of gods and saints and are arranged according to the laws of symmetry. When the motifs had already come to stay in art, they found their way also into the literary tradition, where they are described in great detail (*see* below). It is important to know that the number of miracle motifs used in the representation of the Jinas differs from period to period and from region to region.

We select for our analysis the central Jina and the seated Jinas to his left and to his right. The highly stylised *Ashoka tree* is visible above the central Jina (foliage on both sides) and also above the seated Jina to the right. The *shower of flowers* is probably represented by the divine figures hovering above the Jina and flanking the triple parasol roof (*see* below): We notice in the case of the central Jina two divine *couples*, and in the case of the two lateral seated Jinas two *single* figures (male figures). The divine couples occupy a prominent place in the composition. The garlands, mainly in the hands of the male figures, link the motif with the 'shower of flowers' as listed in literature. As usual, the *heavenly music* is not represented, whereas the *fly-whisks*, the *throne*, and the *halo* are all included into the iconographic programme. However, we do not see detached fly-whisks hovering in the air, but fly-whisks in the hands of human figures. The throne (shown along with the two seated Jinas) takes the form of a lion-throne, i.e. a throne resting on two supports in the form of lions. Between the two lions, a dharmachakra ('wheel of the law') is represented. It is seen from the edge, and it is adorned with

150. Detail of the niche composition of ill.**149**. (Courtesy GÜNTER HEIL)

151. The so-called 'mother of the Jina'. Gwalior Fort.(Courtesy GÜNTER HEIL)

ribbons issuing on both sides from the hub. In Central and Eastern India, the lion-throne appears in the medieval period even below standing Jinas. The halo is omnipresent in Indian iconography and requires no comment. Two *drums* are visible above the halo in the case of the central Jina, and in the top left and top right corners of the panels with the two seated Jinas. The last 'miracle' is the *parasol*. It takes in the case of the Jina normally the form of three superimposed parasol roofs.

In literature, the miracle motifs as just described are connected with a specific event in the biography of the Jinas. Whenever a Jina was about to deliver a sermon, the gods built for him a circular auditorium, or *samavasarana*, where he was to occupy a raised seat under an Ashoka tree in the centre of the structure. Here the saint was not only honoured by an impressive arena, which was occupied by his listeners, but also by the said emblems. It must be added that the samavasarana is based on the concept of a tree sanctuary (provided with emblems of royalty) which survives in Jina iconography in unequivocal form in the tree above the Jina. Needless to add that the Jina in the samavasarana is always seated, while art shows the Jina both in seated and standing postures. The connection between Jina image and samavasarana concept is obvious, but it cannot be called very close. Not all motifs follow the miracle type. This applies, for example, to the additional Jinas (medium size or small size), which are shown quite often and which are very prominent in the case of our composition.

The subsidiary Jinas of the composition include a standing Parshva (fourth subsidiary Jina from left), and there is a similar standing Parshva at the 'entrance' to the rock-cut niche (right side only). Parshva images differ images from of the other twenty-three Jinas basically on account of the cobra motif. The *hoods* of a cobra form a '*hood-circle*' with seven or five hoods behind the head of the Jina, and the superimposed *coils* of the animal appear to the left and to the right of his body. The legend tells us that the Jina Parshva was once attacked by a hostile demon who hurled stones from above at the Jina. At that critical moment, a benevolent snake-god came to Parshva's rescue and spread his

108

152. Kubera and Ambika as Jaina divinities; two miniature Jinas appear in the crowns of the trees, Gwalior Fort. (Courtesy GÜNTER HEIL)

hoods as a protective shield over the meditating saint. This is the Jaina legend (concept and legend exist also in Buddhist art and literature), but actually Parshva is a form of the Jina, which reflects the influence of ancient Indian snake worship, a popular substratum whose influence is seen in Hindu, Buddhist, and Jaina iconography. A divine snake was mostly shown as a human being combined with a multi-headed snake, and the snake worshipper could thus recognize in the Jina Parshva the snake-god of his fathers and forefathers.

Out of the six Jinas we can identify only three, one Rishabha (second subsidiary Jina from left) and two Parshvas (*see above*). Rishabha is recognized by his peculiar hair style, which again has a corollary in legend. Three Jinas, including the one in the centre, remain unidentified. The cognizances which enable us to identify all twenty-four Jinas are important in principle but only comparatively rarely shown in art. The Rishabha figure presents along with four minor Jinas a pentad within the pentad. In Jaina dogmatics, all twenty-four Jinas have the same religious rank, and differences in the scale as found on most multiple compositions are merely an artistic device. To the left and to the right of the central Jina we notice two panels with Jaina *deities* at the bottom level. The panel to the left shows an unnamed divine group ('tutelary couple'), and the panel to the right a goddess (Jaina Ambika). The motifs as such are very common in Jaina art: *see* ill.**152** (Ambika) and ill.**157** (tutelary couple and Ambika). However, the way in which they are included into our composition is unconventional.

Illustration **151** (*opposite*) shows a motif which shall be designated as 'resting queen'. The motif is well known from Hindu art, where the queen is always shown along with a child and is in some cases to be identified as Devaki-with-Krishna. In Jaina art, we find only very few specimens, and the child is shown nowhere. The motif has been identified by some as 'mother of the Jina'. No doubt, the mother of the Jina is often shown in Jaina miniatures from Western India (1100–1500), but the paintings do not help us to identify the sculptural motif which thus remains unexplained. In our photo, the left leg of the queen is bent and the right leg is placed upon it. The female figure to the left, much smaller than the queen, seems to massage the right foot of the queen, but it is not clear what exactly she is doing.

109

A second female attendant figure is shown behind the queen's head. In the back-wall of the niche we notice an unusual ensemble of motifs. A Jina image with lion-throne and fly-whisk bearers is flanked by two-plus-two figures, probably all worshippers and including at least one emaciated ascetic (extreme left). Further up we notice the remaining elements of the Jina image: garland-bearing couple ... drum ... triple parasol with Ashoka tree ... drum ... garland-bearing couple. There is a marked contrast between the main group, which forms a harmonious whole, and the disconnected figures in the rear.

Illustration **152** shows a niche with two Jaina deities, which adjoins the queen's niche to the right. We see Kubera to the left and Ambika to the right. Both deities are well known from Brahmanical iconography, Kubera being in Hinduism the Lord of Riches and Ambika being preceded by the mother-goddesses of Hinduism. Some motifs in the composition are identical with or related to motifs surrounding the Jina (tree etc.), others are peculiar to Kubera and Ambika respectively. We mention only the latter. Kubera carries a money-bag, now mutilated, in his left hand, while his right hand, which is gone, probably held a citron (up to the end of this paragraph, 'left' and 'right' are *left and right as seen from the figure*). An overturned jar, with coins pouring forth from its mouth, is shown below Kubera's left knee. The goddess Ambika keeps a child on her left knee, while a second, apparently elder child is standing to her right. The goddess is sitting on a lion (its head is seen below her right knee), and her feet are placed on a lotus which rests on the lion's back. Not all, but most of these elements belong to the standard iconography of the two deities. A banana plant separates the two figures and indicates that they are not directly connected, but are to be understood as attendant deities of the Jina who is in this case not a part of the composition. In the early period (up to 950), Kubera and Ambika are often shown in the lower register of the Jina images to the left and to the right (*see* ill.**155**). Besides, Ambika and (occasionally) Kubera appear in Jaina art also as independent deities. Strange to say, neither Kubera nor Ambika occupy very prominent places in Jaina *literature*.

Gods and goddesses of every description surface in most phases of Jainism, but they are outside the soteriological plane, that is outside Jainism proper. They cannot help man to reach salvation.

Jaina images at Deogarh

We have now to turn to Deogarh. The Jaina temples of Deogarh boast of a great number of images, virtually the greatest concentration of Jaina images in the whole of India. Apart from the basic difference between 'early-medieval' and 'medieval', we notice various shadings of style, including rather pronounced differences in the physiognomy of the different Jina figures. In addition to the Jina images we find numerous images of Jaina

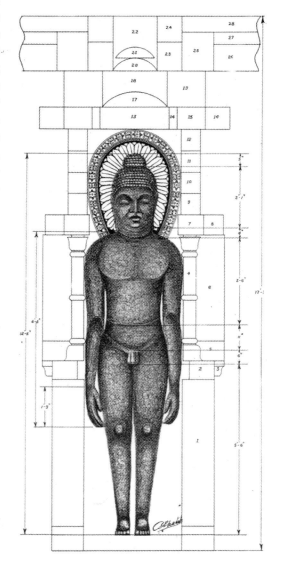

153. The great Shantinatha (height of the figure 3.73 m) in Temple No.12 at Deogarh: organisation of the image.

110

154. The great
Shantinatha.
(Photograph by
RAYMOND
BURNIER)

divinities, and there
are also images of Jai-
na *monks*. Miniatures
figures of various di-
vinities embellish the numerous pillars found in the temple compound. The great number of images
is not the result of any concentrated scheme, but due to donations made over the centuries by pious
Jainas, some rich and some without adequate means. This also explains the fact that some of the
images show little artistic merit. Below we will mainly describe three first rate Jina images, belonging
to Temples Nos.12, 15, and 21 respectively. The first two images demonstrate the art of the early-
medieval period, while the third belongs to the medieval period.

The first image is the great Shantinatha in Temple No.12. Built before 862, this temple consists of
a quadrangular structure which is crowned by a tall shikhara (tower). The quadrangular structure comprises the sanctum and a circumambulatory passage. Some time before 1350, a large pillared hall was
built in front of the temple, and at a still later date (we do not know when) a 'portico' was prefixed to
the pillared hall. (*See* ill.**158**, **159**, and **162** for Temple No.12 and its extensions, and ill.**153** and **154**
for the Shantinatha image.) Temple No.12 has but few Jina figures on its outer walls. Contrary to
Hindu temples, where the figures on the outer walls leave no doubt as to the Hindu character of the
building, Jaina temples have a 'neutral' exterior. There may be wall figures of every provenance, but
they are rarely *clearly Hindu* and rarely *clearly Jaina*. Jina figures in particular are inconspicuous or
missing altogether. As a consequence, the Jaina character of a monument may be recognizable, but it is
never obtrusive – this was the price to be paid for the easily granted permission to erect Jaina temples
under Hindu rulers. Moreover, there were no restrictions as far as the *interior* is concerned. In fact, the
circumabulatory passage of Temple No.12 is jammed with colossal Jina images, and the sanctum
(sanctum plus vestibule) houses, besides the great Shantinatha image, four standing images of the
Jaina goddess Ambika.

If we allot the elements which surround the great Shantinatha to three vertical zones, we can 'read'
the upper portion without difficulty. The VERTICAL ZONE TO THE LEFT has, from top to bottom, a
male garland-bearer, a *rosette*, two leaves (= Ashoka tree), an *elephant* with small figures, a garland-
bearing couple, four figures standing for '*planets*' (numbers one to four*),* and the capital of a pillar

(*see* ill.**154**). The CENTRAL VERTICAL ZONE has, from top to bottom, a drummer (hardly visible in our photograph), two parasol roofs, a vegetable composition, a single parasol roof, another vegetable composition, and the great halo. The VERTICAL ZONE TO THE RIGHT is identical with the zone to the left, but the 'planets' are numbers five to nine, the remaining members of a standard series of nine astral divinities. The miracle group is thus clearly represented with the fly-whisk bearers appearing further down in their appropriate fields (marked as '1' in ill.**153**). The set of 'eight' miracles has been amplified by a few additional motifs (*rosette* etc.), the result being a composition of considerable complexity. There is a marked emphasis on the 'inward' movement of the accessory figures (hovering genii, elephants, fly-whisk bearers), creating the impression that 'gods and men flock together to worship the Jina'. The identity of the Jina (Shantinatha) is not indicated on the image and follows only from a pillar inscription outside the temple. In order to appreciate the impression conveyed to the visitor of the sanctum, one has to consider the size of the Jina composition (5.20 metres) and the semi-darkness of the room with its bare windowless walls. The facial expression of Shantinatha is stern and reserved. Impressive as the great figure is, some visitors will prefer the style of the two flanking fly-whisk bearers and of the four Ambikas – a faint echo of the Gupta age – to the severe expression of the Jina.

The Jina image of ill.**155** is housed in the narrow sanctum of Temple No.15 (*see* ill.**158** and **162**). The composition combines general aesthetic perfection with a convincing rendering of the theme of meditation. The Indian art-historian KRISHNA DEVA observes: "The main image of this temple, a masterpiece of early medieval art, represents a seated figure of Jina, radiating spiritual bliss and effulgence and recalling in its sensitive modelling and serene expression the famous Gupta image of Buddha from Sarnath." In our description we concentrate on the image shown in the illustration but we ignore the superimposed register, which is not visible in our illustration. This unconventional element repeats basically the motifs (standard motifs) of the top area as seen in ill.**155** (garland-bearers etc.). The portrayed Jina has no cognizance, and, contrary to the Shantinatha of Temple No.12, external clues are likewise missing. One wonders what a temple with an unidentified main-idol was called by the worshippers. The motif of the lion-throne is amplified by the addition of a cushion and two blankets. Well-carved figures of Ambika and Kubera are seen to the left and to the right of the throne. A Jina triad *en miniature* appears above each of the two attendant deities. Whereas the two previous Jina images were to some extent construed in an additive manner, we see in this case an integrated whole where each part contributes to the general effect of the composition. This is best demonstrated by the motifs above the head of the Jina (parasol roofs etc.) which are arranged so as to form a self-contained ensemble. The carving of the composition is delicate, and some decorated surfaces such as the halo with its flower design must be viewed up close to be properly appreciated. Unfortunately, this image is among the pieces which have been altered in the course of the more recent operations. A *cognizance* (an antelope in this case) *has been incised* into the lower blanket, and the Jina figure (including the halo) has been *darkened* so as to make it stand out more clearly against the pale backslab. Since the medieval period we notice in Northern India the tendency of providing the Jina figures more or less regulary with cognizances, but the incision of cognizances in existing (anonymous) images has never been practised in the past

Temple No.15 has merely a flat roof, but is a solid and well-planned building. By contrast, the small Temple No.21 (*see* ill.**162**), which houses our next image (ill.**156**), is one of those simple Jaina buildings (found at Deogarh and elsewhere) which were only constructed as shelters for Jina images and which cannot claim any artistic merit. An inscription on the 'foot-band' below the lion-throne tells us that a certain monk (or scholar) Gunanandin caused the image of Chandraprabha to be set up. Chandraprabha's symbol, the crescent, is shown in the middle of the tracery course which appears below the 'foot-band'. The trend to attribute separate identity to all the different Jinas is now fully

112

155. Unnamed Jina in Deogarh Temple No.15 – "a masterpiece of early medieval art." (Photograph courtesy *American Institute of Indian Studies*, Ramnagar)

156 (*right*). The Jina Chandraprabha in Deogarh Temple No.21. "Now the image is but a ruin of what it was . . ."

developed, the vehicles of identification being in the first place inscriptions and cognizances (symbols). Moreover, Kubera and Ambika, frequent attendant deities between *c.* 650–950, are now replaced by other divinities. The basic idea is to provide the 24 different Jinas with 24 + 24 different attendant deities, a commendable theoretical scheme which represented the new trend, but was rarely if ever translated by the artists into practice. In contrast to the elephants at the top which have some legendary background, the elephants on which the fly-whisk bearers stand are a purely decorative addition which enriches the new scheme. Stylistically, the Chandraprabha in No.21 is comparatively close to the image in Temple No.15. However, medieval images clearly differ from early-medieval ones, even in those cases where the latter already seem to show the way to the new period. We notice

113

in the case of the Chandraprabha image deep undercutting where the projecting portions create an element of depth which is in contrast with the comparative flatness of the earlier compositions. We also notice an upward movement, a new lightness, in contrast to the earlier images where the figures are, on the whole, firmly planted on the ground. Of course, the 'shyness' of the old fly-whisk bearers is gone, and the figures now seem to stare into the viewer's face. The aesthetic sentiment has changed. It can be added that many *medieval* sculptures at Deogarh are dated and can even be used to date pieces at other places. The Chandraprabha image is preserved only through our photograph. In 1957 the image was still intact, although slight damage had occurred here and there, but "**Now the image is but a ruin of what it was:** the main figure and a number of subsidiary figures have lost their heads." The art-robbers, who ransacked only the medieval images, had brought havoc to one of the most exquisite Jina images of that period.

The images shown in ill.**157** (four *tutelary* couples and one *Ambika*: compare ill.**149**) demonstrate at a glance to what extent the Deogarh images differ both in their subject matter and in their aesthetic value. We see five tolerably preserved images of average quality which are fixed to the Great Wall. This wall (ill. **159**) surrounds an incomplete square, including Temples Nos.12 and 15, which has thus become the central area of the Jaina compound. The images and fragments which are fixed with cement to this wall form an omnium gatherum of Jaina sculptures, including, of course, three or four very old pieces. One wonders where these sculptures had originally been arranged. The image occupying the lower left of ill.**157** (one of the four tutelary couples) is *medieval* and excels in 'linear discipline', while the other four images of this illustration are early-medieval and recall a more gracious tradition. However, the five images are not very original from the point of view of style and iconography.

The tutelary couple of Jaina art as we can study it in ill.**157** is always seated below a tree. A child is shown either on the lap of the female figure alone, or on the lap of both, the female and the male

157. Detail of the Great Wall at Deogarh, a small section of the sculptural remains. (Courtesy GÜNTER HEIL)

114

158. The Jaina temples of Deogarh before restoration and modernization. Photograph
of the *Archaeological Survey of India* (1918).

figure. A frieze with a series of figures appears below the couple. This iconographic type is not
mentioned anywhere in Jaina literature and has been imported into Indian art from Western Asia in
the early centuries of the Christian era. At Deogarh the Jaina goddess Ambika is always shown under
a mango tree, either standing or seated. In ill.**157**, the goddess is standing, as are the four Ambikas in
the sanctum of Temple No.12. The missing upper portion of the slab contained the mango tree.

There are quite a few images, many fragmentary, but almost all of good quality, which have not
been fixed to the Great Wall, but lie in the open air, or in such places as the pillared hall before
Temple No.12. Finally, we have to mention a collection of small-sized and unimpressive Jina images
housed in a shelter in the said pillared hall. This room has been created by the construction of plain
walls between the four central pillars of the hall (see ill.**162**).

Jaina temples at Deogarh

We will conclude the discussion of Deogarh with a look at the central area of the Jaina compound (ill.
158, 159, and **162**). Illustration **158** (*above*), one of the invaluable and rarely published old photographs of the *Archaeological Survey of India*, shows primarily the complex of Temple No.12 —
shikhara temple, pillared hall (vertical arrow), and portico (diagonal arrow), all in axial alignment and

115

159. Deogarh 1994: The 'portico' of Temple No. 12 and the central area of the Jaina compound. (Photo by KURT TITZE)

viewed from WNW. The other temples are Nos.7 (horizontal arrow), 14, 13 (13 behind 14, only the roof visible), 15, 16, 23 (23 = upper diagonal arrow), and 24 (lower diagonal arrow). The site is shown here after jungle clearing but before the execution of preservation measures. The Great Wall as it exists today passes between No.7 and the portico of No.12 (wall section running from north to south) and again between Nos.15 and 16 (section running from east to west). The photograph was taken in 1917/18 during D.R.SAHNI's campaign and must be consulted in combination with a still earlier plan which was drafted in 1887/88 and where we have marked in our reproduction (ill.**162**) the position of the Great Wall (four arrows). The photograph also shows how the comparative monotony of the Jaina group was relieved in Rajput times by the construction of numerous pavilions. Pavilions crown most of the flat-roofed temples, including Nos.15 and 16. In the foreground we notice No.7, a pavilion which stands on the ground and forms an independent architectural unit.

Illustration **159** (1994) shows above all the portico of No.12, which is here seen from SSW. This portico was assembled at an unknown date from re-used parts. The two *front pillars* are medieval and display on all sides exquisite carvings. Of the two *pillars in the rear* (both early-medieval), the one to the right bears an inscription which says that it (the pillar) was erected in 862 near the temple of Shantinatha (No.12). We thus know that No.12 was built before 862, and we also know that its main idol represents the Jina Shantinatha. In the photograph, we recognize the pillared hall before Temple No.12 (from SW), Temple No.14 (also from SW), and above the Great Wall the roof of Temple No.19 with its pavilion. Due to the modern roof which was built after the nineteen-fifties and which rests on its inner side on plain pillars, the visible side of the Great Wall lies in deep shadow.

The Department of Tourism has developed plans "to provide boating facilities in the Betwa River" and (as we also read in the Hindustan Times of 20-3-94) "to revive the traditional facade of the Jain temples through restoration work." Such statements are easily misunderstood. Deogarh has always been open to visitors, both Jainas and non-Jainas. Construction of roads and other measurements have changed the atmosphere of the locality to some extent, but not materially. Alterations in the archaeological substance will mainly be noticed by the specialists. Basically, Deogarh is still what it was, and those who see the place will be impressed by the splendour of its monuments and by the grandeur of primitive nature.

<<<<<◇>>>>>

160, 161. "Deogarh is more than the sum of its published monuments." To approach it by way of the River Betwa, then to follow the bridlepath that leads up the steep cliff past ancient rock-cut sculptures and on through secluded woodland — this would be an ideal prelude to seeing the "virtually greatest concentration of Jaina images in the whole of India".(*see* pages 104 and 110).

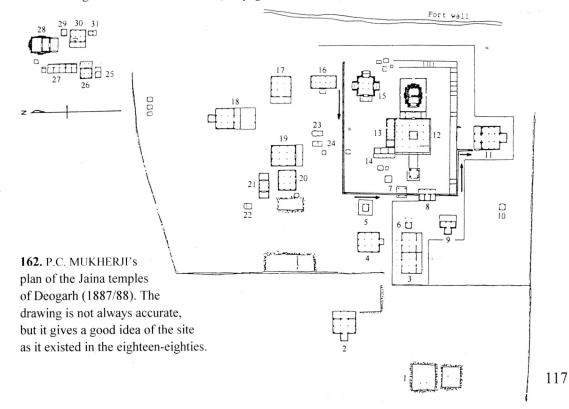

162. P.C. MUKHERJI's plan of the Jaina temples of Deogarh (1887/88). The drawing is not always accurate, but it gives a good idea of the site as it existed in the eighteen-eighties.

117

NOTES AND REFERENCES

I. Bibliography

ANONYMUS (M.B.GARDE?) *The History & Monuments of Gwalior Fort*. Published by the Department of Archaeology, Government of Madhya Bharat, Gwalior. No year. – We have quoted from pp.2 and 25–26 (—> late Jinas).

BANERJEE, N.R., *New Light on the Gupta Temples at Deogarh*, in: *Journal of the Asiatic Society 5. 1963*, pp.37–49. – Vishnu Temple ('Gupta Temple') and Varaha Temple.

BRUHN, K., *The Jina-Images of Deogarh*. Leiden 1969. – Quotation from p.171 (—> the Chandraprabha image of our ill.153).

——.'The Grammar of Jina Iconography I', in: *Berliner Indologische Studien* 8. 1995, pp. 229–83.

CUNNINGHAM, A., *Archaeological Survey of India*, Vol.II. Simla 1871. – *See* pp. 330–96, for Gwalior.

GARDE, M.B., *Archaeology in Gwalior*. Gwalior 1934.

GHOSH, A., (ed.) *Jaina Art and Architecture*. Vols.I–III. New Delhi 1974–75. Refer to pp.175–79 of Vol. I (KRISHNA DEVA) for a condensed survey of the Jaina temples at Deogarh and for a plan of the temple area (p.176). – Quotation from pp.178–79 (—> the image of our ill. 8).

GLASENAPP, H. VON, *Jainism: An Indian Religion of Salvation*. Translated from the the original German by SHRIDHAR B. SHROTRI. Delhi 1998.

IMPERIAL GAZETTEER. *The Imperial Gazetteer of India*. Oxford 1908. – Quotation from p.246 of vol. XI (—> Colonel Baptiste, —> Jaina worshippers).

JOSHI, N.P., "Two Days with the Scholar at Deogarh", in: D. HANDA / A. AGRAWAL (eds.) *Ratna-Chandrika*, New Delhi 1989. *See* pp. 167–74.

MEISTER, M.W., DHAKY, M.A. (eds.), *Encyclopaedia of Indian Temple Architecture. North India. Period of Early Maturity* (*c*. 700–900). Text, Plates. Delhi 1991. – Quotation from p. 48 (—> Gyaraspur).

MISRA, B.D., *Forts and Fortresses of Gwalior and its Hinterland*. New Delhi 1993.

MUKHERJI, P.C., *Report on the Antiquities in the District of Lalitpur, N-W Provinces, India*. Vols.I–II. 1899.

SAHNI, D.R., *Annual Progress Report of the Superintendent, Hindu and Buddhist Monuments, Northern Circle, for the year ending 31st March 1918*, pp. 7–25.

VATS, M.S., *The Gupta Temple at Deogarh*. Delhi 1952. *Memoirs of the Archaeological Survey of India No.70*. – Quotation regarding the —> scenery of Deogarh taken from p. 1 (and selected by M.S.VATS from p.10 of the Jhansi District Gazetteer).

VIENNOT, O., "The Mahishasuramardini from Siddhi(*sic*)-ki-gupha at Deogarh", in: *Journal of the Indian Society of Oriental Art*. New Series Vol. IV/1971–72, pp. 66–77.

WILLIAMS, J.G., *The Art of Gupta India*. Princeton 1982.

II. Acknowledgments and copyrights

Illustrations **149–152**: sculptures on the Fort-rock, Gwalior. – I have to thank once more GÜNTER HEIL (Berlin) who directed my attention to little-known Gwalior sculptures and made the relevant negatives available to me. Refer in connection with our **149–150** also to BRUHN 1995, ill. 12–14. – **153**: *see* BRUHN 1969, ill. 394. – **154**: *see* BRUHN 1969, ill.8 (Photograph: RAYMOND BURNIER). – **155**: *see* MEISTER/DHAKY 1991, Pl .58. –**156**: *see* BRUHN 1969, ill. 211. – **157**: by GÜNTER HEIL – **158**: photograph in the Agra Office of the *Archaeological Survey of India*. 2205. 1917/18. – **162**: from P.C. MUKHERJI 1899, pl. 13. – **159, 160, 161**: by KURT TITZE.

III. Frame of reference

In spite of a few references to changes in subsequent years, we have described in BRUHN 1969 the situation in 1954–57. This applies to our treatment of 319 Jaina images (mainly Jina images) as well as to other details (condition of the temples etc.). In subsequent publications, like the present one, we have still made the 1954–57 situation our basis and ignored later changes. We also plan to publish further Deogarh photographs (temples etc.) in order to record as far as possible the situation during or even before the time of our studies.

See page 5 for the Jinas and their cognizances.

<<<<<<◇>>>>>

118

VIDISHA

Vidisha, situated on the River Betwa and about 100 km south of Deogarh, was one of the first places at which images of Jinas were worshipped. The earliest of them were cut in the walls of the two Jaina caves of Udaygiri, 5 km to the north-east of Vidisha. The first structural temples no longer exist but the torsos of the Jinas – for which those shrines were built – are exhibited in the local open air museum. They are impressive pieces of sculptural art. Vidisha has managed to remain a lively centre of Jaina culture. The percentage of Jainas among its citizens is far above the average.

163 (*above*). Bada Mandir, one of Vidisha's fourteen Jaina temples. The architecture is Mughal. "Bhilsa (a former name of Vidisha) preserves in an open air museum valuable relics of early Jainism and even today the city is populated by many Jainas who have established modern temples" (Klaus Fischer 1957: 6).

164 (*left*). A slightly damaged image of a Jina older than the Bada Mandir in which it is kept. Observe the eight '**miracle motives**', described above by Klaus Bruhn, page 107. Here too they begin with the depiction of an Ashoka tree but then they follow a different sequence.

119

CHANDERI

Chanderi, district Guna in Madhya Pradesh, thirty-seven kilometres west of Lalitpur (*see* map p.100) and renowned for the *Chanderi Handloom Saris* manufactured by a Jaina family enterprise, is an inviting town to visit. The fort on the hill lies in ruins but the approximately five hundred year old Jaina temple is kept in good repair and used for daily worship. It houses a large variety of Jina images as well as a great number of other sacred icons. A nineteenth century shrine, built next to the old temple, contains statues of all twenty-four Tirthankaras.

165.
(For text
see opposite.)

166, 167. Memorial stele (*left*) commemorating the death of an important person. The three incised metal plates called *yantras* symbolize holy scriptures and are auspicious objects of worship. The stele is one of the many art treasures in the Chanderi Digambara Jaina Temple (*below*). On the hill, in the background, the ruined fort.

120

168 (*right*). KHANDAGIRI. Two kilometres south of the temple, past the hillock with the ruined fort on top, lies Khandagiri, Chanderi's actual pilgrim's site. Here, carved into the rock of a vertically rising cliff, are found a number of seated and standing Jinas and a small Bahubali, giving testimony of a once important centre of Jainism.

165 (*opposite above*) and **169** (*below*). A Digambara muni, having first paid homage to the recently cleaned rock-cut Jinas, attends to the request of lecturing to members of the local Jaina community and a group of pilgrims. A close look at the rock face in the rear reveals, on the left, some of the bas-relief figures and, on the right, the decomposed upper torso of a huge Jina.

PAPORA

Papora (also Papoura), five kilometres south of Tikamgarh, is another popular destination for Digambara pilgrims. During late medieval time it was a site of vigorous temple building. By combining old and new elements a rather pleasing type of temple emerged (ill. **170** *right*). The tower, retaining its conical shape, now rested upon a superimposed two-storeyed shrine that showed typical features of Rajput architecture. In all a successful blending of two styles. Influenced by the way Muslim mosques were build, the ground floor now resembled a prayer-hall rather than a temple of old. At the same time the art of figurative sculpture, that had reached impressive heights during previous centuries, continued to decline. But again it should be recalled that the hired builders and stonemasons were no Jainas but members of respective Hindu castes. This is true to the present day.

171 (*below*). Papora, a small 'city' of temples. The long flat-roofed building is a *dharmashala*. The pillars in front, which lack the elegance of the traditional *manastambhas*, are recent additions.

172. Niche with Jina in one of Papora's temples. Not necessarily representative of the large range of sculptures found at this site.

AHAR

173. Ahar, general view of temple-complex.

173, 174 (and **175, 176** *overleaf*). Some time during the 11th century, the Chandella rulers of Khajuraho, who reigned from 1011 to 1241, developed a liking for Ahar, a rural settlement about ninety-five kilometres – as the crow flies – west of Khajuraho, and twenty kilometres to the south-east of Tikamgarh. They had the vision of beautifying this historic place of Jaina worship by building temples and laying out ponds. Judging by the comparatively limited remains, Ahar must have been a haven of beauty and solitude, and was, one should think, a contrast to the 'erotic' Khajuraho of that bygone age. It is still a peaceful and picturesque refuge. The nearest highway is a long distance away. But only one temple tower – reminiscent of Khajuraho – could be restored (*above*). On entering the compound, the visitor beholds what appears to be one large temple surrounded by a high wall. A closer view, however, reveals a compact group of buildings comprising several shrines and an important museum. The Jina in the sanctum of the main temple at Ahar is a Shantinatha of imposing height. In all, Ahar is a place worthy of a monograph.

174. Head of a Jina. Ahar Museum.

123

175. Ahar, two Adinatha images in standing meditation pose. In the palm of each hand they hold a *dharmachacra* ('wheel of the law'). The marble statue, seen on the left, is a modern replacement.

176 (*below*). Close-up of the Jina on the right. The expression of the face is not one of withdrawal from but rather of being fully awake to the world.

*The god of the followers
of the Arhats
is to be represented as
young and beautiful, having
a peaceful countenance
and the 'shrivatsa'-mark
on his chest.*

A sentence from the earliest datable evidence laying down standards for a Tirthankara image. After U. P. Shah in *Jaina Art and Architecture*, Delhi 1975. Vol. III, 466.

KUNDALPUR

177, 178 and **179** (*overleaf*). Kundalpur, thirty-five kilometres north-east of Damoh, with about sixty temples, ranging from plain, flat-roofed shrines built in the eighth/ninth century to widely scattered temples of later dates, is one of the earliest and largest places of Jaina pilgrimage in Central India. Public buses run between the district city of Damoh and Kundalpur during daylight hours. The main temples are closed from midday to about four in the afternoon. A well-kept *dharmashala* provides lodging for pilgrims and visitors who like to linger on in this oasis of natural beauty and religious art and architecture. Illustration **177** (*above*) shows the group of temples closest to the gate.

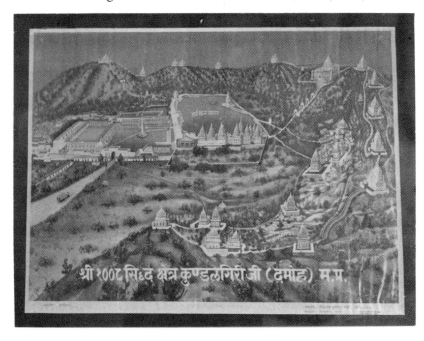

178 (*left*). Layout of the Kundalpur temples as seen by an artist.

The seated Jina in illustration **179** (*overleaf*), having the emblem of a horse, is an image of Sambhavanatha. At some unknown date, the slightly damaged nose led to its removal from the sanctum of a temple. That is Jaina tradition. The two Jinas flanking Sambhavanatha seem to be later additions, chosen for the purpose of obtaining a customary *tri-murtika* (panel of three Jinas).

125

179. Kundalpur. A beautiful image of the third Jina (*see* previous page).

KHAJURAHO

Khajuraho needs no introduction as to its location, history and architecture. Many a western visitor will go away from this rightly famous place with the incorrect view that Jainism is merely a slightly different branch of Hinduism. Is the architecture and art of the Adinatha and Parshvanatha temple, he might ponder, not sufficient proof of resemblance between the two religions? It needs a more thorough look than hurried tourists can spare to take and, preferably, an informed guide to see and comprehend their difference (*see* appendix under Khajuraho).

180. Khajuraho Jaina Museum. Seated Adinatha. Marble. For close-up *see* page 6.

126

181 (*above*). Khajuraho, part view of Jaina temple compound. The Parshvanatha Temple in the centre, built in the tenth century, only a few decades after the Adinatha Mandir (partly hidden behind trees), dominates the skyline. The other buildings are of later centuries. The Shantinatha Mandir (not in the photo), which enshrines a standing Jina of 4.5 metres height has been 'drastically renovated'. Loose sculptures from the ruined Ghantai and other no longer extant temples are exhibited in the Jaina Museum placed outside the compound gate.

182. Parshvanatha Temple, detail of southern façade. Sandstone.

127

SONAGIRI

A convenient way to reach the Jaina temple-hill of Sonagiri is by boarding a south-bound train at Gwalior or a north-bound one at Lalitpur or Jhansi (*see* map, p. 100). After a journey of about sixty kilometres from Gwalior (or forty from Jhansi) the train will halt at a lonely station bearing the name of SONAGIRI. Here, tongas and rickshaws are in attendance to take the pilgrim the last few kilometres to the entrance-gate at the foot of the sacred hill.

The building of the temples which dot the crest and the north-easterly slope of the rocky hill began about the year 1300 and continued for some centuries. The latest structures are of recent date. For on-going transport and accommodation, inquire at the desk in the temple next to the entrance.

183 (*above*). Sonagiri's topmost temples after the annual 'flag-hoisting' ceremony at which thousands of pilgrims gather at this religious site set in a landscape of tranquil beauty. To let one's eyes hover across the whitewashed temples with the orange-gold coloured flags atop their spires is a unforgettable sight. Traditionally, the flags stay hoisted till they are replaced by new ones at the next flag-hoisting ceremony twelve months hence. (Photo: Steffen Kleuser)

128

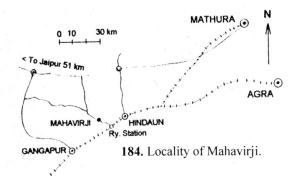

184. Locality of Mahavirji.

MAHAVIRJI

185, 186. The focus of worship and adoration at Maha-virji (connected with Sonagiri by direct bus) is a seated Mahavira of reddish coloured stone (*right*) that lay buried for an unknown period of time. Only after it was dug up early in the 20th century was the present main temple (*below*) built at the expense of an industrial donor. Panels, carved in white marble and fixed to the outer wall of the second storey, relate episodes from the lives of Mahavira and Parshvanatha. Mahavirji, located close to Jaipur, Delhi and Agra, is annually visited by more than a lakh (hundred thousand) of pilgrims. The nearest (9 km) railway station bears the name of Mahavirji.

(Photo: courtesy Temple Manager, Mahavirji.)

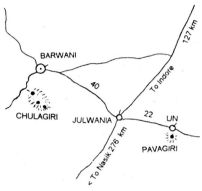

188. Chulagiri and Un.

CHULAGIRI

187 (*above*).The most sacred and highest peak (altitude 641 m) of Chulagiri, also called Bhawangaja, is crowned by a compact temple (*above*) in which every available space along the inner walls is occupied by Jina images, free-standing and in high relief. Hardly a day passes without family groups of pilgrims, after paying homage to the 25.6 m high rock-cut statue of Adinatha (*opposite page*), ascending the numerous flights of steps that take them up to this temple raised on a high plinth. Once there, an all-around grandiose view opens up for them. The centre of worship in this temple are not, however, the Jinas but a pair of footprints, carved from black stone and flanked by two smaller ones, in the inner sanctum. According to a Digambara legend, it was here that Kumbhakarna, the brother of Ravana (*consult* the story of Rama and Sita) and his son Indrajit attained salvation after they had accepted the teaching of the Tirthankaras and renounced violence.

189 (*right*) and **190** (*opposite*). When and by whom this giant representation of the first Tirthankara was hewn into the rather porous rock-face is not known. The average pilgrim is likely to tell you that it has been there for two thousand years and longer. A more probable date is the 10th/11th century AD. The first record of repair work on the statue, carried out at the instance of a Digambara Bhattaraka, bears the date 1503. Illustration **189** shows the image prior to a thorough restoration in 1922. Due to the use of inferior material and the poor condition of the rock, the work had to be done again in 1989/90. In January 1991 thousands of pilgrims gathered at this little known holy site to participate in a solemn reconsecrating ceremony. (Photo: courtesy Publishers of *Arhat Vacana*, Indore.)

130

190. Chulagiri near Barwani, Madhya Pradesh. Restored rock-cut image of Adinatha. The approach to this monument leads through a compound of several temples and a *dharmashala* at the foot of the hill.

PAVAGIRI (UN)

191, 192. Un, a small township in Madhya Pradesh and to Jaina pilgrims better known as Pavagiri, can be comfortably visited from Barwani by taking a morning bus bound for Khargaone and returning in the afternoon. The pilgrims' destination is the temple locally called Gwaleswar situated on a hill at walking distance from the western bus stand (ill.**193**, *opposite*). Another low hill in this remote town is the site of a ruined but still awe-inspiring Jaina temple named by the *Archaeological Survey of India* as Chaubara-Dera 2 (*above*). The Shantinatha image that was found in its sanctum has been removed to the Indore museum. It bears the date 1242 of the Vikram era (AD 1185). Some fairly large Jina statues, badly damaged, have been deposited in the outer hall of a Hindu temple behind the western bus stand.

192 (*left*). The three standing Jinas in the sunken holy of holies of the Gwaleshwar Temple, sculptured of black basalt and highly polished, have escaped mutilation. They are the icons sought out by the pilgrims to be ceremoniously worshipped. The centre one is an image of Shantinatha. A bench facilitates the 'washing' of the statues; for the pilgrims, it is an essential part of *puja* (also *devapuja*).

193. Pavagiri (Un). Gwaleshwar Mandir; in style similar to the ruined Chaubara-Dera Temple (*opposite*). Twelfth century. Several times rebuilt, it has lost much of its original state except the tower, which is missing at the devastated temple.

<<<<◇>>>>

WORSHIP OF THE TIRTHANKARAS (*devapuja*)

The 'unreachable' nature of a Jina renders the presence of any priest or other intermediary, such as one normally finds in traditions more oriented towards the hope of divine intervention, virtually unnecessary in a Jaina temple. Hence the Jaina community has for the most part never developed a special priestly caste analogous to that of the Brahmans in Hinduism. Laymen are encouraged to carry out services on their own, either individually or in a group.(...)

Foremost among the six lay rituals is *devapuja*, worship of the Tirthankaras. This normally takes place before an image of one of the omniscient teachers (any of the twenty-four is considered suitable); such images are most often (but not always) located within a temple.(...)

Construction of images and active veneration of the omniscient teachers whom they represented may well have begun during the Mauryan period (circa 300 BC), sometime after Mahavira had been elevated by many of his followers to the status of a quasi-divine cult figure. But the oldest known Jaina stone inscription suggests that images of the Jinas may have been worshipped at an earlier date. This inscription, commissioned by one King Kharavela of Kalinga (modern Orissa) around 150 BC, tells how that king engaged in warfare to regain a famous image of Ananta Jina (the 14th Tirthankara), which had been carried off by agents of the Nanda dynasty. The Nandas are known to have ruled in Bihar around 400 BC; crediting the veracity of Kharavelas's inscription, therefore, would mean that a full-blown cult of image-worship existed among Jainas even in Mahavira's time.

Padmanabh S. Jaini

From *The Jaina Path of Purification:* 195 and 191/92.

133

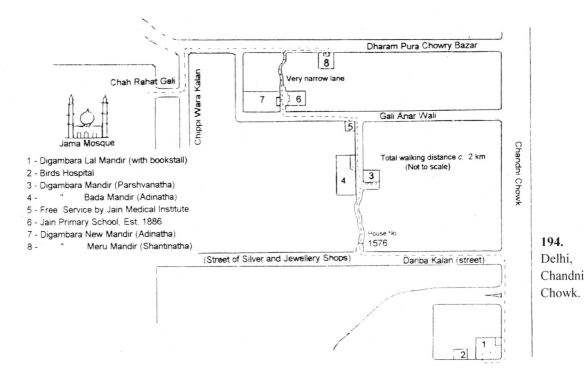

Chah Rahat Gali

Jama Mosque

1 - Digambara Lal Mandir (with bookstall)
2 - Birds Hospital
3 - Digambara Mandir (Parshvanatha)
4 - " Bada Mandir (Adinatha)
5 - Free Service by Jain Medical Institute
6 - Jain Primary School, Est. 1886
7 - Digambara New Mandir (Adinatha)
8 - " Meru Mandir (Shantinatha)

Chippi Wara Kalan

Dharam Pura Chowry Bazar

Very narrow lane

Gali Anar Wali

Total walking distance *c.* 2 km
(Not to scale)

Chandni Chowk

House No
1576

(Street of Silver and Jewellery Shops)

Dariba Kalan (street)

194.
Delhi,
Chandni
Chowk.

DELHI AND HASTINAPUR

With the help of the above map, showing the Chandni Chowk quarter of Old Delhi, foreign visitors to Delhi should be able to trace their way to some of Delhi's eighty or so older Jaina temples. Most visitors to Delhi do not see any of them. Prior to the first sackings of the city by Islamic invaders – the most devastating raid was that by Timur the Mongolian in 1398, when about hundred thousand inhabitants lost their lives – Delhi must have had a number of architecturally important temples. This

assumption is substantiated by the pillars from Hindu and Jaina temples used for building the Qutb Mosque (*c.* 1200). Later, under the more tolerant Mughal rulers (1526–1857), temple building in Delhi began anew. However, very few free-standing Jaina temples were built; it was more opportune to have them tucked away within narrow lanes. The famous Jaina Lal-Mandir (No.1 in ill. **194**) was [erected in 1656.

195. Morning *puja* at the foot of the new (1986) Maha-vira statue atop a prominent hillock at Mehrauli, New Delhi. The statue was sculptured at Karkala in reddish granite (*see* p. 45).

196. Free medical service open to all (*see* ill.**194**, No. 5).

197. Old Delhi, Digambara Meru Mandir, interior (*see* ill. **194**). On the rear cupola,
the symbols of the sixteen dreams announce to the mother-to-be the conception and birth of a
Jina. The mural next to it shows the palace at Ayodyha where Rishabha, the first of the last
twenty-four Tirthankaras, was born.

DELHI'S ATMA VALLABH SANSKRITI MANDIR

North of Delhi, at 20th km Karnal Road – being the first stretch of Highway No.1 from Delhi to Amritsar – there stands, on the left of the road, the probably best-built Jaina temple of the 20th century. The foundation was laid in 1979. Resorting to the ancient art of Indian temple-building, no iron and steel was used for building material because of their limited life span. Thus, the architects and builders are confident that the structural components will last a thousand years and longer. The chosen stone is of a pleasing reddish colour.

The Mandir (temple) is dedicated to Vasupujya, the twelfth Tirthankara, in memory of the late Acharya Vijay Vallabh Suri (1870–1954) who is remembered and admired for his outstanding contributions in the fields of education, humanitarian reforms and religious tolerance. He was among the first supporters of Gandhi's non-violent campaign for independence from British rule. Now his life-like bust (*right*) graces the grandiose auditorium of the new temple. An auditorium that symbolizes with its height of eighty-four feet (one foot for each year in the Acharya's life) the loftiness of Jaina teaching and spirituality.

210. Acharya Viyay Vallabh Suri (1870–1954.

It was a woman – a frequent occurrence in the long history of Jaina temple-building – the late Sadhvi Mrigavati (1926–86) who was the most active propagator behind the scheme of a memorial building to Acharya Vijay Vallabh Suri which is meant to be the nucleus of a 'centre for learning in every sense of the term'. Sadhvi Mrigavati passed away when the temple was still in the process of being built. To honour her, a *samadhi* (meditation) chapel was erected next to the small shrine dedicated to Padmavati Devi (for a photograph of Sadhvi Mrigavati turn to page 18).

Features conducted in the centre comprise – to name just a few –: research on Indology, with emphasis on Jainism; publication of relevant literature in different languages; research on science of nature cure, yoga and Indian medicine; a modern school for boys and girls with accent on character building and industrial training; education in arts and crafts of women of the nearby area, and provision of medical aid to the vicinity. A guest-house provides board and lodging to visitors, research scholars and students from within India and overseas.

136

199. Domed ceiling of the auditorium, sixty-four feet (19.5 metres) in width. Pink sandstone.

200. General view of Shri Atma Vallabh Sanskriti Mandir; on the left the shrine dedicated to Padmavati.

HASTINAPUR

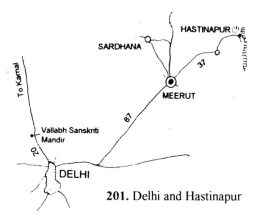

201. Delhi and Hastinapur

Hastinapur, the legendary capital of the Mahabharata epic outside of which the great battle between the Pandavas and the Kurus is thought to have been fought – now just a village about a hundred kilometres north-east of Delhi – is a major place of pilgrimage for both Shvetambaras and Digambaras. It was here, according to tradition, that Rishabha, the former king of Ayodhya, after he had relinquished his kingdom in favour of his two sons Bharata and Bahubali and accepted the life of a homeless ascetic, was offered acceptable food in an acceptable manner for the first time. The fortunate donor was a prince of Hastinapur who happened to know the proper way of giving food to a Jaina monk. The nourishment he offered was sugar-cane juice. Once a year, on the third day of the bright fortnight of the month *Vaishaka* (May/June), thousands of Jaina pilgrims from all over India gather at Hastinapur to commemorate this event.

Wars, floods and vandalism have left nothing standing of ancient Hastinapur. The Ganges, on whose western bank this famous city once stood, has in the course of many centuries found a new bed some distance to the east. During excavations, soon after Independence, a big statue of a standing Shantinatha was found which was dated at 1176. The present temples are of a much later date. Hastinapur is said to be the birth-place of the Tirthankaras Shantinatha, Kunthunatha and Aranatha; their footprints can be seen on a small hill nearby.

With the completion of the Jambu-dvipa shrine (*see* opposite page) in 1985, Hastinapur has become a favourite centre for studying Jaina cosmology and cosmography, an extremely difficult subject to study, not only for Westerners.

The inspiration for "constructing, on scale as far as possible, a model of Jambu-dvipa according to the details available in Jaina scriptures" came not from a mathematical minded male scholar but from the lady ascetic Aryika Jnanmati, a Digambara nun (*see* page 27).

Jambu-dvipa has a diameter of 100,000 *yojanas* (one *yojana* = 8/9 miles or *c.* 13.5 km). It comprises seven islands of which only the inner two plus one half of the third one are fit for humans and five-sensed animals. In the middle stands Mount Sumeru or Meru (there are fourteen more names for it) with a *jambu* tree on top. *Jambu* means rose-apple; thus *jambu-dvipa* may be translated into 'Continent of the Rose-apple tree'. Jambu-dvipa is but the innermost sector of the Jaina universe, and a relatively tiny part of it. For further details consult *The Jain Cosmology* by Colette Caillat and Ravi Kumar, *see* bibliography.

(There is a daily direct morning bus from the main Delhi Bus Station to Hastinapur.)

138

202. Hastinapur. Jambu-dvipa, not a temple, but a model of the 'Continent of the Rose-apple Tree' built in the nineteen-eighties. Stairs lead to the top of the tower which stands for Mount Sumeru (or Meru).

203. View from the top to the islands and oceans contained within Jambu-dvipa.

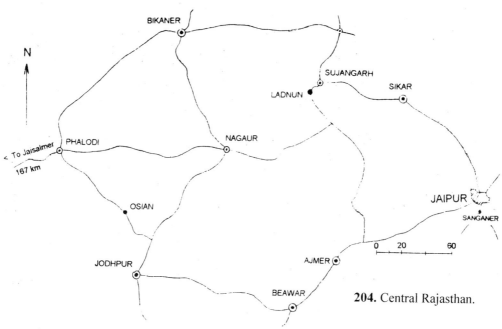

204. Central Rajasthan.

RAJASTHAN

Of all the Indian States and Union Territories, Rajasthan has the highest percentage of Jainas to its total population, namely 1.82 per cent, followed by Maharashtra with 1.50 per cent (*see* appendix). In Jaipur, the biggest city in Rajasthan, there are, one is told, about three hundred Jaina temples, both Digambara and Shvetambara. Most of them are located in the eastern half of the old city; which was designed and founded by Maharaja Jai Singh in 1727. The Jaipur Jaina temples are, like the ones in Old Delhi, not readily spotted from the outside. It is their embellished interiors which makes the visit of some of them an enjoyable experience. Jaipur is famous for its highly-skilled craftsmen.

A large section of the western part of the city is the place where one may watch stonemasons at work; they are Hindu by faith, even those who specialize in producing sculptures for Jaina temples. As there is little demand for individual art at present, the standard of what one sees offered for sale is rather low.

205. Sign to a Jaina temple in which free medical consultation is available (walk downhill from the 'Palace of the Winds' then turn right at the first street).

140

NAMES AND LOCATIONS OF SOME JAINA
TEMLES (MANDIRS) WITHIN JAIPUR CITY:

(1) Chobice Maharaj Mandir at Moti Singh
    Bhomika Rasta (*rasta = lane or street*),
    Jhoari Bazar. Noteworthy for its twenty-
    four seated Jinas arranged in a row.

(2) Tholian Adinath Mandir at Chiwa Lonka
    Rasta, Jhoari Bazar. Has a three dimensional
    model of a *samavasarana* and a large
    coloured dome done in inlaid technique.

(3) Mahavira Mandir at Gopalji ka Rasta. A
    sculptured elephant points the way to
    the entrance.

(4) Shri Moriyan Mandir at Achary Lonka Rasta,
    High cupola; pillars adorned with wooden
    carvings representing musicians and
    dancers; many Jina images.

(5) Parshvanath Mandir at Kawasji ka Rasta
    (ill.**205**).

(6) Bhodichand Mandir at Chiwa Lonka Rasta.

For Shvetambara temples inquire at the Shvetambara Mandir situated near the railway station, on
the left of the road leading to the city.

206. Minor gods in their celestial vehicles and
god Shakra, riding his elephant Airawata, are
on their way to greet the arrival of a
Jina. Here they point to the entrance
of the temple.

207. Historic City of Jaipur.

Most Jaina temples are located
in the area comprising the sectors
marked 1, 2, 3 and 4

5 - Hawa Mahal ('Palace of the Winds')

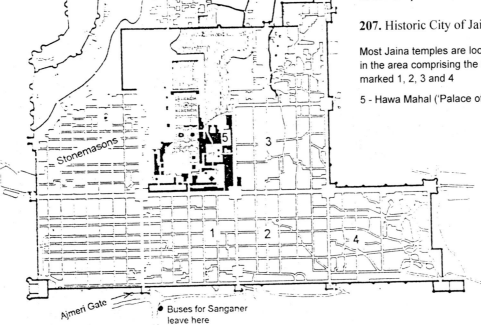

141

SANGANER

The township of Sanganer ten kilometres south of Jaipur (take a bus near the Jaipur Ajmer Gate), is of great interest to students of Jaina art. In the local Shvetambara temple it is the painted interior that attracts one's attention; whereas the Digambara Sanghiji Mandir (*above and left*) abounds in exuberant carvings in marble of a style that pleasingly counterpoises the filigree and 'rococo'-like art of Abu. 'Jaina art lacks life and diversity', this often-voiced comment is here refuted. Unfortunately, only a few temples of that period (11th to 13th century) have survived.

208 (*above*). Sanganer, Sanghiji Mandir. 12th. cent.

209. Close-up of one of the scenes surrounding the inner entrance of the temple.

210. Ajmer, Nasiayan Jaina Temple; part view.
The 25 m high *manastambha* was added in 1953.

AJMER

Ajmer's main attraction is – for the Jainas – the prominently situated Nasiayan Digambara Temple, or rather the two-storied *Svarana Nagara* Hall behind the temple, better known as the *Museum*. Both the temple and the museum were built and are still owned by the Sony family of Ajmer. The temple, dedicated to Rishabha or Adinatha in 1865, was constructed of red sandstone in a matter of a few years, but it took twenty-five years, from 1870 to 1895, to fashion – by artisans at Jaipur – the thousands of individual parts required to assemble a three dimensional replica of the story of Rishabha in accordance with an old manuscript by Acharya Jinasena.

The thought to have such a three dimensional model for eduational purposes occurred to Seth Moolchand Soni, who was born in 1830, only after the completion of the temple. His death in 1891 prevented him from seeing his ambitious work in its finished state.

In many Jaina temples one sees painted or figurative representations of the 'five auspicious events' (*pancha-kalyanaka*) in the life of every Tirthankara: conception, birth, renunciation, enlightenment, and salvation (*moksha* or *nirvana*). The one at Ajmer, now over a hundred years old, is by far the largest and most artistic plastic representation of that much-loved mythological narrative.* A specially designed hall of 24.3 m by 12.2 m had to be build to display it effectively. It is open to visitors of all religions every day all the year round for a very small entry fee.

* At Hastagiri near Palitana in Gujarat a new complex of five Shvetambara temples is nearing completion,
which in a grandiose way represents the 'five auspicious moments' in the life of Adinatha.

143

LADNUN

A few day's sojourn in the Rajasthani town of Ladnun (pronounced: Lahrong), situated halfway between Jaipur and Bikaner (or Ajmer and Bikaner) and also accessible from Jodhpur by direct bus, can be recommended without reservation. It offers, apart from some noteworthy temples and the Terapanth *Vishva Bharati Institution* founded by Acharya Tulsi in 1970, a welcome change from noisy city-life. At the time of our visit, back in 1994, Ladnun was free of smoky three-wheeled motor-rickshaws; instead gaily painted horse-drawn tongas dotted the clean streets and lanes.

Jainism has a long history in Ladnun. Some of its temples – in all there are five Digambara and two Shvetambara ones – are said to date back to the tenth century; their superstructures, however, are of later centuries. Relatively many Jaina families, both Shvetambara and Digambara, are found amongst the citizens of this prosperous-looking town. Most of the Shvetambaras are followers of the Terapanth sect which was founded by Acharya Bhikshu in 1760. There are today about 300,000 adherents of the Terapanthi community and *circa* 550 nuns and 150 monks.

Our stay at Ladnun coincided with a gathering in the neighbouring city of Sujangarh of over twenty thousand Terapanthis and of nearly all the monks and nuns of this India-wide group within Jainism. Acharya Tulsi, their ninth spiritual leader and a native of Ladnun (borne in 1914), was to confer the acharyaship he had held for fifty-eight years on to Acharya Mahaprajna who is now their tenth pontiff.

During Acharya Tulsi's long acharyaship – he was eleven when he was initiated into monkhood and twenty-two when he became the youngest acharya ever – Ladnun acquired the distinction of growing into a seat of Jaina learning and teaching, mainly ethical teaching. It pained him to see how the desire for ever more material

144

211 (*opposite*). Restored temple tower, piercing the roof of a modern building above the sanctorum of this twelfth-century Shantinatha Mandir. The building has an ancient underground room containing beautifully carved doorjambs and lintels, some fairly old Jina images, and a highly venerated Sarasvati, goddess of learning.

212. Ladnun. *Manastambha* in front of a temple built in 1935. A master-piece of modern sculpturing. White marble.

possessions took preference over honouring the traditional moral values. He began his crusade by instilling a new spirit, based on old Jaina virtues, into the hearts and minds of his monks and nuns without himself becoming a fundamentalist in the modern sense of the word. Then, in 1949, two years after India gained independence, he launched his Anuvrata Movement which he wanted to be understood as a supplement to the Freedom Movement of earlier years: a movement for righteous living. The message of Anuvrata, addressed to lay-people, stood and still stands for a 'code of conduct aimed at developing the character of an individual' (*anuvrata* stands for 'minor' vows pertaining only to non-ascetics).

145

प्रेक्षाध्यान का फलित है आत्मा की आवाज को पहचान लेना। मन की आवाज आत्मा की आवाज नहीं है। मन की आवाज को आत्मा की आवाज मानना भ्रान्ति है। समता या वीतरागता की आवाज ही आत्मा की आवाज है।
— युवाचार्य महाप्रज्ञ

The fruit of Preksha Meditation is the recognition of the voice of the spirit. The voice of the mind is not the voice of the spirit. To confuse the one with the other is an illusion. The voice of equanimity and dispassion alone is the voice of the spirit.
— Yuvacharya Mahapragya

213. Board with a message near the 'House of Meditation'. Other sayings displayed along the campus lanes are quotations from Mahavira, the Buddha, Jesus, Mohammed, Guru Nanak, Socrates and others.

214. Muni Kishantal, a leading teacher of Preksha Mediation (*preksha* = to perceive carefully and profoundly).

In the nineteen-seventies, when *Jain Vishva Bharati* was formally established in a sprawling area outside his birth-place Ladnun, another visionary dream of the late Gurudev Tulsi begun to bear fruit. Today it is a large and still growing complex of buildings in a setting of trees, bushes and flowers. There are schools, facilities for study and research, a library, a centre of Ayurvedic medicine, a hospital, an auditorium, a printing shop, a meditation retreat, student hostels, guest-houses, and the like. It is a modern campus-like ashram in which foreign travellers and students, be they young or old, male or female, are welcome and free to participate in meditation retreats and to study Jainism at their own pace (*see* appendix).

146

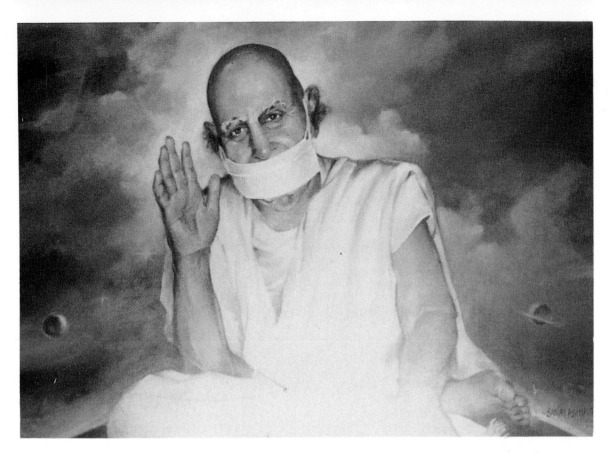

215. Portrait of Acharcha Tulsi, released in 1994. (Shri Gurudev Tulsi died in June 1997.)

In the course of our interview, Shri Tulsi said a number of profound things. I remember in particular, "If you don't disappoint your desires, they will disappoint you". Before we said goodbye to Shri Tulsi and his happy disciples, I questioned him about the problem of achieving happiness here on earth (...). In effect Shri Tulsi answered that the body is a good servant but a bad master. To be truly happy man must obey the voice of ahimsa *or non-violence.* Woodland Kahler (past Chairman International Association of Vegetarians, London).

216. Sujangarh near Ladnun, February 18th, 1994. Yuvacharya Mahaprajna expressing thanks to the audience for accepting him as their tenth Acharya.

BIKANER

The desert city of Bikaner was founded, with the valuable help of Jaina families, in 1488, at a time when in north India Indo-Islamic art had firmly established itself. The best known and best preserved four Jaina temples situated at the eastern outskirts of the city are important examples of this period. It is mainly their interior which shows Islamic influence, whereas their exterior is still dominantly Indian.

As these temples are partly hidden behind walls, it is the so-called *Havelis* (privately owned mansions) which at first catch the attention of the sightseeing visitor to Bikaner. How many private Jaina shrines there might be in these palace-like buildings can only be guessed. Their number may well go into the hundreds. According to the census of 1971 there were 18,266 Jainas (mostly Shvetambara) among the 188,518 inhabitants of Bikaner (V.A. Sangave *Jaina Society Through the Ages*, Delhi, 1992: 31).

With the re-modelling, in 1994, of a large *Haveli* into a first-class hotel by an old Bikaner Jaina family, in the process of which care was taken to retain the character and charm behind the fantastic façade, overseas visitors are offered the opportunity

217 (*above*). Bikaner. Bhandasar Temple, sacred to Parshvanatha. Building began early in the sixteenth century by a merchant named Bhanda. An outstanding example of Indo-Islamic architecture.

of experiencing and enjoying the atmosphere of a historical Jaina residence. There is a chapel with exquisite Jina statuettes and murals, a library with books on Jainism, a restaurant in which pure vegetarian food is prepared and served, and there is, wherever one looks, locally produced art of a very high standard (for address *see* appendix).

218. Altar in the private chapel of the Bikaner Jaina Hotel in the centre of the old city.

219. Beautifully designed balconies open out to the inner courtyard of this Bikaner *Haveli*, now a hotel run on Jaina values.

JAISALMER

Jaisalmer, the other desert city, is about three and a quarter centuries older than Bikaner. Even more ancient is Lodurva, seventeen kilometres north-west of Jaisalmer. Once a royal city, Lodurva was overrun by Muslim forces and totally destroyed in 1152. The present temple, dedicated to Parshvanatha, is of a later date. About halfway to Lodurva, on the southern side of the road, there lie, amidst natural beauty, extensive ruins of Jaina buildings. Restoration work is in progress.

An impressive architectural feat is constituted by the main temples inside the fort of Jaisalmer. They are dedicated to Parshvanatha, Adinatha, Shantinatha, Sambhavanatha and Mahavira. Having of necessity been erected within a very limited space, the southern complex could be taken for one large shrine. This three-dimensional closeness of the four temples is in no way oppressive but rather inspiring. Each time, by taking a few steps round a corner or up or down a staircase, something different catches one's eyes. "There are," states a semi-official leaflet for visitors, "about seven hundred Jina idols over here, seven libraries with rare palm-leaf manuscripts, and eighteen *upashrayas*" (rooms for religious teaching and for providing temporary shelter to monks and nuns). One subterranean library is open to visitors.

Jaisalmer was about the first place where western scholars gained entry into Jaina libraries. This in turn led to the publication of two volumes of *Jaina Sutras* in English translation in Max Mueller's famous series of *Sacred Books of the East* (*see* bibliography). That was as far back as 1884 and 1895; but only now, over a hundred years later and still rather tentatively, a few western writers have begun to popularise the labour of the scholars for the benefit of the general reader. This guide is an example of what can be done, some day soon, to provide readable books on Jaina philosophy, art, ethics and culture for the shelves of every bigger library in western countries. At present there would be not one in a hundred libraries of which this could be said, simply because of the lack of such books at reasonable prices. Many thousands of foreign tourists have visited Jaisalmer's famous library as well as the temples at Mount Abu and Ranakpur during the last few decades, but back home very few of them will find one single book on Jaina religion, art and architecture on the shelves of their nearest library (a regrettable contrast to the general availability of books on Buddhism).

Unlike Bikaner, Jaisalmer's once large Jaina community has dwindled to a few families. The partition of the subcontinent into Pakistan and India put an end to Jaisalmer as a centre of trade and commerce. However, hardly a day passes without a steady coming and going of Jaina pilgrims. It is by way of their donations that the local authorities are able to keep the entrusted sacred buildings, most of them were built in the fifteenth century, in good repair.

220. Jaisalmer. Jaina temple-complex within the fort, built in sandstone. Fifteenth century.

221. Mutilated Jina on outer wall of the ruined Jaina buildings halfway between Bikaner and Lodurva.

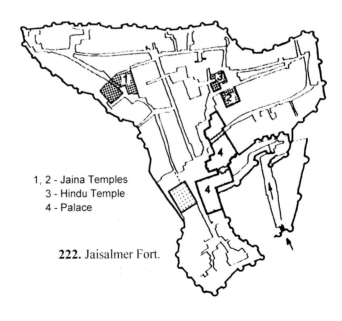

1, 2 - Jaina Temples
3 - Hindu Temple
4 - Palace

222. Jaisalmer Fort.

151

OSIAN

The Mahavira temple of Osian (also Osia or Osyan), located on the western edge of the town and a long way from the Hindu temple-hill, has found entry into about all the mayor books on Indian art and architecture. The same cannot be said, regrettably, of other, equally splendid Jaina temples. The easy access from Jodhpur by rail and road – a distance of fifty-two kilometres – may have something to do with it. The main reason for the scholars' attention to this shrine is, however, its significance as one of the very few still extant prototypes of a new and more elaborate temple-style that was to develop into such masterpieces as the Parshvanatha temples at Khajuraho, Sadri and Ranakpur.

The Mahavira temple at Osian was built, according to an inscription, in the last quarter of the eighth century, at a time prior to the bigger intrusions of Muslim forces, in the course of which many temples were reduced to rubble. Unfortunately, none of the original Jina statues of the Mahavira temple have come to light; also the tower above the sanctum is of a later time and style; the date given for this addition or restoration is 1016.

Though there are only a few Jaina families left in Osian, this well documented temple is still in active Shvetambara worship. "The Osian Mahavira temple," writes J.C. Harle on page 144 of his already cited book on Indian art, "is a thriving place of worship in contrast to the abandoned and sometimes misused temples just considered." A school, open to children of all religions, has been established and given shelter in a house built next to the temple.

223. Osian. Mahavira Temple, detail of temple façade. Eighth century, last quarter. Note the natural postures of the human figures.

152

224. Osian, part view of the Mahavira Mandir with the Hindu Temple-Hill in the background.

225. Student *pujaris*, Hindus by faith, practise for a religious ceremony scheduled for the following day in the famous Osian Mahavira Temple.

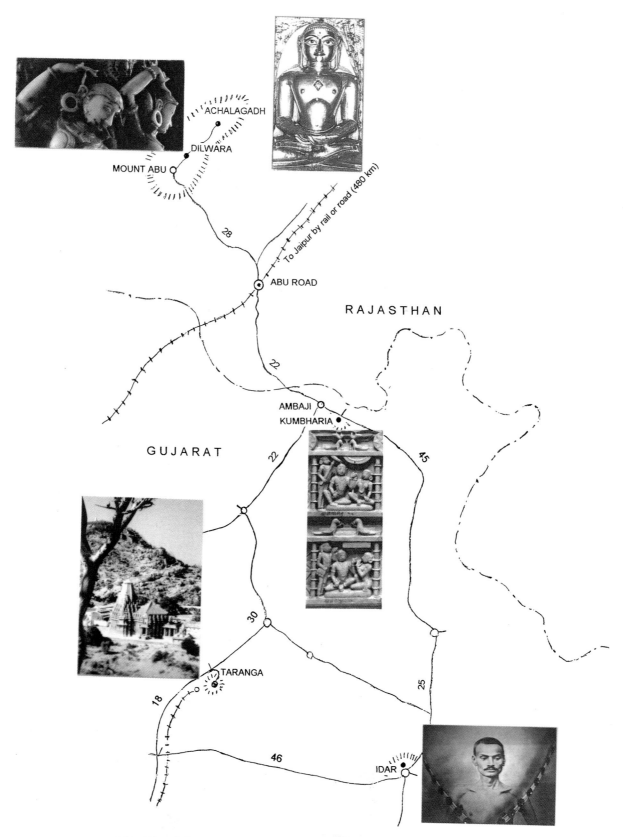

226. 'Grand Tour' of five sacred Jaina sites.

'Grand Tour'
of five Sacred Jaina Sites

This chapter is both a logical sequence of the previous one as well as an itinerary for travellers with limited time at their disposal, be they overseas Jainas on business or simply tourists. Those who follow the suggested tour will be amazed at what there is to be seen in so short a time and without having to sit in a vehicle for longer than a few hours at a time.

Starting from Abu Road, a town which can comfortably be reached from Delhi by fast night trains (but also by luxury buses from cities like Jaipur, Udaipur and Ahmedabad), the round tour devised here can be done very cheaply using public buses. For people pressed for time or travelling in a group, it is advisable to charter a jeep for the total tour. This can be done at Abu Road bus-station or up at Mount Abu town. Having a car at one's disposal means no waiting for buses and no hiring of short-distance transport at Dilwara, Ambaji and Idar.

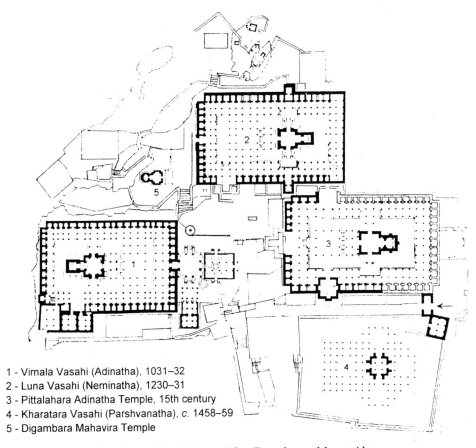

1 - Vimala Vasahi (Adinatha), 1031–32
2 - Luna Vasahi (Neminatha), 1230–31
3 - Pittalahara Adinatha Temple, 15th century
4 - Kharatara Vasahi (Parshvanatha), c. 1458–59
5 - Digambara Mahavira Temple

227. Plan of the Dilwara Jaina Temples on Mount Abu.

HOLY ABU

It was holy Abu, first visited in December 1968, and the sight of the giant statue of Bahubali at Shravanabelagola early in 1969 that awakened in me the desire to return some day in order to see and learn more about a religious force capable of inspiring the human mind to envisage such grandiose works of art.

At my first visit to Abu I was lucky enough to purchase one of the last copies of the 1954 English edition of the late Muni Jayantavijaya's *Holi Abu*, about the best guide to this famous mountain. "Once upon a time," to quote Muni Jayantavijaya, "the great Jaina monk Dharmaghosha Suri came upon Chandravati (the now devastated but once rich and famous city at the foot of Mount Abu; *the editor*) and at Vimala's request, decided to spend the rainy season in this lovely city. The day-to-day preaching of the monk led Vimala to introspection and deeply religious thoughts. Vimala ultimately requested the teacher to prescribe to him some act of atonement for the great sins of killing and such others committed in statecraft. The monk said that no *prayashitta* (rite for atonement of sins) was prescribed for sins committed knowingly and deliberately. However, since Vimala had sincerely repented for them and asked for atonement, the teacher advised him to undertake repairs at Abu, the holy place of pilgrimage. Vimala decided to follow the advice and undertook the great task."

Vimala, encouraged by his wife Shrimati, who was a devoted follower of the Jaina religion, aimed at something more lasting that what Muni Jayantavijaya wanted him to do. He decided to build a grand temple to Adinatha on Mount Abu near the village of Dilwara; and being an influential minister to the king of the Solanki empire, he disposed of all the needs necessary for such an ambitious task. The consecration ceremony of the finished temple, today known as Vimala-vasahi (*vashai* = temple), was performed in 1032. The 'Hall of Elephants' (*hasti-shala*) in front of the temple was added about hundred and thirty years later.

Two centuries after the construction of the Vimala temple, when the Solanki-dynasty was still reigning over Gujarat from the capital Patan, two ministers to king Bhima II, the brothers Vastupala and Tejahpala, erected a number of Jaina and Hindu temples of which the one at Dilwara on Mount Abu, known as Luna-vasahi or Tejahpala temple, is the most famous. It is stated that Tejahpala built this temple for the spiritual welfare of his wife and son.

In the central sanctum of Luna-vashai, a big seated Neminatha, sculptured in black basalt, was installed, the consecration of which took place in 1230. A mere eight decades later, in 1311, these first two Jaina shrines at Dilwara were badly damaged by Muslim raiders. "All images of the Tirthankaras," writes the author of *Holy Abu*, "were broken to pieces or badly mutilated and even the outer carvings

228. Luna-Vasahi Temple. Dedicated to Neminatha 1230/31. Light and cleanliness are two characteristic aspects of the Dilwara Jaina temples on Mount Abu.

of the main sanctum and their front halls did not escape destruction." Thus, before passing judgement on the artistic value of the Jina statues, it should be borne in mind that most of the Jinas worshipped in these and other temples are not the original ones but replacements made to order by the hand of non-Jaina sculptors at a time when the standard of the sculptural arts was on the decline.

Some ten years after the raid by Muslim invaders, a wealthy Jaina merchant by the name of Pethada led a group of pilgrims to the Dilwara temples and initiated extensive repairs to the Luna-vasahi shrine at his own cost; and since mutilated Jinas are not retained in Jaina temples, he installed a newly made image of Neminatha in place of the damaged one.

The date of erection of the Pittalahara temple, also known as the shrine of Bhima Saha, falls between 1316 and 1433 according to the author of *Holy Abu*. It was never

229. Luna-Vasahi, ornamental ceiling with pendant. White marble.

finished. Its attractions are the statues in both stone and metal, especially the image of Adinatha to whom the temple is dedicated.

The three temples of Dilwara so far mentioned are built of white marble. The *chaumukha or chatur-mukha* (four-faced) temple, placed outside the enclosure, consists of grey sandstone. Its probable year of completion is 1458/59.

230. Adinatha, cast in bronze; main image in the temple built by Bihma Shaha. A replacement of the original statue. It is a so-called *pancha-tirthi*, a sculpture showing five (*pancha*) Jinas with subsidiary figures.

158

231. Achalagadh, group of Jaina temples perched on a north-eastern ridge of Mount Abu.

ACHALAGADH

To behold the Jaina temples of Achalagadh – seven kilometres north-east of Dilwara, but still on Mount Abu – is an absorbing sight. Pilgrims who take advantage of taking a room in one of the two *dharmashalas* should not miss to greet the rising sun from the upper storey of the renowned Chaumukha shrine that has within its topmost sanctum four big Jina statues, three of Adinatha and one of Shantinatha.

In the Dilwara temples, it is the artistically and minutely wrought white marble that demands our attention and admiration; the Achalagadh shrines, in contrast, abound in works of art cast in metal. These statues range from the beautiful Jina images occupying the central sanctums to a variety of small-scale figures representing, in the shrine dedicated to Kunthunatha, a *samavasarana*: a mythical assembly arena due to be build by the gods whenever a Tirthankara is about to deliver his first sermon. Some of the bronzes are thought to be fairly old. Muni Jayantavijaya counted 173 Jina images in the Kunthunatha temple.*

Frequent buses run between Mount Abu town and Achalagadh.

* Another *samavasarana*, made of metal and thought to be about four hundred years old, is found in the Neminatha temple at the seaport town of Ghogha, 21 km from Bhavnagar in Gujarat.

KUMBHARIA.

The five temples at Kumbharia, three kilometres beyond the popular holy Hindu site of Ambaji and the second destination of our 'grand tour', are a delight to the pilgrim with a camera. A written permit to photograph is freely obtainable from the manager of the temples.

The first impression that awaits the visitor to Kumbharia is an air of tranquillity which pervades the extensive temple compound located a short way off the road. Some kind of blessing seems to have saved these five temples – the first was consecrated in 1061, the last in 1231 – from destruction at the hands of vandals, a fate that befell an unknown number of shrines which once dotted this area, then named Arasana. One source speaks of over three hundred Jaina temples of which nothing was left standing. It was here that the white marble required for building the temples on Mount Abu and other places was mined; it is still being excavated in great quantities.

An inscription in the Mahavira temple, the earliest of the five, reads: "On Monday, the 9th of the bright half of Phalguna, in Samvat 1118 (AD 1061) at a place known as Arasana, the image of Vira (Mahavira), to the memory of whom the place is sacred, was consecrated (...)." The other four temples are dedicated to Shantinatha, Parshvanatha, Neminatha and Sambhavanatha respectively. All are in active worship for the benefit of pilgrims; as many of them travel long distances, the management provides lodging and cooking facilities. The nearest town is Ambaji, about 2.5 kilometres to the west.

232. The figurative carvings at Kumbharia resemble those seen in the Dilwara temples, but the structural lines follow a sober angular design. The marble used is of a yellowish tone.

160

233. Kumbharia. Neminatha Temple, consecrated 1136.

"The next* Jaina temple of this style is the magnificent marble temple of Mahavira built in 1061 at Kumbharia, which has also four other Jaina temples.(...) The interior of the temple is exquisitely finished and excels even the Vimala temple at Abu in porportion and unity of conception."

Krishna Deva

"The Kumbharia (Mahavira) temple also contains in one of its ceilings long panels showing figures of the mother and father of each of the twenty-four Tirthankaras, all having inscribed labels giving their names.(...) The panels in the temple at Kumbharia are masterpieces of art in rendering miniature figures of gods, men, women, animals, trees, etc., in marble. Artists of this region in the eleventh and twelfth centuries were experts in the minute chiselling of soft marble." **

U. P. Shah

* Next in time to the Vimala-vasahi temple (1031-32) at Dilwara on Mt. Abu (the editor).

** *See* page 230. Both quotations from A. Gosh *Jaina Art and Architecture*. Vol. II, 302 and 307/8 respectively.

234. Idar, Digambara Jaina Temple raised on rugged ground high above the town.

IDAR

Idar is a pilgrim's centre for both Shvetambaras and Digambaras unlike Kumbharia which is exclusively Shvetambara. Its importance as a holy place (*tirtha*) is confined to being the birth-place of some outstanding acharyas and laymen of distinction. It attracts comparably few visitors, but this should change once Idar's attractions become better known.

The pilgrim who does not mind the physical exertion of a not too over-arduous ascent – part of the trail leads through the basements of the deserted royal castle half-way up the mountain – will, on reaching the end of the trail, be wonder-struck at the sight of two temples. The first one lies perched on a high bed of natural rock, the other partly hidden in a grove of trees and bushes, both watched over by rocky mountain peaks. A grand view, and once again the western traveller to holy Jaina places will be impressed by the Jainas' lucky hand when it comes to choosing a site for religious worship. Both temples, one Digambara the other Shvetambara, offer facilities for staying overnight.

Idar, having a sizeable Jaina community that bears witness to the town's long

162

235, 236. Idar, Shvetambara Shantinatha Temple on the hill. The text below, fastened to the wall near the [entrance, relates the history of the temple.

history as a stopping place on an ancient trade route, was for centuries the seat of a Digambara Bhattaraka. The *matha* still exists in a fair state of repair. There are libraries with important collections of illustrated old Jaina manuscripts. Scholars associated with the study of such documents are made welcome at Idar.

Up on the mountain, it is the meditative calmness and scenic setting of the two temples that captivate the pilgrim's mind and heart. In Idar town, at the foot of the mountainous range, it is the temples tucked away in tidy narrow streets which are worth a visit. The sacred images in these shrines have something about them

163

that seems to be peculiar to Idar – the liking for silver, for instance. Idar is another place yet to be discovered by students of Jaina art. It takes some asking to locate the various temples – five Shvetambara and three Digambara – but it is a rewarding pastime to walk the town's lanes and streets lined with small workshops specialising in handicrafts. With some luck one may be able to locate the person who has the key to Idar's famous Jaina library which is known by the name of Anandji-Mangalji-ni Pedhi-na Jnan Bhandara. Its most precious possession is a palm-leaf manuscript depicting thirty-four *Kalpa Sutra* miniatures ascribed to the last quarter of the fourteenth century.

237. Idar town . Altarpiece made of metal showing a seated Parshvanatha surrounded by two standing and twenty-two seated Jinas.

164

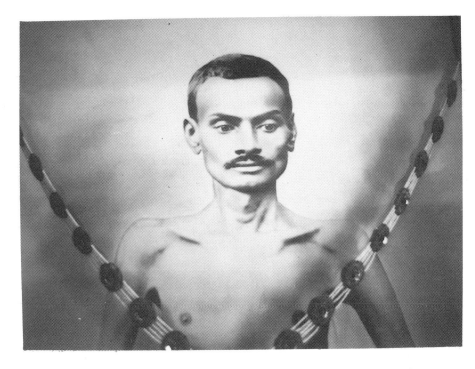

THE SHRIMAD RAJACHANDRA ASHRAM AT IDAR

In recent times an ashram in memory of Shrimad Rajachandra, alias Raychandbhai Metha, the teacher and friend of Gandhi, has been built on the crest of a rocky hill about nine kilometres west of Idar. Students of all ages, religions and nationalities who desire to make themselves acquainted with the teaching of this thinker and teacher, as yet little known in the west, are offered board and lodging.

Shrimad Rajachandra was a Sthanakavasi Jaina, which means that there is only a library hall for study and meditation in the ashram, no temple. "The spiritual climax of Rajachandra's life is regarded by his followers as having taken place on a hill out-side Idar, a small town in north Gujarat. There he practised intense austerities and preached to seven Shvetambara monks who had become his disciples (...)." (Dundas 1992: 226). Shrimad Rajachandra, author of some books, was born in 1867 in the small Gujarati port of Vavania. He died early in life in Rajkot in 1901. Considering his life and work as a spiritual teacher, one is inclined to call him a mystic. Many of his letters to friends and disciples have been collected and published.

*   *   *

HE WAS MY REFUGE:

> *I have tried to meet the heads of various faiths, and I must say that no one ever made on me the impression that* [Rajachandra] *did. His words went straight home to me. His intellect compelled as great a regard from me as his moral earnestness, and deep down in me was the conviction that he would never willingly lead me astray and would always confide to me his innermost thoughts. In my moments of spiritual crisis, therefore, he was my refuge.*

Mahatma Gandhi
(after Dundas 1992: 226)

TARANGA HILL

The photograph on the opposite page should suffice to show that there is more to see at Taranga than just another temple. Still, if it was only this one sacred edifice and the nearby Digambara shrine with the lofty *manastambha* in front of it, a much more tiresome journey than the one from Idar would be justified. Situated so close to Idar, Taranga Hill can be reached by car within a few hours; by public bus it takes somewhat longer. Once there, every moment spent at this jewel of a place means being in touch with what matters so much in one's life as a human being.

Buddhists seem to have been the first religious occupiers of Taranga Hill. An image was unearthed that was identified as a representation of the Mahayana Buddhist goddess Tara. From the worship of this idol the name of Taranga is likely to have been derived.

Later it was Digambara Jainas who settled on this isolated hill with it's three rocky peaks. Then at some time in the twelfth century, Kumarapala, the Solanki king residing at Patan, who was himself a Shvetambara Jaina, selected this site for the erection of an exceptionally beautiful temple in honour of Ajitanatha. Some years earlier he had a temple built to Adinatha on Mount Shatrunjaya near Palitana.

Built of light sandstone, the Taranga temple measures 45 metres in length by 30.4 metres in width and reaches up to a majestic height of 30.6 metres. In its plan and design it resembles the Neminatha temple on Mount Girnar and the above mentioned Adinatha temple on Shatrunjaya. The temple on Mount Girnar is lower in height and less ornate, and the Shatrunjaya Adinatha temple has lost some of its original features in the process of restoring damage caused by Muslim raiders. Thus, most visitors will agree with Harihar Singh, author of *Jaina Temples in Western India*, who named the Ajitanatha temple of Taranga (dedicated 1164) the "grandest and loftiest temple in Gujarat." The white marble statue of Ajitanatha in the main sanctum measures 2.75 metres in height.

During the last major renovation works the roofs and the stone carvings on the outer walls were cleared of thick layers of white paint, a praiseworthy undertaking. Recently a new block of comfortable guest-rooms has been added to the existing ones. Meals are served twice a day.

On the highest elevation of the three-peaked hill there stands a so-called *tonk*, a small building in the style of a Muslim grave. Built by Digambaras, it houses a marble statue of Mallinatha (ill. **241**), the nineteenth Tirthankara who the Shvetambaras believe to have been a woman. To accompany the *pujari* on his daily morning round up to this picturesque spot is a vigorous hike that opens beautiful bird's-eye views of the temples below.

239. Taranga Hill. Ajinatha Temple, dedicated 1164. Sandstone. Left of the big shrine
the Digambara temple complex. The *tonk* with the Mallinatha statue shown in illustration **241** is
visible in the background on the centre hill. More such tonks containing Jina images dot the
top of the rocky peak from which this photo was taken.

240. Taranga Hill. Interior of a temple outbuilding containing a sculptural model of *Nandishvara-dvipa*, that mythical island of fifty-two sanctuaries, thirteen in each of the four directions, where the gods gather whenever the birth of a Tirthankara is to be-celebrated. No humans live on that island.

241. Stele with Jina Mallinatha around which a domed chapel (*tonk*) has been built on the highest of Taranga's three peaks.

242. Plan of the Taranga Ajitnatha Temple.

168

243. Taranga Ajitanatha Temple; view of the tower from the
west. The balcony-like structures are not accessible from within, they are
ornamental devices.

RAJASTHAN

(continued)

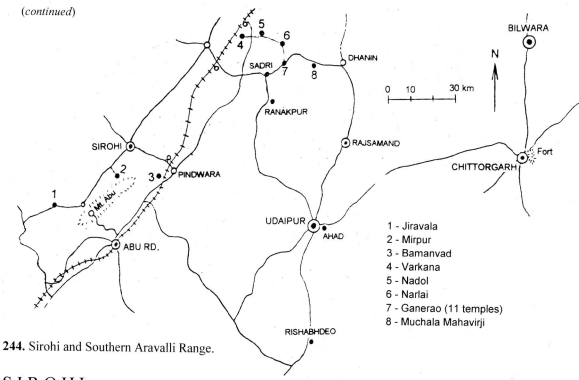

244. Sirohi and Southern Aravalli Range.

1 - Jiravala
2 - Mirpur
3 - Bamanvad
4 - Varkana
5 - Nadol
6 - Narlai
7 - Ganerao (11 temples)
8 - Muchala Mahavirji

SIROHI

With its two Jaina *dharmashalas* and a well-conducted bus station, Sirohi is a convenient stopover for travellers who are inclined towards discovering for themselves lesser known, but in no way inferior, holy Jaina sites in the vicinity of this ancient city that was founded in about the fourth century BC under the name of Shivapuri. From 1405 onward, after the devastation of Chandravati at the southeastern foot of Mount Abu by Muslim forces, it was the capital of Sirohi State, up to Independence in 1947 when it was incorporated into Rajasthan.

In Sirohi itself there are sixteen temples, all Shvetambara. The earliest of the thirty-four inscriptions discovered in these temples dates from 1167. But most of the shrines were built in

245. Sirohi. The new *dharmashala*, located next to a Hindu temple in the main bazaar street. The other, more secluded, Jaina *dharmashala* is found in a big traditional building close to the temples shown in ill. **246**.

170

the sixteenth/seventeenth century. The best known is the Parshvanatha temple. The partly deserted palace of the Sirohi royal family, towering above the old part of the town where most of the Jaina temples are situated, is closed to the public.

To illustrate the view of Sirohi being a suitable place for undertaking short excursions, there is, to start with, seven kilometres from Sirohi Road towards Abu Road a prominent hill with a large complex of temples called Bamanvad. It is sacred to Mahavira and a popular destination for Shvetambara pilgrims. The earliest inscription on this hill dates from 1292, but there are remains which are much older. An extensive re-renovation took place in 1979. Lord Mahavira's footprints are worshipped on top of the hill.

Jiravala Parshvantha, another temple connected with Sirohi by direct bus, is thought to be one of the oldest sacred Jaina sites in Rajasthan. Located on a mountain range near Revdar, sixty-five kilometres to the south-west of Sirohi, it is a rewarding place to visit. There are in that remote temple, installed in fifty-two small sub-shrines (*devakulikas*), 108 Parshvantha images, each bearing a different name, a peculiarity not found anywhere else in the country. The principal idol, also representing Parshvanatha but only eighteen centimetres in height, is believed to have been made of sand mixed with milk.

246 (*above*). View of Sirohi from the height of the old palace. All the towers and cupolas seen in the photo belong to Jaina temples. The lofty one in the centre is the 'four-faced' Parshvanatha Mandir.

171

MIRPUR

The architecturally most important building near Sirohi is the main temple of a group of four at Mirpur, also known by its former names of Hamipur or Hamiryadh. A bus-ride of about fifteen kilometres to the south-west, then a half-an-hour walk along a track leading towards the Abu mountain range, and the pilgrim will find himself transported into a world where nature reigns supreme. However, the "dense forest inhabited by bears, tigers and other animals of the jungle," mentioned by Jodh Singh Mehta in his book *Abu to Udaipur* (Delhi, 1970: 106), has all but disappeared and is no longer a threatening danger to pilgrims on foot. Centuries ago, Mirpur was the site of a fortified town inhabited mainly by Jaina traders. Little is known about it. Amazingly, four temples have been left standing whereas all the other buildings have vanished. The largest of the four is kept in active worship, thanks to the Seth Kalyanji temple managing body of Sirohi who also saw to it that rooms for pilgrims, a kitchen, and shelters for visiting ascetics were constructed round the remains of a garden-like courtyard.

Having taken a public bus from Sirohi and walked the last stretch on foot, we happened to reach the Mirpur temples on the day before the annual ceremony at which all the Jina images are re-anointed. Before we left later in the afternoon, we were asked to come again the next day and take part in the festivities and to taste of the food offered on such occasions. There would be music and dancing, we were told, and Acharya Gunaratna Suri and his monks would be present too. Needless to say, we gladly accepted the invitation. Everything we could wish for would be there: a medieval temple of great beauty, a monk of high standing, a large symbol of Mount Meru wrought in silver together with all the utensils we would be able to see used in their proper way by worshippers of a religion we had come to admire. Music and dance would add a crowning touch to it. In short, the unexpected chance was offered to us to see and hear what M. C. Joshi, in Vol. II of *Jaina Art and Architecture*, page 260, set forth in the following words (using the past tense): "The medieval Jaina shrine appears to have functioned as a centre of arts and hub of socio-cultural life intended to lead the commoner from falsehood to truth, from lower to higher truth and ultimately to the last goal of the life of a *shravaka*, that is *moksha.*"

247 (*above*). Two of Mirpur's four Jaina temples. The right one is the best preserved.

172

248. Mirpur. The *pujari,* a Hindu by faith, performs the ceremony during which a miniature Jina, allegorically placed on top of an image representing Mount Meru, is re-anointed. This rite is followed by reconsecrating all the other Jinas in the temple to the accompaniment of music and singing, and sometimes, as on that occasion, also dancing.

249. Whenever possible an acharya is invited to preside over an important ceremony; here it is Acharya Gunratna Suri (*Suri* is a Shvetambara honorific comparable to acharya).

250, 251. Mirpur. In the book entitled *Festivals, Fairs and Fasts of India* (Delhi, 1996), the chapter on Jaina festivities opens with the remark: 'Jaina festivals lack gaiety'. Unbiased guests at Jaina religious celebrations will go away with a different impression, as can be seen in the above two photos. *See* also chapter *Music and Dance in Jainism.*

252. Ceiling mural in the smallest of the four Mirpur shrines. It shows motifs rarely seen in Jaina temples.

174

CONCORD IS MERITORIOUS

His Sacred and Gracious Majesty the King does reverence to men of all sects, whether ascetics or householders, by gifts and various forms of reverence.

His Sacred Majesty, however, cares not so much for gifts or external reverence, as that there should be a growth of the essence of the matter in all sects. The growth of the essence of the matter assumes various forms, but the root of it is restraint of speech; to wit, a man must not do reverence to his own sect, or disparage that of another, without reason. Depreciation should be for specific reasons only, because the sects of other people all deserve reverence for some reason or another.

By thus acting a man exalts his own sect, and at the same time does service to the sects of other people. By acting contrariwise a man hurts his own sect, and does disservice to the sects of other people.(...) Concord is meritorious.

King Ashoka (*c.* 290–32 BC). Rock Edict XII.

Speaking ill of others;
praising oneself;
concealing the good qualities of others
and proclaiming in oneself good qualities
which one does not possess:
this causes influx of bad karma.

Speaking well of others and
praising their good qualities without
drawing attention to one's own virtues;
cultivating humility in company with others,
and to eschew pride in one's own achievements:
this causes influx of good karma.

Mahavira
Tatvartha Sutra, VI, 25, 26

SADRI

There is a direct daily bus that leaves Sirohi bus station in the morning and arrives at Ranakpur in the afternoon. From there it goes on to Udaipur. The last halt before reaching Ranakpur is Sadri. Readers of this guide are advised to alight at this pleasant township, ask their way to the nearby Shvetambara Jaina *dharmashala* and book a room there for a few days. Scattered throughout the picturesque vicinity of Sadri there are a number of holy sites worthy of being visited. The best known is the famous temple of Ranakpur, only nine kilometres to the south. Others are – to name just a few – Narlai (eleven temples); Nadol, an ancient place 'where once resounded every evening 999 bells indicating 999 temples' (today there are ten); the Varkana Parshvanatha temple built in 1154, and Muchala Mahavirji, a solitary temple set amidst hills twelve kilometres east of Sadri.

Sadri itself has fourteen Jaina temples, the earliest of which were built in the tenth/eleventh century. The latest, a so-called 'glass' temple, was constructed only recently.

253. Sadri, Parshvanatha Temple. Detail of south-eastern façade. Sculptural art of the best. *Circa* end of tenth century.

176

254 (*above*). Sadri, Parshvanatha Temple. Another section of the outer wall. Located in a residential street in the centre of the town, this small shrine is easily overlooked.

255. Close-up of a niche with a strikingly beautiful figure of a dancer.

RANAKPUR

The grandest of the Jaina temples built after 1300 is the Adinatha Vihara (*vihara* = temple) at Ranakpur. It covers an area of 3720 square metres and its twenty-nine halls are supported by 420 pillars, none of which are alike. Building began in 1389, and took fifty years to complete.

It was the fortunate constellation of four outstanding personalities to which we owe this marvel of a temple. First there was the Shvetambara Acharya Somasundara Suri, a great religious leader of his time. Close to him stood a young layman by the name Dharana Shah who was much devoted to the acharya and on his way of becoming minister to Rana (= king) Kumbha, being the third in the said constellation. Rana Kumbha, though not a Jaina by religion, looked favourably on Dharana Shah's plan for erecting a temple equal to the one he was shown in a dream. Eventually he, King Kumbha, was to give him the land needed to build the temple. Fourthly there was Depaka (or Depa), an unconventional architect whose imagination matched the visionary dream of Dharana Shah. The latter, by the way, took the vow of lifelong celibacy at the age of thirty-two, but being a minister to the king and committed to financing his ambitious project, he never became a monk. (> *page* 180)

256 (*above*). Ranakpur Adinatha Temple. Situated in the Aravalli Hills on the eastern bank of a small river, eighty-nine kilometres from Udaipur. There is a tourist bungalow close to the temple.

257. Ranakpur Adinatha Temple. View into one of the twenty-nine halls carried by carved pillars.

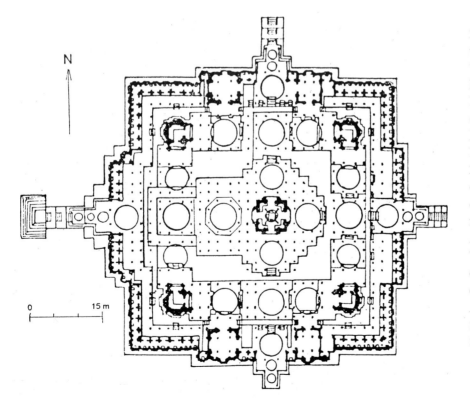

N

0   15 m

258. Plan of the Ranakpur Temple also known as Dharna Vihara (after Cousens). Likened to lotuses, the 29 halls can be compared to a cluster of this much adored Asian plant. The consecration ceremony was celebrated by Acharya Somasundara Suri in 1441.

259. With her eyes fixed on the Jina in the sanctum, a Shvetambara nun softly recites a prayer of devotion. The Ranakpur Vihara is more than an architectural feat. But it needs one's presence at an evening *puja* to get a glimpse of the religious aura that arises in this majestic shrine whenever – that is about every evening – pilgrims gather in the pillared hall before the sanctum in order to pay homage to the seated Jina by offering adoration, singing hymns and by finally waving lighted ghee wicks in front of the statue which for them represents the perfect teacher and *paramatma* ('supreme soul'). It is during this final act of worship that the inlaid eyes of the Tirthankara image – they being a Shvetambara peculiarity and regarded by many Westerners as an oddity – emit rays of light that bestow an appearance of life upon the face of the idol. At this stage the foreign guest will no longer be a mere onlooker but a welcome and wholeheartedly accepted participant in this moving rite.

260 (*below*). Seated Parshvanatha, main altar-piece in the Ranakpur Parshvanatha Temple.

Strange to say, this grandiose temple, though it remained largely spared by fanatic iconoclasts thanks to an order by the great Mughal emperor Akbar at the request of a Jaina monk, was left to decay in later centuries. There came a time when pilgrims no longer dared to visit the temple for fear of wild animals and dacoits. At long last, after the administration of the temple was handed over to the Anandji Kalyanji Trust, a thorough restoration, taking eleven years to complete, began in 1933.

Foreign visitors to Ranakpur should note that the so-called 'high priest' of the temple is not a Jaina but a Vishnuite Hindu. This extraordinary arrangement applies to almost all Shvetambara shrines. Regarding Ranakpur, the 'priestly' position is passed on from father to son, and this since fourteen generations within the same family.

At the beginning of the performance of a play at the court of princes in India in the Middle Ages, the reader used to step out upon the bare boards and relate to his audience what he saw about him in his mind's eye; his words then called to life corresponding images in their consciousness, and they served as decorations and wings. The public was credited with so much imagination that it was capable of retaining in its mind imaginary surroundings as an ever-present frame of reality. – Udaipur seems to me to have been created by similar evocations, to be real in the same sense. Udaipur seems so improbable in its beauty that I stand in the midst of it, look at it and enjoy it as if in a dream.

Count Hermann Keyserling (1880-1946)
Indian Travel Diary of a Philosopher, Bombay, 1969.

UDAIPUR

Udaipur, so named after Udai Singh who founded the present city in 1572 – Chittorgarh had fallen to the Mughals five years earlier – has animated the romantic trait of many a foreign traveller to the present day. The above cited Hermann Keyserling, a well known German philosopher, began his journey round the globe from west to east with Ceylon and India in 1911. At that time Jainism was well on the way of recovering from a long period of decline, Ranakpur, however, was still in a neglected state. One wonders what Keyserling might have noted down in his *Travel Diary* if someone had urged him to go and see that grandiose building – as well as the four ancient Jaina temples at Ahad, three kilometres east of Udaipur's Delhi Gate. Still, since its foundation Udaipur has been and still is, though largely unnoticed by foreign visitors, a city with a large and active Jaina community in which all denominations are represented. There are close to forty Jaina temples in the city, about all of which are in active worship.

The Shitalanatha Shvetambara Mandir, sacred to the tenth Tirthankara and located close to the Clock Tower in the heart of the city, is said to have been founded on the very day and year as the Royal Palace. Construction of he nearby Jagdish Hindu temple began about sixty years later. The 'glass' temple, as the Shitalanatha Mandir is usually called, is much larger than its position in a narrow street does suggest; it has a library and two big rooms for Jaina ascetics. Westerners interested in the Jaina religion should not hesitate to inquire – in this or any other temple – whether there is a monk or nun in temporary residence and if it would be all right to call on him or her.

On the opposite side of the same street, called Bada Bazar, a short distance hence, there are some more Jaina temples. Located near Bandor House in a lane deviating from the Clock Tower to the south, there is an old Digambara Adinatha temple which has an exact replica of Sammeta Shikhara carved in marble at the scale of one inch to one hundred feet; a unique piece not to be found elsewhere in India

Behind the Chetak Cinema in the vicinity of Chetak Circle, a major landmark of

Udaipur, there is found, set in a quiet garden, a big Shvetambara temple named Sethi ki Badi Mandir the front wall of which is adorned with murals typical of this city. Another Jaina temple worth visiting is known by the name of Chougan ka Mandir, situated on the road from Chetak Circle to Swaroop Lake. The special attraction of this temple is the marble statue of a seated Jina (ill. **263**) which is worshipped as the first Tirthankara of the next time cycle. There are two more temples within the same compound, dedicated to Shantinatha and Mahavira respectively, as well as a secondary school, a club, a Jaina *bhojan-shala* (kitchen and eating-hall), and the Shri Vijaya Shanti Shiksa Bhavan.

The road from the Dehli Gate to Ahad (also Ahar), the site of four ancient Jaina temples, passes through Ashok Nagar. In Road No. 10 of this suburb there is a Digambara temple in which super-size enlargements of coloured photographs depicting Jaina holy places are on permanent display (some of them are by the present author). As the local taxi and rickshaw drivers do not seem to be well conversant with the locations of Udaipur's Jaina temples, it is advisable to ask for a guide at the Shvetambara *dharmashala* in Hathipol Road or at the Digambara *dharmashala* nearby.

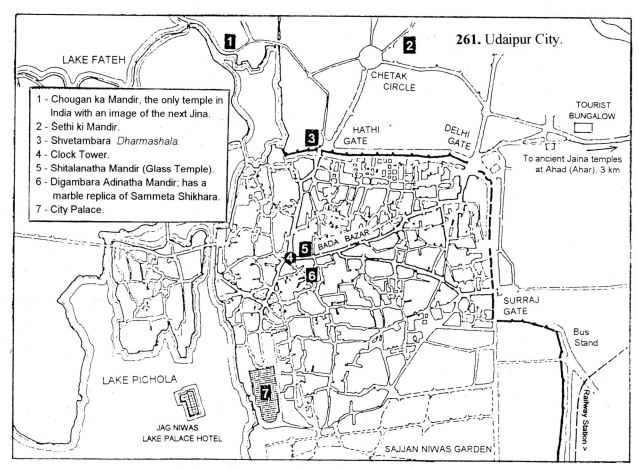

261. Udaipur City.

1 - Chougan ka Mandir, the only temple in India with an image of the next Jina.
2 - Ṣethi ki Mandir.
3 - Shvetambara *Dharmashala*.
4 - Clock Tower.
5 - Shitalanatha Mandir (Glass Temple).
6 - Digambara Adinatha Mandir; has a marble replica of Sammeta Shikhara.
7 - City Palace.

262. View of Udaipur with City Palace, seen from across Pichola Lake.

263. Chougan Mandir, Udaipur. Image of the future Tirthankara named Padma Nabh Prabhu; mid eighteenth century. He will be, it is believed, the next incarnation of the soul of Shrenika who was the ruler of Rajgir at the time of Mahavira. His birth is due in the third phase of the next half-cycle of time, which will be an upward swing. No other Jaina temple is known with an image of the next Tirthankara. (To the Buddhists, king Shrenika is known under the name of Bimbisara who, later in his life, was imprisoned by his son.)

183

RISHABHDEO MANDIR

264, 265. Two views of Rishabhdeo Mandir. Situated sixty-five kilometres from Udaipur on the road to Ahmedabad, it is one of the most popular Jaina temples in Rajasthan. Since it is claimed as a place of worship not only by Jainas (predominately Shvetambara) but also by Hindus and especially by Bhils, who visit the temple in great numbers, it stands under the jurisdiction of the State of Rajasthan. This explains the armed guards. Tradition has it, that on some remote day it was a Bhil who, guided by a dream, discovered a black stone-image of Rishabha hidden in a tree. Eventually it came to be installed and consequently worshipped in this temple. The dark-skinned Bhils continue to see in the black coloured statue an idol that has always belonged to them, whereas the Jainas date the image back to the time of Rama and Sita. For some time it was installed in a temple at Ujjain.

Vowing to undertake a pilgrimage to Rishabhdeo and to actually embark on it, is seen by the Bhils and other pilgrims as a way of getting one's wishes fulfilled.

Non-stop buses for this popular site leave Udaipur Bus Station about every hour.

184

CHITTORGARH

266. Nothing will be said here about the many battles and the bloodshed associated with Chittorgargh Fort. In the end, after more than a thousand years, this abruptly rising plateau remotely shaped like a whale when seen from the air, has found peace. Thus, a photograph emanating today's peaceful atmosphere of the Fort has been chosen to head this chapter. It shows the Kirti Stambha or 'Tower of Fame' that was built in the twelfth century by a Digambara merchant named Jija and dedicated to Adinatha. Erected on about the highest elevation of the plateau and rather removed from other buildings, it rises to a height of 22.8 metres; the Mahavira Temple next to it is of a later date. Some centuries after, in 1440, Rana Kumbha, probably inspired by the Jaina 'Tower of Fame', ordered the building of his famous 'Tower of Victory'. Which of the two towers is architecturally the more elegant, is an open question; some experts favour the Jaina Kirthi Stambha.

Each of the seven storeys of the 'Tower of Fame' is differently moulded and carved. A winding staircase leads up to the top pavilion; however, the original statue of the first Tirthankara for which it was designed is missing. Both the Kirthi Stambha and the Mahavira Temple beside it, which is thought to have been built in the thirteenth century and restored in recent times, stand under the jurisdiction of the Archaeological Survey of India.

You cannot save the world, but you can cultivate your garden, which the Jainas know to be the soul.

Michael Tobias

267. Chittorgarh Fort. One of the profusely sculptured Shvetambara temples of the Satbis Deora group. In the rear the Museum.

268. Map of Chittorgarh Fort. Length 5.6 km, elevation above city 153 m.

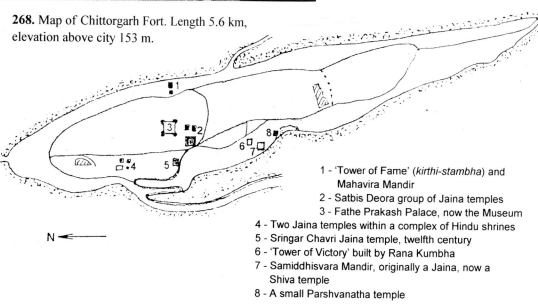

N ←

1 - 'Tower of Fame' (*kirthi-stambha*) and Mahavira Mandir
2 - Satbis Deora group of Jaina temples
3 - Fathe Prakash Palace, now the Museum
4 - Two Jaina temples within a complex of Hindu shrines
5 - Sringar Chavri Jaina temple, twelfth century
6 - 'Tower of Victory' built by Rana Kumbha
7 - Samiddhisvara Mandir, originally a Jaina, now a Shiva temple
8 - A small Parshvanatha temple

186

GUJARAT

Three of Gujarat's sacred Jaina sites – Kumbharia, Idar and Taranga – have already been featured in the 'Grand Tour' chapter (p. 154). Of the many other places only a few can be mentioned here.

Gujarat – Gandhi – Jainism: three names that form a kind of 'trinity' in the minds of many Indians and non-Indians. Carlos G. Valles, S.J., a Spaniard by birth and a Gujarati by choice, writes in his *Sketches of God,* written and published in Gujarat (1987), page 140: "Gandhiji hailed from Gujarat, and in this state (which is mine) Jain influence is particularly felt because, due to historical reasons, most of the Jains in India live here*, and, though in numbers they are a very small minority, their presence is felt in their faith, their prestige and their zeal. It was through these channels that Gandhiji learned from Jainism the doctrine of non-violence; with it he obtained India's independence through peaceful means. The greatest historic deed of our times, a country becoming independent without a war of independence, drew its basic inspiration from Jainism."

* Naming Gujarat as the state with the most Jainas is quite common among both Indians and non-Indians. However, it is Maharashtra which has the highest number of Jainas, about twice as many as Gujarat, which, after Rajasthan, takes third place. For distribution of Jainas in India, *see* appendix. *The editor.*

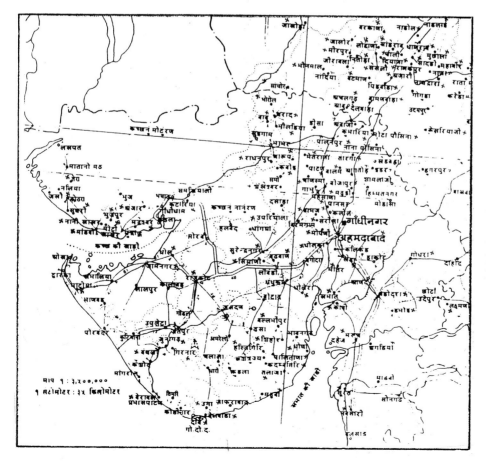

269. Detail of a map of India in Hindi showing the State of Gujarat. Each swastika denotes a temple or religious site sacred to Jainas, in the case of Gujarat mostly to Shvetambaras. (Courtesy T. T. Maps & Publications Ltd., Madras.)

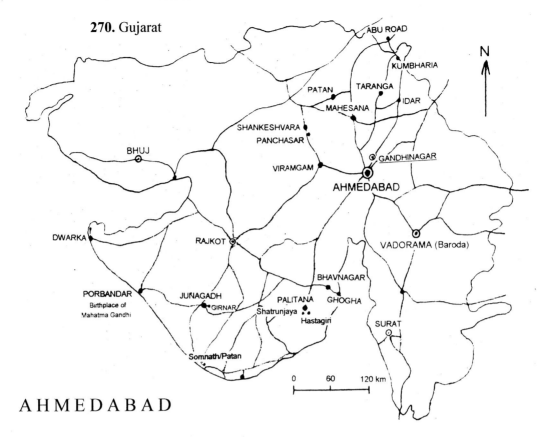

270. Gujarat

AHMEDABAD

Though founded by a Muslim, Sultan Ahmad Shah, in 1411, Ahmedabad has more Jaina temples than mosques within its historic city wall. Astonishingly, a guide published by the *Archaeological Survey of India* (2nd ed. 1992), entitled AHMADABAD, does not mention a single Jaina monument. A Parshvanatha temple which was built by Shantidas Jhaveri, a wealthy Jaina merchant of Ahmedabad, was confiscated by Aurangzeb, then governor of Gujarat, in 1645 and turned into a mosque. Later, by order of emperor Shah Jahan, the father of Aurangzep, the temple was given back to Shantidas Jhaveri. However, because of the desecration and rebuilding, it could not be used again as a Jaina shrine.

A frequent sight in the narrow streets of Ahmedabad's inner city are small pavilions placed on pillars and mostly built of wood. Many of them are artistically modelled and carved. They are Jaina 'inventions' meant for feeding birds and simply called *parabadis* (pigeon-houses). Another peculiarity, found in Ahmedabad's Jaina temples, are large underground chambers designed for worship.

To undertake a pilgrimage to Sammeta Shikhara, that most sacred mountain in far away Bihar, is – and especially was before the age of modern transportation – beyond the means of many Gujarati Jainas. To alleviate this handicap, Jaina laymen erected a fitting substitute: a temple that has in its centre a huge replica of the holy mountain. Known as Sammetshikara temple, it has become a popular sight; also for tourists.

188

271. Ahmedabad. Karnavati Tirtha, so named by the local Jainas; but because of its location in the Hatheesing Vadi (*vadi* = suburb), outside the Delhi Gate, it is called Hatheesing Jaina Temple, especially in guides and maps. With its two storeys, fifty-two *devakulikas* and several underground chambers it is the largest Jaina temple in the city. It is sacred to Dharmavanatha, the 15th Tirthankara. Building began in the second quarter of the nineteenth century by Sheth Hatheesing, a Jaina layman; when he died, his wife Harakunvar spend a huge amount of money to have the temple completed. The festive inauguration, lasting for twenty-one days, took place in 1848.

It is not easily located. A knowledgeable rikshaw-driver is required; hiring a taxi would not be a good choice, because of the narrow lanes. Once there, more Jaina temples can be discoverd on foot in this area.

272. Portico of the Hatheesing Temple. Detail of the lower façade seen from the east. Sandstone.

189

I found the Jains to be such warm, welcoming, and fundamentally well-adjusted and happy people that I felt that I had to pursue the religious roots of their obvious wellbeing.

John E. Cort (1989: 4)

PATAN

The study and the translation of Jaina scriptures by western scholars has a history of almost two hundred years. Understandably, this long preoccupation with written words led to a dry and unexciting, even grim picture of Jainism; a portrait that is still perpetuated by editors of books on the world's religions as well as by writers of tourist guides. For those of us who are not happy with this harsh evaluation, it is a welcome change to chance upon a personal observation like the one in the above prefix made by a member of a new generation of scholars. At long last, prolonged fieldwork is to become an important part in the study of this widely undervalued religion. The 'happy people', referred to by John E. Cort in his published Ph. D. dissertation, are the Jainas of Patan, North Gujarat.

The best known Indian of our time, Mahatma Gandhi, was a Gujarati by birth. As to the rulers of Gujarat, they were mostly Rajputs from neighbouring regions and, after the founding of Ahmedabad, Muslim sultans of foreign descent. Long before that, from around 300 BC, Gujarat was part of the Maurya empire whose capital was Pataliputra (now Patna in Bihar). A list of fourteen edicts, cut into a boulder near Junagadh at the order of Ashoka, the last great king of the Maurya dynasty, can be taken as a testimony of the presence of both Buddhism and Jainism in Gujarat during that remote time.

Still further back, there lived in Gujarat the legendary Shri Krishna as well as Neminatha, the twenty-second Jaina Tirthankara. The two, it is believed, were related to each other, but both were born outside Gujarat. Still, it can truly be said that Gujarat has produced great personalities in the realms of intellectualism, spiritual learnedness and asceticism, and it attracted, which is equally noteworthy, rulers who were prepared not merely to tolerate men of learning and ethical stead-fastness, but to have them in their courts as counsellors.

One such ruler, king Jayasimha Siddaraja of the Solanki (also Chaulukya) dynasty, who reigned from 1094–1143, had the famous Jaina writer-monk Hema-chandra (1088–72) in his court, though he himself was a worshipper of Shiva. Under Kumarapala, Siddaraja's immediate successor, who ruled for thirty-two years (until 1175) and who retained the counsel of Hemachandra, many Jaina temples were erected, at places like Shatrunjaya, Girnar, Taranga Hill, Kumbharia and Mt. Abu.

The capital of the Solanki kings was Anahilvad Patan, now simply Patan, then ranked as one of the finests cities on the Indian subcontinent (there is another Patan near Somnath in the south). Of the royal glory, architecturally, little has survived. But the Jainas of Patan (then made up of both Shvetambaras and Digambaras, but since the mid-twelfth century only of Shvetambaras), have managed to survive all vicissitudes in good numbers. The last exodus, a voluntary one, started after Independence when many Jainas of Patan and other places in Gujarat decided to settle in Bombay. About all of these migrants seem to have retained their religion and language. In his book *Liberation and Wellbeing: a Study of the Svetambar Murtipujak Jains of North Gujarat* (*see* bibliography) John E. Cort lists a number of Jaina religious, social and charitable institutions found in present-day Patan, some of them having a long history behind them.

On the way to Patan, Mahesena, a city 93 km north of Ahmedabad, offers itself as a place of sojourn. Before entering this city, the motorized traveller from Ahmedabad is greeted by a new temple built in traditional style and situated in an elevated position. The Jina in its sanctum measures 3.68 metres in height. Within Mahesena city there are fourteen Jaina shrines, and among them, located in the main market-place, an old temple sacred to Parshvanatha.

273. Patan (the figures were prepared by Arthur Duff; courtesy John E. Cort).

274. Area around Panchasar Temple.

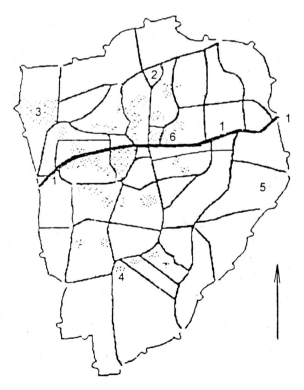

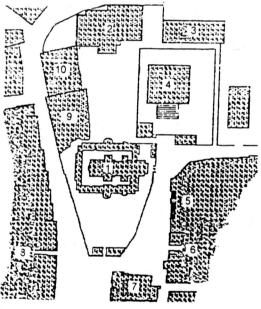

Shaded Areas = Traditional Jaina Neighbourhoods
1 - Main Bazaar
2 - Panchasar Complex
3 - Salvi Vado
4 - Rajka Vado
5 - Samalji Parshvanatha Temple
6 - Sagar Upashray

1 - Panchasar Parshvanatha Temple
2 - Temple Complex comprising five Shrines
3 - Panchasar Dharrmashala
4 - Hemachandra Institute and Library
5 - Quarters reserved for Monks
6 - Astapad Dharmashala and Temple
7 - Quarters reserved for Nuns
8 - Dharmashala and Parshvanatha Temple
9 - Vardhman Tap Ayambilshala
10 - Upashray and Manibhadra Vir Shrine

191

275. Patan, Panchasar Parshvanatha Temple. Rebuilt in the sixteenth/seventeenth century, after
it was devastated by Muslim invaders. According to *Shree 108 Jain Tirth Darshanawali,* a recent book
in Gujarati with short English translations, "There are 84 big temples and 134 shrines
in 55 streets" in Patan.

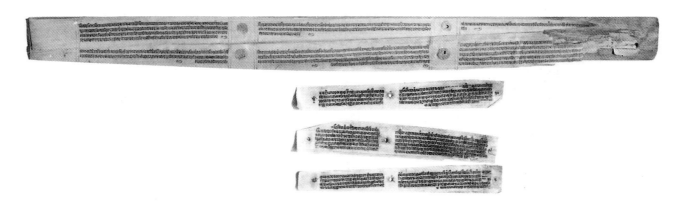

276. Hemachandra Institute and Library, Patan.
Palm-leaf manuscripts, selected for preservative measures.

192

277. Patan. The presiding Jina in the Panchasar Parshvanatha Temple. Clad like a king for the occasion of an important festival. White marble; height *c.* 1.2 m.

278. Portrait of Acharya Hemachandra (1088–1172) in the ante-room of the Institute named after him. Hemachandra, author of many learned works, was credited with the epithet 'Omniscient One of the Kali Yuga'. He was not a recluse but a respected adviser to two successive Patan kings. One of his literary compositions, entitled *Yoga-shastra*, which can be called a 'Treatise of Behaviour', he specifically directed at Kumarapala, the second ruler he served. His aim was to convince the young king of the beneficiary tenets of Jaina life. He largely succeeded. Under the reign of Kumarapala, Gujarat came close to being an exemplary Jaina kingdom. Seen from this angle, it looks plausible that a man like Mahatma Gandhi was born in this state centuries later.

279. Parshvanatha Shankesvara Temple. Part view.

SHANKESHVARA

Shankeshvara (*see* map ill. **270**) is a historic Jaina site comprising an old temple within a fortified enclosure, some new to very new temples, about a dozen *dharmashalas,* a bus stand, and one long street lined with shops. Usually called Parshvanath Shankeshvar, it is the most popular place of pilgrimage next to Palitana in Gujarat. It is the marble image of a seated Parshvanatha in the sanctum of the old temple that the pilgrims desire to see. Worshipping this statue in the proper frame of mind is believed to dissipate one's miseries.

Little is known about the early history of this locality as a holy Jaina *tirtha.* Popular belief dates the beginning back to Shri Krishna's time, when, it is thought, a layman named Ashadhi installed Jina idols in three places named in old records as Charoopa, Stambhapura and Shankesvara. In 1098, during the time of the Patan king Jayasimaha (mentioned above, p. 190), the state's minister-in-chief had the fort and the temple repaired. Early in the fourteenth century, Shankeshvara, like many other places in Western India, was raided and badly damaged by soldiers of the Delhi Sultan 'Alau-u'd-Din Khilji, but the statue of Parshvanatha was rescued and kept hidden. Rebuilding began in the seventeenth century under the Mughal emperors.

194

*O lord of peaks Shatrunjaya! How can even wise people describe in brief your
qualities? Due to the influence of this* tirtha, *there is auspicious mental modifica-
tion of men who come on pilgrimage. A pious man eliminates sin by placing on his
limbs dust from the carts and the feet of the horses, camels and men in a congregation who go on pilgrimage to you. (...) O you whose glory is praised by Indra!
You should be praised, O land of perfection with mind, speech, and body.*

From a fourteenth century *Guidebook to various Pilgrimage Places*
by Muni Jinaprabhasuri. Translated by John E. Cort.*

MOUNT SHATRUNJAYA

Lamenting over misfortunes, be they of personal or of general nature, is not to the
liking of believers in Jainism. Laments like those of Job or Jeremiah in the Jewish
Bible are not found in the Jaina canon. After the temples on the summit of Shatrunjaya were sacked by Turkish Muslims in 1311 – Muni Jinaprabhasuri, the author of
the above quotation, was then in his fiftieth year – the first reaction by leading Jainas
was not the thought of revenge but of how to repair the damage and to replace
the desecrated images. True to this determination, rebuilding began within two years;
but most of what one sees on Shatrunjaya today is of a much later date.

From the outside the 'new' Shatrunjaya – the hill 'which conquers enemies' –
looks like a fortress yet apparently there never was a garrison to defend it. (With
'enemies' our vices are meant that cause bad karma.)

Climbing the 3750 steps on a bright early
morning during the winter months of November
to March is in itself already an experience that
remains in one's memory. Articles of leather or
fur must be left behind or deposited at the
appropriate places near the entrance. Owners of
cameras should inquire whether a written permit
to photograph is still required, and if so where it
may be obtained (*see* appendix).

For the Shvetambara Jainas Shatrunjaya is the
earliest and, next to Sammeta Shikhara in Bihar,
the most sacred mountain. Traditionally it was
Adinatha or Rishabhanatha, the first Tirthankara
of our age, who is said to have sanctified the hill

280. Shatrunjaya. Pilgrims are expected to bath and don clean
garments before paying homage to the image of Adinatha in
the holy of holies. Here it is a newly married couple.

* In *The Clever Adulteress*, edited by Phyllis Granhoff. Delhi, 1993: 251.

195

by visiting it to deliver his first sermon. However, it was not Rishabha, as sometimes stated, who died and attained salvation on Shatrunjaya but his grandson Pundarika; thus Shatrunjaya is also called Pundarikagiri.

Bharata, the father of Pundarika and half-brother of Bahubali, is likewise credited with having frequented Shatrunjaya and established a *tirtha* about nine kilometres south of Palitana. There, on a hill near the river, a new complex of five temples is nearing completion bearing the name Hastagiri, meaning 'elephant hill'. Tradition has it that at this spot Bharata and his elephant obtained release from *samsara*, the cycle of perpetual rebirth.

Palitana is the name of the township which has, in close proximity, both a bus and a railway station. From here horse-drawn tongas take the visitor through the town and then along a straight road to the Jay Taleti Mandir at the foot of Shatrunjaya. The last mile of this long road is lined with *dharmashalas,* temples, a museum and houses for monks and nuns respectively. In 1656 the Mughal governor of Gujarat, a Muslim, gave custody of Palitana to the Jaina merchant Shantidas Jhaveri.

For pilgrims swift of foot there are three circumambulatory routes. The shortest leads round the temples along the outer wall; the other follows the foot of the mountain. The third, about forty kilometres long, frequents en route five temple sites where pilgrims may stay overnight before continuing their holy walk. The major event of the year takes place on the day of the full moon in the month of Phalgun (Feb./March) when some ten thousands of pilgrims circumambulate Shatrunjaya hill, the 'Lord of Peaks'.

281. Shatrunjaya. Large panel showing a seated Tirthankara surrounded by a multitude of smaller Jinas. It symbolizes a holy mountain. At the top left a *samavasarana;* on the opposite side a diagram depicting the Jaina cosmos in form of a human figure (*loka-purusha*).

196

282. Part view of Shatrunjaya. Top right the Adishwara Temple, the main shrine of the '180 large temples and 872 small shrines.' These two figures, as any others found in publications, should not be taken at face value. There are no standard criteria for describing a temple as big or small.

283. Site plan of Shatrunjaya.

1 - Main Temple of Adishwara (Adinatha)
2 - Sammeta Shikhara Temple
3 - Bahubali and Bharata Temple
4 - Pundarika Temple
5 - Shet Motishaw Tonk
6 - Balabhai Tonk
7 - Chaumukha Temple
8 - Shantinatha Temple

Kund = water tank

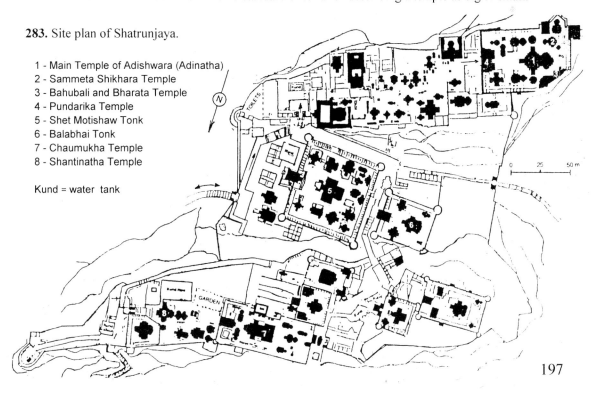

197

GIRNAR

284 a. Plan of the Neminatha Temple, built in *c.* 1128. The surrounding *devakulikas* were added later. The walled enclosure measures 139 metres in length by 58 metres in width. The Neminatha image in the sanctum is of polished black basalt. A special feature of this temple is a panel of 108 well-carved footprints.

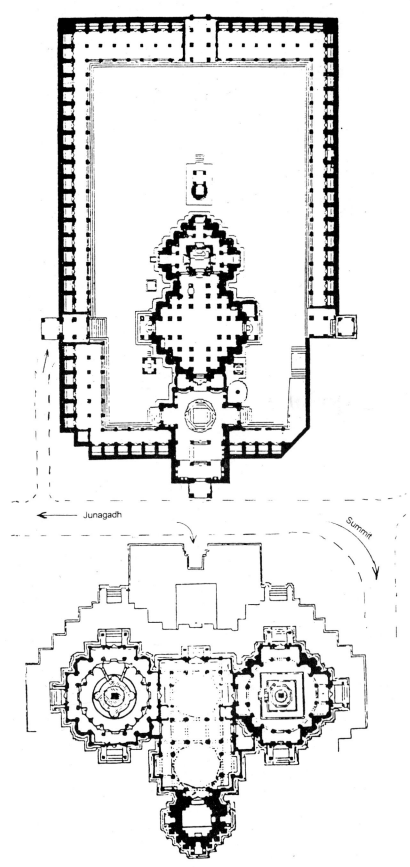

← Junagadh

Summit

284 b. Plan of the three-shrined Vastupala Temple (1231), so named after its builder who was chief minisiter for Gujarat at that time. According to an inscription, Vastupala built one of the shrines, the one dedicated to Adinatha, for his own good, the second one 'for the good of his dutiful and illustrious wife Lalita Devi', and the third sanctum 'for the good of another illustrious wife', Sokhu Devi by name.

285. Mount Girnar, about six kilometres east of Junagadh, is a gigantic five-peaked rock formation of volcanic origin, rising steeply on all sites to a height of 1117 m above sea level. As to the famous sixteen Girnar Jaina temples, it is the fact that they do not crown the top of one of the peaks (all five summits belong to the Hindus) but are located on a protruding ledge about half-way up the western flank of the mountain which makes them one of most beautifully situated groups of temples in India.

At this height of the ascent – after the four thousandth step – the now level track passes through the extensive temple compound, but the high walls on both sides disclose nothing of the architectural richness behind them. It is only when looking back from the next elevation that the perfect layout and splendour of the temples is revealed to the beholder.

The main temple, built in 1128 of black granite, is dedicated to Neminatha, the twenty-second Tirthankara. Being of royal descent, as all the twenty-four Tirthankaras were, Arishtanemi (Neminatha's given name) had become disgusted with the cruel customs of his time when he saw – it happened on the way to his marriage to a daughter of the king of Dwarka – hundreds of fenced-in animals condemned to be slaughtered for the guests at his wedding. Sensing his involvement in these unjust doings, he discarded all his regalia and walked away. At Girnar, in the 'Thousand Mango Grove' half-way up the mountain, he pulled out his hair and took up the life of a Jaina monk. His bride followed his example and became a nun. Again it was on this mountain that he reached the highest state of enlightenment, and finally attained liberation.

To go on pilgrimage to a place credited with such sacred history is considered very meritorious; still more to build a temple at such a site. This explains the great number of buildings at places like Shatrunjaya and Girnar. Some of the Girnar temples are not accessible, due to their bad state of repair.

199

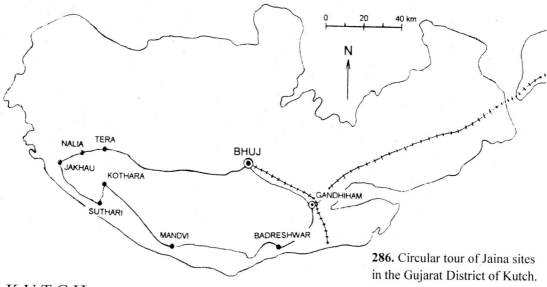

286. Circular tour of Jaina sites in the Gujarat District of Kutch.

KUTCH

"The off-the-beaten track semi-island of Kutch is a region where age-old customs have only recently been touched by modern civilization. The gates of the walled city of Bhuj – now connected by rail, road and air with the mainland – used to be locked from dusk to dawn until very recent times."

Such meagre information, cited from a publication for tourists, is about all the foreign tourist will find in his travel guide under the heading of Kutch, the western-most district of Gujarat. That means that only a few feel tempted to go and see for themselves what this remote corner of India has to offer.

For those who do go, it will be a surprise to learn that the district of Kutch, having a population of about 1.3 million, is the one with the highest density of Jainas of all the districts within the Indian Union. According to Vilas A. Sangave's *Jaina society through the Ages* (Delhi 1992: 31) the percentage of Jainas of the total population of the district of Kutch was 6.72; for India as a whole 0.48 per cent (1971 census).

The map above shows the locations of some major Jaina pilgrimage centres of Kutch. Some of the sites have a long Jaina history; but the present temples date, with a few exceptions, from the nineteenth and twentieth century. The temple of Bhad-reshwar, situated close to the sea, is such an exception. It was built or rebuilt in the middle of the thirteenth century by a so-called 'merchant prince' by the name of Sheth Jagdusha who was a great philanthropist. Since that time nine major renovations have been carried out in the process of which the fifty-two *devaculikas* have been added, yet the plan of the main shrine has remained unchanged (ill. **288**).

Mandavi, the main port of Kutch, has seven Jaina temples as well as some libraries containing valuable manuscripts. The Suthari Parshvanatha temple, set in the heart of Suthari town, the next centre of the pilgrimage circuit, is an imposing two-storeyed building richly embellished both inside and out. Devi Padmavati is one of the divinities worshipped in this temple.

The Jaina shrine at Kothara, occasionally described as a 'skyscrapper' temple, rises to a height of seventy-four feet (22.5 m). When approaching Jakhau, the following destination of the Kutch Jaina circuit, the visitor is taken unawares by the sight of a majestic complex of nine temples. Of the Jina images enshrined in these temples, 126 are made of stone, eighty of metal, two of quartz and one of gold. At Jakhau the road turns east, and soon the city of Naliya comes into view where the visitor is welcomed by a three-in-one temple, a spacious building lavishly decorated with gilded carvings and mosaics made of coloured glass. A special feature of this temple, dedicated to Jina Chandraprabha, is a display of 138 *siddha-chakras* (saint-wheels) 132 of which are made of silver, four of other metals and two of sandalwood. Next comes Tera, a town with two Jaina temples. One was built in 1858; the construction of the other goes back about three hundred years. Finally there is Bhuj, the capital of Kutch, where there are three Jaina temples, all built in the nineteenth century.

287, 288. Bhadreshwar Mahavira Temple, plan and general view. A booklet containing detailed information is available at the office. For pilgrims accommodation is provided.

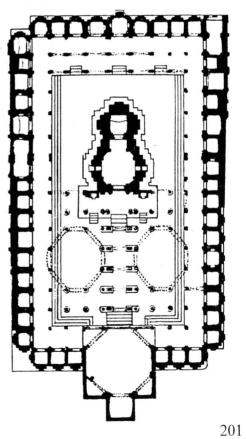

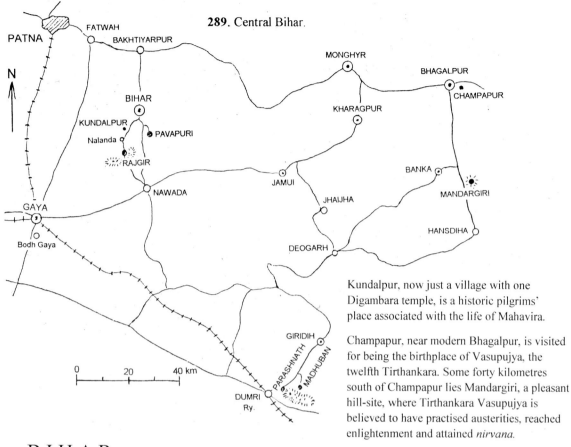

289. Central Bihar.

Kundalpur, now just a village with one Digambara temple, is a historic pilgrims' place associated with the life of Mahavira.

Champapur, near modern Bhagalpur, is visited for being the birthplace of Vasupujya, the twelfth Tirthankara. Some forty kilometres south of Champapur lies Mandargiri, a pleasant hill-site, where Tirthankara Vasupujya is believed to have practised austerities, reached enlightenment and attained *nirvana*.

BIHAR

Bihar – a name derived from *vihara* meaning temple – is the cradle of two great religions: Buddhism and Jainism, the elder of the two. Its capital Patna, in olden times Pataliputra, was the political centre of India for nearly a millennium, from about 400 BC to 500 AD. Ashoka, the greatest king India has seen, ruled his vast empire from this city. Relatively much is known about ancient Bihar, thanks chiefly to Buddhist and Jaina sources, and travelogues written by Chinese pilgrims to the land of the Buddha, which have come down to us. There lies much unused material for historical novels and films. Coinciding with the militant expansion of Muslim rule to West and East Bengal (the latter now being Bangladesh), the land of Mahavira and the Buddha fell into oblivion. Though Bihar's present Jaina population amounts to only little more than twenty-seven thousand (1981), it contains within its borders some historic places which almost every Jaina, irrespective of sectarian leanings, longs to visit at least once in his or her lifetime; foremost those where Mahavira was born, lived and died, and above all Sammeta Shikhara (also known as Parashnath Hill), at an altitude of 1360 metres the highest mountain in Bihar.

RAJGIR

If some day the world's leading advocates of animal rights should require a suitable site for a monument to commemorate the beginning of what by now has become a world-wide concern of millions of people – the protection of all that lives – Rajgir, anciently Rajagriha, in Bihar would be the place to choose.

In Sister Nivedita's* *Footfalls of Indian History* (Calcutta, 2nd reprint 1980: 149/51), we read: "We know the age of a heresy by the tenets it contradicts, and in repudiating the authority of the Vedas, Jainism proves itself the oldest form of non-conformity in India.(...) Only by accepting the Jaina tradition, moreover, as to the influence which their Gurus had upon the Buddha, are we able to account satisfactorily for the road taken by Him [the Buddha] from Kapilavastu to Bodh-Gaya through Rajgir. He made his way first of all to the region of the famous Jaina teachers. If, again, there should be any shred of truth in Sir Edwin Arnold's story (presumably from the *Lalita-Vistara*) that it was at Rajgir that He interceded for the goats, the incident would seem under the circumstances the more natural. He passed through the city on His way to some solitude where He could find realisation, with His heart full of that pity for animals and that shrinking from the thought of sacrifice, which was the characteristic thought of the age, one of the great preoccupations, it may be, of the Jaina circles He had just left. And with His heart thus full, He met the sacrificial herd, marched with them to the portals of Bimbisara's palace, and pleaded with the king for their lives, offering His own in their place.** Whether this was actually so or not, it is certain that one of the great impulses of the day lay in the rebellion against the necessity of the Vedic sacrifice; one of its finest sincerities, in that exaltation of the personal experience which made it seem natural to found on it a religion. That a man's religious conviction must be the result of his own private realisation of truth is an idea so old in India as to lie beyond the Upanishads themselves. But that such a realisation had a right to be socialised, to be made the basis of a religious sect, is a principle which was first perhaps grasped by the Jainas. (...) The religious teacher of those days lived retired in the forest clearings and gathered round him, not a sect, but a school, in the form of a few disciples. Jainism, with its sudden intense revolt against the sacrificial idea, and its sudden determination to make its pity effective for the protection of dumb animals, was the first religious doctrine to call social forces to the aid in India, in other words, it was the first organised sect or church." (> *page 206*)

* Sister Nivedita was born in Ireland in 1867 as Margaret Elizabeth Noble but the latter part of her life she spent in India as a follower of Ramakrishna and a teacher, mostly in Calcutta. She died at Darjeeling in 1911.

** Bimbisara and his son Ajatasatru appear in Jaina texts as Shrenika and Kunika or Kuniya respectively. *See* also ill. 263.

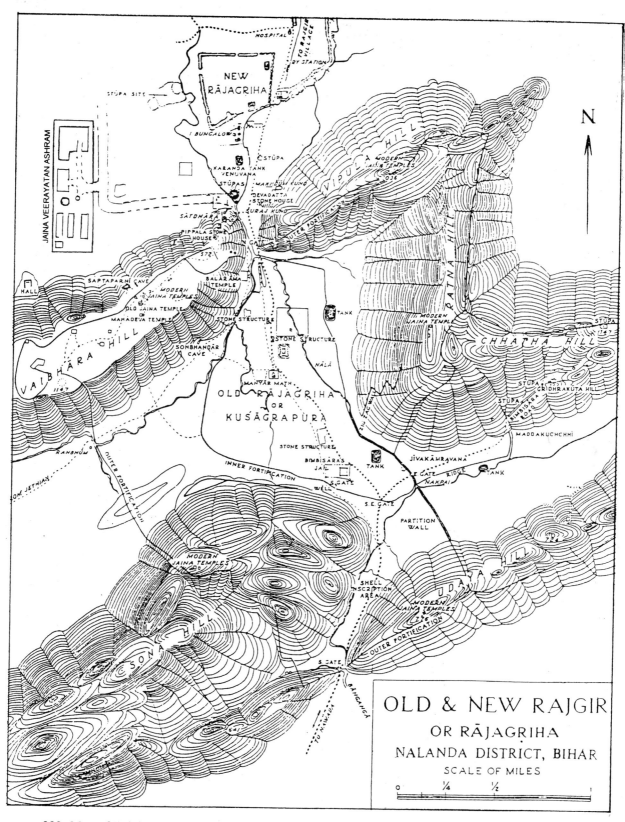

290. Map of Rajgir. Reprint from a recommendable publication entitled *RAJGIR*, published by and available from the Archaeological Survey of India, Patna Circle, Patna. The added layout of the Jaina Veerayatan Ashram is not to scale. (Courtesy the Archaeological Survey of India.)

204

291. Rajgir. A modern Digambara temple on top of Vipula Hill.

292 (*below*). Outline of a seated Jina on the inner rear wall of the eastern Sonbhandar Cave, excavated in the southern scarp of the Vaibhara Hill. Third or fourth century AD. The roof of this part of the cave has collapsed but is still intact in the western half of the cave.

293. Defaced Jina images on the inner wall of the eastern Sonbhandar Cave. (Courtesy Archaeological Survey of India.)

205

The Chinese traveller Hiuen Tsang who visited Bihar in the seventh century described Rajgir as a prosperous city. At that time, the Jainas apparently occupied one half of the city, the Buddhists the other. In modern times, the ruins of an ancient Adinatha temple were discovered on top of Vaibhara Hill and partly restored. Some of the niches surrounding the central chamber of this temple contain images of Tirthankaras, important finds for students of Jaina art. The inscriptions date back to the fifth and eighth century. The other Jaina shrines nearby, one large and some small ones, are modern structures, as are the temples on the four other hills.

In recent times, Rajgir's appeal to Jaina pilgrims and travellers received an additional attraction – the Veerayatan Ashram whose large campus extends out into virgin land at the eastern foothills of Vaibhara Hill. The inspiration for this charitable venture came from the late Sthanakavasi Muni Gurudev Amar. That it became a reality within a few years was due to the devoted determination of Sadhvi Acharya Chandana and her small group of nuns (*see* pages 216/17). Besides the Eye Hospital, the 'temple of worship' in this unique ashram, there is a permanent three-dimensional exhibition depicting the life of Mahavira, which by now has been seen by more than half a million visitors. Rajgir was a favourite place of sojourn for Mahavira who is known to have spent as many as fourteen rainy seasons in this ancient city. Munisuvrata, the twentieth Tirthankara, was a native of Rajgir.

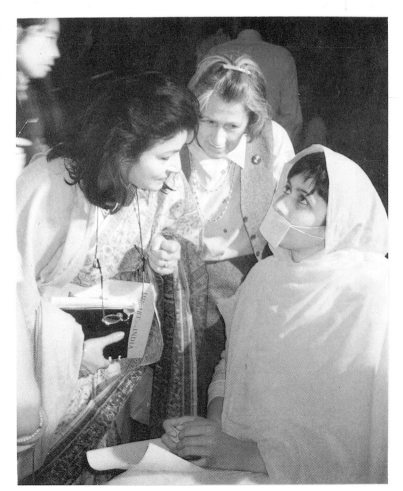

294. Sadhvi Shilapi, the first Jaina nun ever to study at a western university (namely Comparative Religion at King's College, London), joined the Veerayatan Ashram in 1986 and took *diksha* in 1991. This photo was taken at the opening of the exhibition *The Peaceful Liberators – Jain Art from India* at the Victoria and Albert Museum, London, November 1995.

295. A pair of footprints, cut from black stone in high relief and enshrined in this scenically situated Mahavira Mandir at Pavapuri, is the austere yet appropriate memorial of Mahavira's attainment of *nirvana*. Every year at Divali, the day of his death, a big fair of lights is held at Pavapuri.

PAVAPURI

Pavapuri in Bihar is the place where Mahavira died in 527 BC at the age of seventy-two. It was, in the words of the *Kalpa Sutra* translated by Hermann Jacobi: "In the fourth month of that rainy season, in the seventh fortnight of Kartika, on its fifteenth day, in the last night, in the town of Papa, in king Hastipala's office of the writers, the Venerable Ascetic Mahavira died, went off, quitted the world, cut asunder the ties of birth, old age, and death; became a Siddha, a Buddha, a Mukta, a maker of the end of all misery, finally liberated, freed from all pain. (...) In that period the Venerable Ascetic Mahavira had an excellent community of fourteen thousand *Shramanas* (monks) with Indrabuti at their head; thirty-six thousand nuns with Kandana at their head; one hundred and fifty-nine thousand male lay votaries with Shankhashataka at their head,(and) three hundred and eighteen thousand female lay votaries with Sulasa and Revati at their head."

Present-day Pavapuri consists of two villages separated by a mile – Pava and Puri. The latter is the Jaina *tirtha*. Besides the Mahavira Mandir shown above there are several other temples, among them an older and a new *samavasarana* shrine. As the bus service to and from Pavapuri is not very reliable, an overnight stay in a *dharmashala* is recommended.

296. View of Madhuban at sunset.

MADHUBAN AND SAMMETA SHIKHARA

Madhuban, the easternmost Jaina 'temple-city', embedded among trees at the foot of Parashnath Hill (better known as Sammeta Shikhara or Sametshikhar), comes to life hours before sunrise. As early as three in the morning the first pilgrims, the youngest safely tied to the back of an adult, set out on their long uphill hike by the light of torches. By the time of their return in the afternoon, they will have walked about twenty-seven kilometres: nine up, nine round the five peaks, and nine back to Madhuban.

Joining a group of pilgrims on their way to the top of this holy mountain is an unforgettable experience for the newcomer to Jainism. The upper nine kilometres – they ought to be walked barefooted – are laid out in such a way that they guide even the inexperienced pilgrim to all the twenty and more holy spots marked by small shrines (*tonks*) containing footprints, but leave the highest elevation (1360 m above sea level) to the very last. It is this last summit, visible from afar and readily recognized by its lofty temple, at which Parshvanatha is believed to have attained *nirvana* at the age of one hundred. That was some time in the eighth century BC. Within the temple, in an underground cell, it is once again the Jaina symbol denoting *nirvana* – a pair of rock-cut footprints – onto which the pilgrims focus their rites of worship (*see* the footprints of Acharya Kundakunda, ill. **100**). (*Continued page 210*)

208

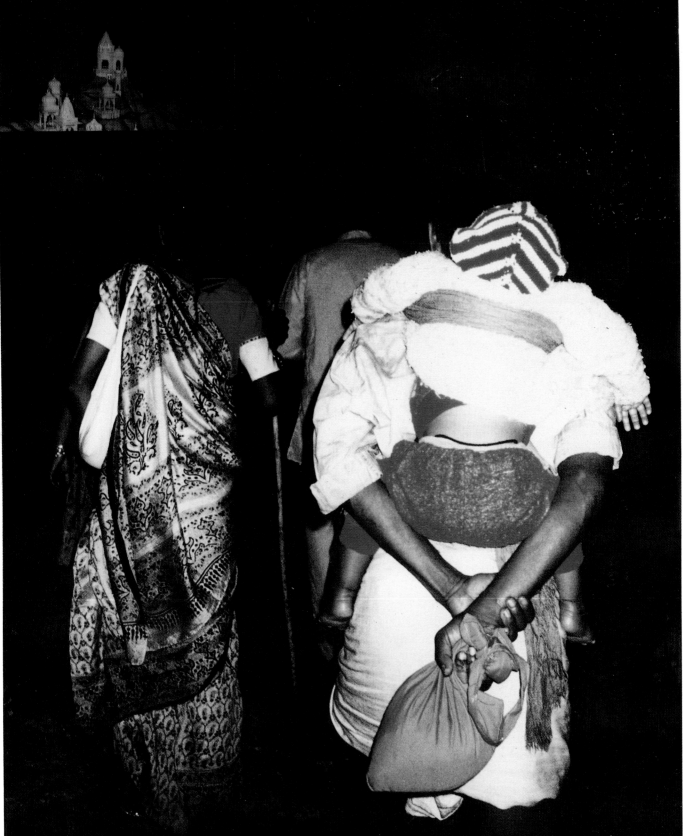

297. The long-awaited day has come for this family group of pilgrims — the ascent of holy Sammeta Shikhara. At daybreak, the summit with its lofty temple tower will loom high in the distance.

Twenty out of the twenty-four Tirthankaras of our era are thought to have found liberation on this mountain, a location far removed from today's centres of Jaina culture. Going by the joyous mood in which the pilgrims set off in the small hours of the night and the happy faces with which they return, though physically exhausted, leaves no doubt that in Jainism the tradition of going on pilgrimages has lost nothing of its religious significance. – May the mentioning of this observation by a Westerner be a fitting conclusion of this section of this book in which most of the important Jaina sacred sites are presented side by side, regardless of their affiliation to any particular sect.

298. Sammeta Shikhara. It is the white-washed super-structure of the Lal Mandir and the *Tonks* dotting the eastern slopes, which reflect the day's first rays of light.

299. Main Jina in the Parshvanatha Lal Mandir. Due to earthquakes and other havocs of nature, no original buildings on top of Sammeta Shikhara have survived.

300. Parshva Tonk, the last destination of the Sammeta Shikhara circuit that takes the pilgrim to all the hallowed spots at which twenty Tirthankaras and some of Mahavira's disciples attained *nirvana*.

301. Letting oneself be carried in a simply constructed palanquin, called *doli*, is a welcome means of transport for the weak and old and a needed source of income for the bearers, men of the indigenous people living in this area.

211

302. Moodabidri in Karnataka. Educating the young was and is of major concern to the Jainas. In this respect they had no misgivings about largely adopting the British schoolsystem.

303. BIRDS HOSPITAL, an annex to the Digambara Lal Mandir in Old Delhi (*see* ill. **194**).

304. Another social service is announced by the Jaina Matha (1989). Though far outnumbered by the Hindus, the Jainas of Shravanabelagola are, guided by their leader Karmayogi Charukeerty Bhattarak Swami, the driving force in the fields of charity, education, and health service. These services are available for the benefit of all the citizens of the town.

Social Service at Shravanabelagola
under the guidance of
H.H. Karmayogi Charukeerty Bhaṭṭarak Swamiji
Shravanabelagola

• *Adoption of ten villages in the vicinity of Shravanabelagola for development,*
• *Free distribution of Sewing Machines to the unemployed and tricycles for the handicapped,*
• *Nursery, Primary and Higher Primary Schools, College of Pharmacy and Polytechnic,*
• *Numerous Medical Camps, Children's Camps and Eye Camps held on various occasions,*
• *Charitable Ayurvedic Hospital and Pathological lab,*

• *and now Mobile Hospital !!*

Do your duty and do it as humanely as you can – this, in brief, is the primary principle of Jainism.

Vilas A. Sangave

CHARITABLE AND SOCIAL TRADITIONS IN JAINISM

When it comes to providing shelter and medical aid to the needy and injured, the Jainas do not distinguish between humans and animals. The first European travellers in India were astonished at the sight of houses for sick animals.* These nursing homes for birds and animals called *panjarapolas*, maintained by donations, still exist. Their exact number is not known; in Gujarat alone there are about sixty-five of them.

"The last of the five main vows," writes Vilas A. Sangave in his *Jaina Community* (p. 219/20), "is noteworthy as it indirectly aims at economic equalisation by peacefully preventing undue accumulation of capital in individual hands. It recommends that a householder should fix, beforehand, the limit of his maximum belongings, and should, in no case, exceed it. If he ever happens to earn more than that, he must spend it away in charities, the best and recognised forms of which are distribution of medicines, spread of knowledge, provision for saving the lives of people in danger, and feeding the hungry and the poor. Obviously, these vows are of great social value as they accord a religious sanction to some of the most important public and private interests and rights which are, in modern times, safeguarded by the laws of the state."

The observations and photographs featured in this chapter have not been made and taken by way of a subsidized research project on the practice of charity in Jainism. No such project, it seems, has yet been conducted. The following photos and observations simply illustrate what an open-minded and open-'eyed' visitor to the religion of non-violence is likely to encounter, be it in a lane in Old Delhi (ill. **196**) or outside the gate to a solitary old Jaina temple somewhere in Uttar Pradesh (*see* overleaf).

* Fa-Hien, a Chinese Buddhist who visited India at the beginning of the fifth century of our era was astonished at the free hospitals and other charitable institutions he noticed. In his journal, translated by James Legge (*Indian Literature,* p. 336), he recorded, "Throughout the whole country the people do not kill any living creature, nor eat onions or garlic." These remarks rather point to Jaina than to Buddhist influence upon the people.

EYE-CAMP FOR THE POOREST OF THE POOR

A group of Jaina lay people from Lalitpur in Uttar Pradesh has raised a sufficient sum of money to conduct a so-called eye-camp. We were invited to join a team of two doctors, one male one female, and their helpers on their way to the camp.

After a drive of about twenty-five kilometres in a north-easterly direction we reached a walled-in temple near a hamlet by the name of Sironji. Out in the open, between the temple wall and a newly raised building destined to be a museum, a row of large Jina statues, all badly damaged, has been set up (*below*). Inside the new building we noticed scores of smaller images and temple fragments waiting to be catalogued and exhibited.

It was the last day of the camp. Before it began, ten days ago, the news was spread to the tribes-people in the area to have all those suffering from fading sight brought to the temple for examination on such and such a day. The ones who could be operating on would need to stay in the camp. Everything would be free of charge, regular meals and after-care medicines included

In a simple, almost bare room, under the light of a torch, stitches were pulled and reassuring advice given by the doctors whereas their helpers renewed bandages and distributed medicines. Everything went smoothly; no paperwork was involved. With everyone having been treated, a last free meal was consumed in the open outside the temple wall. Then, by the last rays of the sun, the bare-footed patients with their white bandages round their heads, the oldest guided by the hands of small children, dispersed in all direction along narrow tracks.

Visibly pleased and relieved with the work done, the two physicians and we others sat down to a meal in the temple courtyard. It was, we two guests thought to ourselves, unbureaucratic charity at its best.

305. Sironji near Lalitpur. A row of Jina images – de-capitated but still conveying the Jaina ideal of serenity. The statues are reminiscent of the art of Deogarh (*see* p. 100). Lovers of Jaina art should not miss visiting the temple and the new museum at Sironji (U.P.).

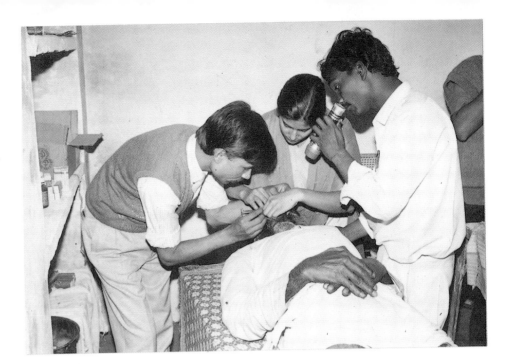

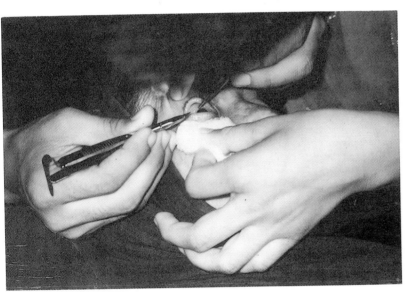

306 – 308. Compound of the Sironji Jaina Temple, showing snapshots made on the last day of an eye-camp organised and paid for by the Lalitpur Jaina community.

THE VEERAYATAN ASHRAM AT RAJGIR

Offering help to the needy is common to all Jaina sects. The above featured eye-camp was conducted by a Digambara community. Some weeks later, at Rajgir in Bihar our last place of sojourn on our way to Parashnatha Hill, we found hospitable lodging and board in the Veerayatan Ashram run by nuns belonging to the Sthanakavasi denomination. The first time we stayed in this 'Socio-religious Institute', as it is designated in a brochure, happened to be early in 1989. At that time the late Muni Amar Maharaj was still alive. It was he who in a dream saw how at Rajgir, that historic place where Mahavira spent many a rainy season, an oasis of truly religious life was meant to come into being.

It was a young nun who dedicated her life to the not easy task of making Muni Amar's dream a reality. She would hardly have succeeded, in spite of her exceptional abilities, had it not been for the adherence of many Jainas to the last of the five Great Vows cited above (pages 20 and 213) and named *aparigrahavrata*, meaning "voluntarily setting a limit to one's possessions and spending any income above the set limit on matters of religion and charity". Without this continuous flow of donations this socio-religious oasis could not have grown and flourished the way it did in so short a time.

Once the purchase of a large plot of waste land at the western outskirts of Rajgir was completed, the then 36-year-old Sadhvi Chandana – since her fourteenth year a nun – laid the foundation of Veerayatan. It was the auspicious day of Parshvanatha's birthday in 1973. The spiritual guidance continued to come from Muni Amar Maharaj who stayed at Rajgir till his death in 1992.

Considering today's remoteness and rather neglected state of Rajgir – of old it was a famous royal city and an important commercial centre – Sadhvi Chandana, now respected by her subordinate nuns and her many lay followers as Acharya Shri Chandanaji, accomplished a miracle. Within a few years her 'Temple of Worship' – a modern eye hospital – was built. Sthanakavasi Jainas, it should be noted, do not have temples.

By the time of our second visit early in 1994, over 43,000 eye surgeries had been performed in this hospital of a hundred beds. Of late, the medical service has been extended to polio and

309. Blackboard in the Veeyaratan Eye Hospital showing the number of completed operations.

VEERAYATAN

RAJGIR

NETRA JYOTI SEVA MANDIRAM
FROM 1974 TO 1993 DECEMBER
42,285 FREE OPERATED
197 TH CAMP WILL START ON 11 TH FEB. 1994

196 TH CAMP IS IN SESSION

OUR PATIENTS ARE OUR FAMILY MEMBERS

DONATE RS. 551 FOR ONE OPERATION

10 TH POLIO CAMP WILL START ON 16 TH APRIL 1994

orthopaedic patients. Artificial limbs, spectacles and medicines, and all operations and treatments are free of charge. Almost all patients – over a hundred each month – are non-Jainas. Their introduction to the religion of non-violence is the common greeting of each new day by listening to the melodious voice of Sadhvi Sumati Kunwar.

Veerayatan of Rajgir, started and built up by just five dedicated nuns – by 1995 their number had grown to ten – "is the first Jaina institution where the concept of service to mankind is not only preached by monks and nuns but also practised by them."* Visitors of all creeds and nationalities are welcome. Two long rows of guest-rooms, set in a garden of trees and flowers at the foot of the historic Vaibhara Hill, and a number of other facilities ensure a comfortable and peaceful stay. Elderly inhabitants of Rajgir remember this area as a hide-out of criminal gangs. All this has been changed by a muni's dream and the vision and determination of a Jaina nun.

310. Veerayatan Charitable Eye Hospital, Rajgir. Men, women and children from near and far queue up for admission. The token fee is Rs. 2/-.

"What makes Veerayatan even more impressive is that it was set up due to the dedication of five Jaina nuns who worked in virtual isolation as there was no Jaina community anywhere nearby to support them morally. Furthermore, they managed to transform not only the location into a paradise but also the hostile attitude of the local people. Today Veerayatan is a major source of livelihood for many locals from clerical staff to gardeners and from cooks to washerwomen." From an article by Payal Kumar in *The Hindustan Times*, Feb. 5, 1995.

* Quoted from an Veerayatan publication.

217

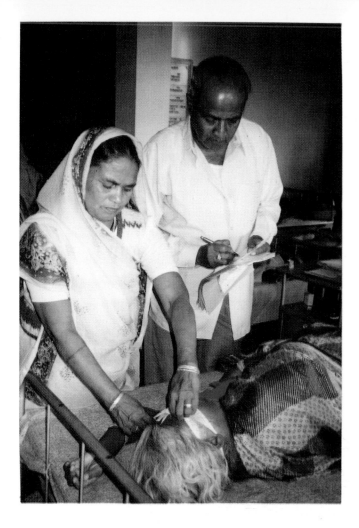

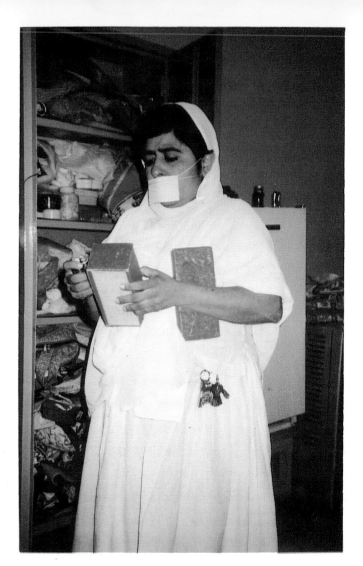

311 – 313. Veerayatan Eye Hospital, Rajgir. Daily routine competently attended to by the medical staff and local people trained at the hospital. Sadhvi Chetna (*above*), holding a diploma in allopathic medicine (obtained after she became a nun), is the affectionate and serene 'mother superior'. Motivation and dedication are the key to this admirable 'Temple of Worship'. Pure vegetarian food is supplied by the hospital.

The Indian woman is the living embodiment of peace, service and devotion. She holds the torch-light of humanity in this dark world. Her heart overflows with love, compassion, forbearance and fortitude. She scatters flowers in place of thorns.

Muni Gurudev Amar
(From his book *Amar Vani*, 1988: 139)

THE JAINA WOMEN'S ASHRAM AT SHOLAPUR

In Jainism, nothwithstanding the rather stringent rules of conduct, there is room for unconventional innovators, male and female. This liberal outlook enhanced by the trust in the potential resourcefulness of human nature can be traced back to Mahavira who was one of the great innovators of his time. He was the first, it seems, who granted women the right to form their own ascetic orders.

In 1925, in the city of Sholapur in Maharashtra, a then teenage Jaina woman by the name of Sumatibai Shah chose for herself, inspired by Gandhi and Acharya Shantisagar, the life of a *brahmacharini*, that is to voluntarily live like a nun without actually being one. To have opted for nunhood would have restricted her in making her own resolutions and putting them into practice.

With the financial help of an aunt and other members of her pious family, Sumatibai Shah set herself to work, namely – in her own words – "to convert every Indian woman into a warrior, to fight against injustice done to her, to stand on her own legs, to offer her heart to the needy and to make her an ideal citizen of India." At that time, educating the female population in a land like India was no subject for public concern and discussion, but this was what she intended to do.

In due course the first classrooms of a girls' school were erected on a piece of land that used to be a cremation ground. And from that time onward she never stopped scheeming for new educational and charitable additions to her Jaina Women's Ashram, such as a hostel for girls who had lost their parents or whose families lived away in the country; a health centre; a printing press run exclusively by women; classes for bookkeeping, typing and tailoring; a library, and a meditation hall. She even had a Mahavira shrine built to her own plans.

The strength needed to hold all these many activities together and to plan still further ones, that strength which has never failed her during these many decades, she draws from her beloved religion, the faith as it was taught by Mahavira and which continues to be embodied in saints such as the late Acharya Shantisagar (1873–1955) of whom she was a devotee. The benefits resulting from her tireless endeavours are there for all those who participate in or take advantage of her work, regardless of their respective religion or caste.

Visitors to this exemplary institution of charity, envisaged and given shape by a frail lady, are offered lodging and board. For those who travel from Karnataka to Ellora or vice versa, Sholapur (also spelled Solapur) is a commendable stopover place. An old Digambara Adinatha temple, located within walking distance from the Padmashri Sumatibai Shravika Ashram, is worth a visit; and Kunthalgiri, that sacred temple-hill where Acharya Shantisagar ended his life by the rite of *sallekhana* in September 1955, lies about eighty kilometres north of Sholapur.

314. Classes for the girls of Padmashri's school begin with a spiritual prayer.

315 (*below*). The principal of the school. He, too, is responsible to Padmashri Sumatibai.

316. Padmashri at her daily morning *puja*.

DHARMASTHALA — A UNIQUE MODEL OF CHARITY

For those of us who for some reason or other have lost faith in humanity, a visit to Dharmasthala in Karnataka (*see* map, p. 28) should help to activate one's immunity to this kind of modern ailment. But it would have to be a stay longer as a halfday sightseeing tour. One's request to stay overnight is readily complied with by being offered lodging in one of the many rest-houses for pilgrims. Westerners are advised to inquire at the office of the Secretary to the Heggade.

Dharmasthala, located among wooded hills at the foot of the Western Ghats, is not one of those modern ventures one sees advertised as new solutions of man's perennial problems. Having a history of over eight hundred years, Dharmasthala may be looked upon as the realization of a utopian dream which has not failed its founders.

The main ingredients of utopia are all there. There is, first of all, the enchanting landscape which ought to be approached at the hour of sunrise when layers of silvery mist withdraw into nothingness while the sun's rays penetrate deeper into the low-lying valleys calling the birds and animals of the forest to life on a new day.

Watching – at the other end of the day – the setting of the sun beyond the giant statue of Bahubali, the Jaina symbol of saying no to violence and worldly power, is another sight to be seen and absorbed by the pilgrim to Dharmasthala.

Another component in the make-up of Dharmasthala is its model character "as an experimental ground for practising what Indian sages propounded the idea of '*vasudhaiva kutumbakam*', the whole world is my family" and its "proclaiming to the world the spirit of oneness of all religions."* "Dharmasthala" to quote from another leaflet, "is the perfect embodiment of the word 'Dharma'. As elusive of description, yet possessing a wealth of meaning to all who come in faith. The word 'Dharma' traditionally means religion, ritual, duty, righteousness, alms. It also implies justice, truthfulness, freedom from fear, faith, solace, fulfilment and peace."

Thus, the main temple of Dharmasthala is dedicated to *Manjunatha* (another name for Lord Shiva); the priests are Vishnuite Brahmins who traditionally worship Vishnu whereas the worldly lord, so to speak, is a Jaina. At present this is Shri Veerendra Heggade (born in 1948), the twenty-first of a long hereditary line of outstanding religious leaders and administrators.

True to a message delivered in form of a dream by celestial messengers, to the first Heggade, a Jaina chieftain then named Pergade, Dharmasthala developed into and has remained, throughout these many years, a haven of religious tolerance, charity and hospitality. This is all the more remarkable in view of the fact that during these centuries India was beset with inner warmongers and foreign invaders.

Today's visitors to India seem to be prone to hurrying from one old fort to

* From: *The Holy Kshetra Sri Dharmasthala*, 1982: 48.

another; whether of their own accord or simply in compliance with a general trend is an open question. Acquainting oneself, as an alternative, with a human enclave like Dharmasthala which does not lie in ruins like most of those 'houses' of warfare but lives on as a well-nigh utopia of religious tolerance, charity and learning – to do this can indeed restore one's belief and trust in man's potential to building a better world.

Providing lodging and meals to all pilgrims irrespective of creed, caste, sex and nationality has become a main concern of Dharmasthala's Jaina Heggades, and because they have never developed a liking for political power and personal luxury, all their administrative skills have gone into expanding their charitable activities towards building and maintaining hospitals, schools and colleges, research institutes, training centres for different arts, educational classes and workshops for people living in villages round about Dharmasthala, and other charitable institutions.

Direct bus services connect Dharmasthala with cities and towns such as Bangalore, Mysore, Mangalore, Karkala, Moodabidri, Hassan, Shravanabelagola and other places.

317. The Bahubali of Dharmasthala at sunset. Having had it sculptured from a single granite rock at Karkala (1967–70), hauled to Dharmasthala in 1973 – a distance of 72 km along a winding road – and set up on the chosen hillock in 1975 was a gigantic feat. The inauguration (*mastakabhisheka*) of the 15.8 m high statue took place in February 1982.

222

318. The Chandranatha Jaina Temple of Dharmasthala.

319. Dharmasthala. Annapoorna Dining Hall. Constructed to feed three thousand guests. Annapoorna is the name of the Hindu Goddess of Food. 'In the tradition of generous hospitality, initiated by the founder, every pilgrim at Dharmasthala is an honoured guest – whatever his or her caste, creed or culture. Everyone is provided with free food and shelter.' (Both photos courtesy Veerendra Heggade, Dharmasthala.)

BAHUBALI — A SAINT'S HERITAGE

As a holder of an academic degree of education from the university of Bombay, the late Acharya Muni Samantabhadra committed his life to educating the young. The spreading of knowledge, we have seen, is a duty for the Jaina; it belongs to *dana*, the giving of gifts.

Acharya Samantabhadra, who lived half his life under British rule, wanted to see the colonial school system supplemented by imparting traditional Jaina values to the younger generations. This self-set aim imbued him with the idea of starting a school on the guidelines which used to be practised in the pre-colonial *gurukulas* (residential schools guided by a spiritual teacher). It was in 1934 that he started his experiment with just five pupils in a somewhat dilapidated temple on Kumbojagiri, a holy hill about twenty kilometres east of Kohlapur in Maharashtra. A year before, Samantabhadra had joined the Digambara ascetic order as a *kshullaka* (junior monk who wears three pieces of clothing).

The number of families wanting to send their children to this school increased from year to year. As the ground available on top of the hill allowed no further extension, Muni Samantabhadra decided to build a school at the foot of the hill. Assisted by the State Government and helped by generous donations from Jaina lay people, a huge educational complex arose on the chosen site now consisting of several two-storey buildings of classrooms, houses for teachers, quarters for the *gurukula* inmates, a large kitchen, administration offices, a printing shop, a gymnasium, toilets, and the like. Among the recent additions is a guest-house with a library and a bookstall.

Care was taken to retain the serene character of the surrounding environment. Only in the mornings and afternoons is there a busy coming and going of buses which bring the approximately one thousand boys and girls from the outlying villages to school and take them home again after classes.

The *gurukula* proper counts about three hundred inmates, only they – all boys – receive religious instruction and must come from Jaina families They wear simple white clothes and are known as *brahmacharis*. The girls and boys from the villages may be of any religion or caste. The curriculum of the school must comply with governmental guidelines, and the teachers are paid by the state.

On the slope of the hill above the school a uniquely designed temple has been built, crowned by a Bahubali statue of light Rajasthani marble. This colossus, erected in 1963 and measuring eight and a half metres in height, marks the revival of the Jaina monumental art of statue sculpturing which until then had lain dormant for some centuries. Since then, dozens of huge Jina and Bahubali images have been installed at sacred Jaina centres throughout India; a welcome source of income for

(continued page 226)

224

320. General view of the Bahubali Temple, Gurukula and Educational Campus.

321. A closer view of the rear terraces of the temple and the Bahubali statue. On the left of the upper terrace a three-dimensional replica of the sacred mountain Sammeta Shikhara in Bihar.

sculptors at places like Karkala in Karnataka and Jaipur in Rajasthan (these stone-masons, it should be noted, belong to a special Hindu-caste and are no Jainas).

It was within the precincts of this temple that Acharya Muni Samantabhadra put his mortal body to rest by observing the rite of *sallekhana* – by slowly reducing the intake of nourishment. He died fully awake on the 18th of August 1988. In December of the same year he would have been ninety-seven years of age. From 1952, when he became a fully ordained Digambara monk, he never wore a piece of clothing, never sat down to a meal, never used a vehicle. The heritage he left behind is there to be marvelled at by everybody whose path takes him to this model of a *gurukula* at the foot of this sacred hill better known nowadays by the name of Bahubali. For Shvetambara pilgrims to this site the place of worship is a renovated old temple sacred to Parshvanatha on top of the hill. There is a *dharmashala* annexed to this temple.

322. The late Acharya Muni Samantabhadra in his cell with window opening to the 8.5 m high Bahu-bali statue.

323. August 1988; thousands of devotees pay their last homage to the saint whose dead body, seated in meditation posture, is carried to the cremation ground. (Both photos courtesy Sanmati Publication, Bahubali/Kolhapur.)

Panjarapolas

324. A Jaina *Panjarapola* (shelter for cattle) in Panchasar, a village near Shankhesvara in Gujarat. When the cow of a Hindu has grown too old for giving milk he usually no longer feeds her but lets her roam about as she likes; under no circumstance would he kill her. To rescue these deserted animals from starvation or being killed by non-Jainas or non-Hindus has become a religious duty of the Jainas for as long as they can remember. This is done by providing shelters in which the animals are fed and cared for by paid low-caste Hindus and sometimes even Moslems. The expenses for running these shelters are met by committees who collect donations mostly from Jainas but also from wealthy Hindus and governmental sources.

*   *   *

KINDNESS TO ANIMALS

From the JAIN DECLARATION ON NATURE which was presented to His Royal Highness Prince Philip, President of the World Wide Fund for Nature (WWF) International, on the 23rd October 1990 at Buckingham Palace: The transgressions against the vow of non-violence include all forms of cruelty to animals and human beings. Many centuries ago, Jains condemned as evil the common practice of animal sacrifice to the gods. It is generally forbidden to keep animals in captivity, to whip, mutilate or overload them or to deprive them of adequate food and drink. The injunction is modified in respect of domestic animals to the extent that they may be roped or even whipped occasionally but always mercifully with due consideration and without anger.

Except for allowing themselves a judicious use of one-sensed life in the form of vegetables, Jains would not consciously take any life for food or sport. As a community they are strict vegetarians, consuming neither meat, fish nor eggs. They confine themselves to vegetable and milk products.

By taking the basic vows, the Jain laity endeavour to live a life of moderation and restraint and to practise a measure of abstinence and austerity. They must not procreate indiscriminately lest they overburden the universe and its resources. Regular periods of fasting for self-purification are encouraged. (Acknowledgement is offered to Dr. L. M. Singhvi, the author of the Declaration.)

*O Lord of Saints! may thy feet
which dispel the pitchy darkness
of ignorance like a brilliantly
lit lamp, ever stay in my heart, as
if they were fixed, nailed, rooted,
or permanently reflected therein.*

*May thy feet, O Noble Jina,
the friend of all living beings,
be my refuge.*

A Jaina Prayer

SYMBOLS, MANTRAS AND PARABLES
IN JAINISM

Padukas

Stone-carved pairs of feet (*padukas*), mostly in high relief, are one of the oldest and most common emblems worshipped by Indians in general and Jainas in particular. They usually mark the spot, apart from those seen in temples, at which an ascetic of renown is believed to have died; a corresponding inscription will often be found nearby. It would be wrong, however, to assume that *padukas* are to the Jainas what tombstones are to the Chinese or the Christians. It is not death that they symbolize, but the soul's conscious departure from the mortal body, an event which does not just happen as death usually does to most of us. The death of a saint is seen and understood as the culmination of life brought about through years of dedicated effort.

Pairs of stone-cut feet related to a Tirthankara – there are twenty of them on Sammeta Shikhara in Bihar – symbolize final liberation usually called *nirvana* or *moksha*. Those footprints which commemorate saints born into the present age in which, according to Jaina teaching, attainment of *moksha* is not possible, may be likened to sign posts or stepping-stones on the path to purification, a path that calls for at least one more incarnation as a human being. This would apply, for example, to the footprints of Acharya Kundakunda near Ponnor Hill in Tamilnadu (ill. **100**). It is the spirit, as expressed in the inserted prayer (*opposite page*), that makes the *paduka* such a beautiful and timeless symbol of adoration where adoration is due.

Symbolizing the Five Auspicious Events in the life of a Tirthankara

In Jaina art no attempts have been made to portray the passage of a Tirthankara's soul from the *nirvana-bhumi* to the *siddha-loka* – from the place of death to the permanent abode of the liberated soul. This transformation, which is believed to take place within an extremely short span of time, cannot be perceived by our senses. Thus it is the *paduka* which, in a way, symbolizes the last of the five auspicious events in the life of every Tirthankara. These five happenings are: (1) Incarnation in the mother's womb; (2) birth and first bath on Mount Meru performed by Indra, king of the gods; (3) initiation into monkhood called *diksha*; (4) enlightenment and first sermon; and fifthly, as already mentioned, attainment of *nirvana* or *moksha*.

Accounts of these five principal events in the life of a Jina, called *pancha-kalayanaka*, are enumerated in old manuscripts, especially in the *Kalpa Sutra* by Bhadrabahu. The oldest copies of this book are written on palm-leaves, later ones

325 (*opposite*). Tirumalai, Tamilnadu.

also on paper. Most of the extant copies date from about 1050 to 1750. In consequence of a continuous demand for this invariably illuminated book, especially popular with Shvetambaras, Jaina pictorial art became well known and gained high rating within the field of Indian miniature painting.

Less well known than the miniatures from the *Kalpa Sutra*, which one sees displayed in museums the world over and reproduced again and again in books of Indian art, are the representations of those auspicious events worked in stone and metal and found in Jaina temples all over India. The following illustration shows part of a ceiling décor in the Mahavira temple at Kumbharia in Gujarat.

326. Detail of ceiling depicting the first of the five auspicious moments in the life of a Tirthankara.

On the left, resting on a cot, is the sleeping mother-to-be of a Tirthankara. On her right are symbols of the approaching fourteen dreams she is about to dream. In the *Kalpa Sutra*, translated from Prakrit into English by Hermann Jacobi (here abridged and slightly edited), each dream opens with lines that keep ringing in one's ears: "Then Trishala saw in her first dream a fine enormous elephant, possessing all lucky marks, who was whiter than an empty cloud, or a heap of pearls, or the ocean of milk . . . (2) Then she saw a tame lucky bull, of a whiter hue than that of the mass of petals of the white lotus, illumining all around by the diffusion of a glory of light. . . (3) Then she saw a handsomely shaped, playful lion, jumping from the sky towards her face; a delightful and beautiful lion whiter than a heap of pearls. . . (4) Then she, with the face of the full moon, saw the goddess of famous beauty, Shri, on top of Mount Himavat, reposing on a lotus in the lotus lake, anointed with the water from the strong trunks of the guardian elephants. . . (5) Then she saw, coming down from the firmament, a garland charmingly interwoven with fresh Mandara flowers. . . (6) And the moon: white as cow milk, or a silver cup. Such was the glorious, beautiful, resplendent full moon which the queen saw. . . (7) Then she saw the large sun, the dispeller of darkness, the destroyer of night, who only at his rising and setting may be well viewed. . . (8) Then she saw an extremely beautiful and very large flag, a sight for all people. . . (9) Then she saw a full vase of costly metal, splendent with fine gold, filled with pure water, and shining with a bouquet of water lilies. . . (10) Then she saw a lake, called Lotus Lake, adorned with water lilies. . . (11) Then she whose face was splendid like the moon in autumn, saw the milk-ocean, equalling in beauty the breast of Lakshmi, which is white like the mass of moon-beams. . . (12) Then she saw a celestial abode excelling among the best of its kind. It was hung with brilliant divine garlands, and decorated with pictures of wolves, bulls, horses, men, dolphins, birds, snakes. There the Gangharvas performed their concerts, and the din of the drums of the gods, imitating the sound of big and large rain-clouds, penetrated the whole inhabited world. . . (13) Then she saw an enormous heap of jewels. . . (14) And a fire. She saw a fire in vehement motion, fed with much-shining and honey-coloured ghee. . . – After having seen these fine, beautiful, lovely, handsome dreams, the lotus-eyed queen awoke on her bed while the hair of her body bristled for joy."

According to Digambara tradition a Jina's future mother sees sixteen dreams of which the first seven correspond to the ones of the Shvetambaras. The eighth comprises a pair of full vases with lotuses, the ninth is a pair of fish, the tenth a celestial lake, the eleventh an agitated ocean, the twelfth a golden lion-throne, the thirteenth a *vimana* (celestial car), the fourteenth a palace of the king of snakes (*nagendra-bhavana*), the fifteenth a heap of jewels, and the sixteenth a smokeless fire.

The symbols of these sixteen dreams may be seen carved on door-lintels of Digambara temples, at Khajuraho for instance, or, as it became the mode of later centuries, painted in form of murals (*see* ill. **196**).

The dreams symbolize the incarnation of the Jina in the mother's womb. The birth, the second auspicious event, is represented by showing the mother, either lying or sitting, with the child close to her breast. The symbol of *diksha,* the initiation into monkhood, has the figure of a monk sitting cross-legged and plucking out his hair with one hand, a ritual named *kesh lonch* (Sanskrit: *kesha-luncana*). For illustrations of this rite *see* pages 96 and 97.

The attainment of omniscience, termed *kevalajnana* (knowledge involving awareness of every existence in all its qualities and modes), the fourth of the five auspicious events and the focus around which the religion of the Jainas has become concentrated, has led to the unique and most elaborate symbol in Jainism – the *samavasarana.* Fortunately, this symbol has not been reduced to a standardized module. Countless architects, temple-builders, sculptors and painters were free to use their imagination as long as they kept to a few basic elements such as having a Jina in the centre, preferably a seated one. The *samavasarana*, when seen as a flat painting, must not be confused with a tantric mandala. During all these centuries, Jainism, unlike Buddhism, has managed to steer clear of tantrism. Jainas

327. Palitana. Samavasarana-Temple, dedicated 1986.

may believe in phenomena that are close to magic, but they would never subscribe to a belief that sees in sexual union a way of enlightenment.

The aim of a representation of *samavasarana*, be it an old painting or a modern temple of enormous size, is to arouse in the mind of the beholder the picture of a Tirthankara's first sermon. Whenever, according to Jaina mythology, a Tirthankara attains enlightenment and is about to deliver his message, god Indra (also called Shakra) orders the erection of a huge auditorium with flights of steps leading from the four points of the compass up to the central platform where the nude Tirthankara, sitting or (rarely) standing under an *Ashoka* tree, proclaims his message to the assembled audience consisting of monks and nuns, kings and chieftains, lay people in great numbers as well as four-legged animals, birds and even snakes, fishes and turtles. After the sermon, the auditorium vanishes the way it was built and the Jina sets out on his mission of preaching the doctrine of non-violence and the other ethical precepts.*

Attaining *moksha*, the fifth and final event in the life of a Jina, defies concrete representation. Thus the rock-cut footprints may, as already suggested, be taken as a symbol of that invisible and lastly unexplainable metamorphosis without actually representing it. The same could be said of those peculiar metal icons (*left*), displayed in Digambara temples, which show the stencilled outline of a human figure. They are meant to exemplify the non-material state of the soul (*siddha*) in the highest heaven called *siddha-loka*.

328. Image of a *Siddha*. 1910, North Karnataka. (Courtesy Marg Publications, Bombay.)

* For a detailed account of the *samavasarana* see the chapter by Gopilal Amar in *Jaina Art and Architecture*, Vol. III, 529–533. G. Amar concludes his entry with the remark: "As a matter of fact, symbolizing even in a large structural form the vast and complex area like the *samavasarana* is more or less impossible for an architect or a sculptor to achieve." Nor for a painter to paint, it may be added.

329. *Samavasarana*: an assembly of beings who have come to hear a Tirthankara preach the Doctrine. 1800, Rajasthan. (Picture and text courtesy R. Kumar, co-author of *The Jain Cosmology*, 1981: 44/45.)

"The assembly is taking place on a huge circular mound. The area is enclosed by a wall, and cut across by four monumental staircases, which give access from the four points of the compass. At the crossing of the triumphal ways which they form, at the exact centre of the assembly and of the circular open space situated at its middle, stands the pillar from which the Tirhankara preaches the Doctrine.

   The illustration shows the vast central platform, demanded by tradition. It is surrounded by three successive circular rings. On the middle ring there are wild animals, their mutual hostiliy laid aside. On the inside ring gods and goddesses, princes, layfollowers and monks are assembled.(...) While evoking the charms of the tangible world, the artist also focusses our gaze on the prophet and attracts our attention to his unsurpassable teaching."

The eight objects of auspiciousness: *Asta-mangalas*

The earliest representations of the eight objects of auspiciouness, cut into slabs of stone, have been found at Mathura among the remains of the Kushana period (64–225 AD). In the course of time they became popular objects of worship in Jaina temple rites but progressively more in the form of engraved metal platters and coloured paintings on cloth and paper rather than of stone-cut panels. Originally each of the eight symbols had its own meaning. The mirror for instance was meant for seeing one's true self. Today they are rather looked upon as a 'eight-in-one' symbol, the worship of which, when offered in the right frame of mind, is believed to be a good omen. The current *asta-mangala* symbol is not rigidly fixed but occurs in various shapes and arrangements.

330. *Asta-Mangala*, the eight objects of auspiciousness; Shvetambara tradition: (1) *swastika*, (2) *shrivatsa*, mark on the chest of the Jina, (3) *nadyavarta*, a diagram , (4) *vardhamanaka*, powder-flask, (5) *kalasha*, full vase, the two eyes represent right knowledge and right faith, (6) *bhadrasana*, a high seat, (7) pair of fish, (8) a mirror.

The Digambara tradition gives the following set of *asta-mangalas*: (1) *bhrngara*, a type of vessel, (2) *kalasha*, the full vase, (3) *darpana*, the mirror, (4) *camara*, the fly-whisk, (5) *dhvaja*, the banner, (6) *vyajana*, the fan, (7) *chatra*, the parasol, and (8) *supratistha*, the auspicious seats. (After U. P. Shah in *Jaina Art and Architecture*, 1975: 492.)

Amity and fearlessness

331. The emblem, showing a tigress suckling the calf of a cow and the cow suckling the young of the tigress has become a favourite symbol with Digambara Jainas in this century. The story goes that some time in the eighth century, at a deserted place where Moodabidri stands today (*see* p. 47), a muni from Shravanbelagola saw a tiger and a cow drinking from a common trough while feeding their young as described above. The panel pictured here was seen by the present author above the gate of the Jaina Basadi at Nandani near Kolhapur (*see* map p. 28), which was built, according to the Bhattaraka of the locality, in 935. This sculpture, though perhaps of later date, would still be one of the earliest specimens of this attractive motif.

Shruta-skandha Yantra

332 (*left*). An interesting version of the *Shruta-Skandha Yantra* (literally = scripture – assemblage – diagram), photographed in a Tamilnadu Digambara temple. The central pillar symbolizes Sarasvati, the goddess of learning. To show that the earliest scriptures were written on leaves, the artist gave the twelve limbs the shape of palm-leaves; the letterings inscribed on them specify the titles of the twelve main texts (*agamas*) of the Jaina canon. *Shruta-skandha yantras* are usually made of brass or bronze. No two of them seem to be alike.

Sthapanacharya

333. The *Sthapanacharya*, a compound word made up of *sthapana* (installation) and *acharya* (head monk), is peculiar to Shvetambara monks and nuns. It is a small stand of three crossed-sticks, like the letter X, on which five round pieces of sea-shell, wrapped in a cloth, are placed. Each day anew, monks and nuns, no matter of which rank, like to 'install' the *stapanacharya* in front of them as a symbol of their respective spiritual teacher, regardless of whether he is temporarily absent or has already died. Westerners need not hesitate to ask a monk (or nun) they are visiting to show and explain to them the *sthapanacharya* or, for instance, the intricate 'mechanism' of the fly-whisk, the most characteristic symbol of Jaina mendicants, which is, among the Shvetambara, Terapanthi and Sthanakavasi, of woolen tufts, whereas the Digambara prefer peacock feathers for theirs. – The photo shows Acharya Vijaya Vallabh Suri (1870–1954, *see* page 136). The *sthapanacharya* in front symbolized to him the spiritual presence of his guru Acharya Vijayanada Suri, the one who had been invited to participate in the first Chicago Conference of World Religions in 1893, but which he could not attend (*see* page 250).

Siddha-chakra

334. Ajitanatha Temple, Taranga. *Siddha-chakra* (saint-wheel) or *nava-pada* (*nava* = nine). Marble relief embosomed in the outer wall of the eastern one of the two outbuildings situated within the temple compound.

At first, how early is not known, the *siddha-chakra* of both the Digambaras and Shvetambaras was confined to a lotus of four petals, with a representation of the Arhat in the centre. Patterned in this way it may also be called *pancha-parmeshti*, with which the five dignitaries are meant: the *Arhats, Siddhas, Acharyas, Upadhyayas* and *Sadhus*. The eight-petalled *siddha-chakra* (ill. **334**, *above* and **336**, *opposite*), either cut in stone, cast in metal or painted on cloth or paper, appeared in the eleventh century, but by then each of the two big sects employed a different pattern; the Shvetambara named theirs *nava-pada*, the Digambaras *nava-devata*. However, the term *siddha-chakra* is used as the common term for all the different forms of the 'saint-wheel'. Thus the Shvetambaras call the festival, held around the end of winter, at which they offer worship to the symbols representing the 'Five Dignitaries' and the 'Four Essentials', *Siddha-chakra-Mahapuja*. On that occasion colourful *siddha-chakra mandalas* are designed and composed in the temples out of rice and different grains, seeds, and blue and black pulse. For the Shvetambaras the four 'essentials' are: Right Knowledge, Right Faith, Right Conduct and Right Penance*. For the Digambaras they are: the Jina image, the Temple enshrining the image, the Wheel of Law, and the Scriptures.

335. Figure of eight-petalled *Siddha-chakra*.

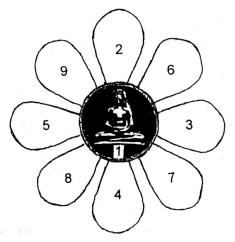

Shvetambara:
    1 - *Arhat*
    2 - *Siddha*
    3 - *Acharya*
    4 - *Upadhyaya*
    5 - *Sadhu*
    6 - *Jnana* (right knowledge)
    7 - *Darshana* (right faith)
    8 - *Charitra* (right conduct)
    9 - *Tapas* (right penance)
Digambara: 1 to 5 as above
    6 - *Chaitya* (the Jina image)
    7 - *Chaityalaya* (temple enshrining the Jina)
    8 - *Dharmachakra* (wheel of law)
    9 - *Sutras* (represented by a book stand)

* Referred to in form of short mantras on petals 6 to 9.

236

336. Matha Temple, Shravanabelagola. Digambara *Nava-devata* metal image.
Height 44 cm. Cast in Tamilnadu and, according to an inscription on the reverse,
presented to the Matha by a layman named Perumal in 1858.

The Jaina faith and universe

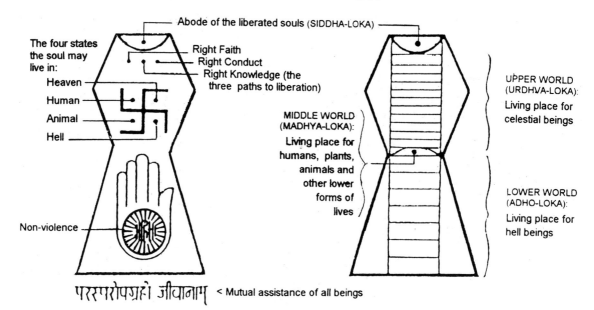

Abode of the liberated souls (SIDDHA-LOKA)

The four states the soul may live in:

Heaven

Human

Animal

Hell

Right Faith
Right Conduct
Right Knowledge (the three paths to liberation)

MIDDLE WORLD (MADHYA-LOKA): Living place for humans, plants, animals and other lower forms of lives

UPPER WORLD (URDHVA-LOKA): Living place for celestial beings

LOWER WORLD (ADHO-LOKA): Living place for hell beings

Non-violence

परस्परोपग्रहो जीवानाम्   < Mutual assistance of all beings

337 a. Prior to the 2500th anniversary of Mahavira's *nirvana* in 1974/75, the leaders of the various Jaina sects found themselves under the necessity of devising a common symbol for the Jaina religion; all other religions seemed to have one. They agreed on the diagram shown above. A new composition of old elements like the svastika and the 'wheel of law'. New is the lettering in the centre of the wheel meaning *Ahimsa*. The phrase in *Devanagari* script below the diagram denotes, 'All life is bound together by mutual support and interdependence.'

338. The eight 'black fields' in the third layer of the *Brahmaloka*. Gouache on paper, eighteenth century. (Courtesy R. Kumar *The Jain Cosmology.*)

The discovery of 'black holes' by our astronomers is of rather recent date. Interestingly, Jaina cosmology speaks of eight 'black fields', which are not, however, described as holes but as thin layers of watery and greatly swollen vegetable fragments (of waste so to speak) that arise from an ocean of the 'middle world' – that part of the universe in which we live – right up to the dizzy hights of the *brahmaloka*, the fifth heaven of the gods. That astronomical event is stylistically depicted in this painting from Rajasthan.

337 b. Diagram showing in a stylized form the Jaina universe based on descriptions in old manuscripts and paintings which emerged in Jaina art from around the sixteenth century onwards. In many of these illustrations which have come down to us, the universe is shown in the shape of a human being (*purusha*), who can be either female or male. Descriptive details of the Jaina cosmos, here and there touched upon in the present book, are found in most English publications on Jainsm.

Two Jaina parables

339. Mural painting covering the rear wall of the Assembly Hall in the Terapanthi Adhyatma Sadhana Kendra, at Mehrauli, New Delhi. The picture on the right illustrates how the mental and moral level of a person can be judged by the colour (*leshya*) of his soul. The popular parable of the 'Man in the Well' is the motive of the picture on the left. Paintings with these contents are found in many Jaina temples.

The tree with the six persons illustrates the six *leshyas* of Jaina philosophy. *Leshya* (tint) is that by which the soul is tinted with merit and demerit. It is of six kinds and colours, three being meritorious and three sinful. Meritorious *leshyas* are of orange-red, lotus-pink and white colours, while sinful *leshayas* are of black, indigo and grey colours. The former lead respectively to birth as man and to final emancipation, while the latter lead respectively to hell and to birth as plant or animal.

The picture illustrates the acts of persons affected with the different tints. With the desire of eating mangoes a person under the influence of the black *leshya* cuts the trunk of the tree; another affected with the indigo chops off big boughs; a third influenced by the grey cuts off small branches; a fourth affected with the orange-red breaks the twigs, a fifth under the influence of the lotus-pink merely plucks mangoes; and a sixth affected with the white picks up only fallen fruit. (After Saryu Doshi in *Homage to Shravana Belgola*, 1981: 35.)

There exist several versions of the popular parable of the 'Man in the Well'. A concise account would run as follows: A merchant lost in the jungle fled from the attack of a mad elephant and now clings to the branch of a tree he has grabbed just in time. Casting his eyes downwards he looks into a black water-hole full of snake-like monsters. Looking skywards he sees a hive alive with bees. Whenever the elephant shakes the tree with his mighty trunk, honey drops down from the hive right onto his tongue. A *deva* (god), passing by in his *vimana*, catches sight of the man in distress and calls out to him that he will come to his rescue. The man shouts back that he need not hurry for he would like to relish the taste of the honey somewhat longer. At the same time, he takes no notice of the two rodents, one white the other black (symbolizing day and night), which keep gnawing their way through the stem of the branch he is hanging on. The god, taking his time, sees the man slipping off the breaking bough and falling into the hole where he is seized by the hungry monsters.

This in a nutshell is the way many a human lives his life. Though being aware of the threatening danger and perceiving the message of a potential saviour, his desire for a few more pleasures of the senses prevents him from taking advantage of the offered help.

Offerings

Whilst invoking the name of the respective Jina during temple worship, the following eight substances are offered: (1) Water, (2) uncooked rice, (3) flowers, (4) sandalwood paste mixed with saffron, (5) camphor, (6) incense, (7) sweets and (8) fruits. The presentation of flowers is practised by some sects but contested by others. Uncooked rice, the primary substance, is chosen for its whiteness and for having been born only once. At no stage in the long history of Jainism have animals been used as offerings.

The breaking of a coconut upon a stone positioned for this purpose in front of the entrance to a temple (*see* ill. **318**) is another rite with a symbolic content. The coarsely knit fibres of the coconut are thought to represent jealousy, greed, lust, selfishness and the like. This coarse layer, corresponding to the layers of karma encompassing one's soul, needs to be broken and removed before one reaches the sweet, nectar-like liquid, which, pure throughout and untouched by any hand, symbolizes that purity of soul one should strive for. The three eyes of the nut, which no other fruit has, stand for Right Faith, Right Knowledge, and Right Conduct: the Three Jaina Jewels.

*   *   *

340. Chart of Meditation on *Namo Arihantanam*; after the late Acharya Sushil Kumar (*see* page 92 in his *Song of the Soul*).

240

The Namokar Mantra – the Song of the Soul

The late Sthanakavasi Acharya Sushil Kumar (1926–1994), the first Jaina ascetic who dared to trespass the rule that bans the use of mechanical transport for mendicants, was a great master of meditation and the science of sound. As a child, though born into a Hindu Brahmin family, he had discovered the power of the Namokar Mantra that was taught to him by a Jaina muni. At the age of fifteen he himself became a Shvetambara Sthanakavasi monk. In his small book *Song of the Soul – An Introduction to the Namokar Mantra*, he writes, "A valuable question to ask yourself is – what is your goal? What do you want to become in this life? To this question, I must answer that the Namokar Mantra is my goal and my life. It is my life and destiny. Through it I can serve and guide along the path of non-violence.(...) So when I came to America (that was in 1975, *the editor*), I decided to teach the science of sound vibration according to the Arihant tradition. The ancient teachings of the Arihantas are very powerful, very clear and true, and the Namokar Mantra is the essence of that knowledge. This small book will simply introduce you to the mantra's power." *

Jainas of all denominations chant and sing the Namokar Mantra in Prakrit, the language in which it was composed at an unknown date many centuries ago. It consists of just five lines of text and two appended lines. They read as follows:

Namo Arihantanam   (I bow to the *Arihantas*, the Jinas, the perfected human beings).
Namo Siddhanam   (I bow to the *Siddhas*, the liberated bodiless souls).
Namo Airiyanam   (I bow to the *Acharyas*, the leaders of the Jaina congregations).
Namo Uvajjhayanam   (I bow to the *Upadhayayas*, the spiritual teachers).
Namo Loe Savva Sahunam   (I bow to all the *Sadhus* (ascetics) in the world).
Eso pancha namokaro savva pavapanasno
mangalanamcha savvesim padhamam havai mangalam. (This five-fold
obeisance mantra destroys all sins and obstacles, and of all auspicious repetitions, it is
the first and foremost.)

"In the Namokar Mantra," Acharya Sushil Kumar continues to say, "we pay homage to the five divine personalities, but they are not separate from us. They are actually symbolic of noble qualities, or states of consciousness, which we are striving to attain. They do not represent different paths to the goal of liberation but rather, various states in the evolution of the soul. If we are spiritual practitioners, then in essence we are *Sadhus*, and we can progress to the ultimate states of *Arihant* and *Siddha*, and attain liberation." **

* Published in 1987 by Siddhachalam Publishers, 65 Mud Pond Road, Blairstown, New Jersey 07825, U.S.A. This is
also the address of the main Ashram founded by the late Acharya Sushil Kumar in the U.S.A.

** Page 28 in *The Namokar Mantra – the Song of the Soul.*.

MUSIK AND DANCE IN JAINISM

Having come to Jainism via Theravada Buddhism, a creed that – leaving aside the monotonous chanting of the monks – permits of no music in its temples. And as in my readings about Jainism I have never come across a comprehensive evaluation of Jaina music, I concluded that there was none. Does not Mahavira advise his monks and nuns to stay away from places where sounds of musical instruments can be heard? "A monk or nun," says he, " should not resolve to go where they will hear sounds of stringed instruments, kettle-drums etc." (*Acaranga Sutra* 2, 11, 1)

Only after I submitted myself to the impulse of going to *see* Jainism instead of just studying it from books, I discovered that there *is* Jaina music and, to my delighted surprise, not just a solemn kind of incantation as someone might expect, whose knowledge of Jainism is confined to having studied its doctrines, but that there exists in Jainism the artistic capacity of producing, not seldom on the spur of the moment, sonorous seas of sounds which at times reach hights of jubilation that stir the participants into stepping forward and dancing.

It woud need someone better versed in matters of music and dance than myself to put this aspect of the Jaina religion into a wider perspective. I must confine myself to the attempt of inducing my non-Jaina readers to go, hear and see for themselves. They would not return disappointed. The best time, next to certain major ceremonies such as the consecration of a new idol, is in the early evening when the temple-rite of *arati*, a ceremonial adoration of the Jina with kindled wicks, is performed.

"We have", to quote from a lecture by the late Kumari Parul Troliya, "little knowledge and record of contributions to music by Jainas. There are several creations like Gita Vitaraga in Sanskrit and Kannada along the lines of Jayadev's 'Gita Govinda'. (...) Jaina poets like Mahayogi Anandhan, Chindananda, Banarasi Das, Dyanstrai, and others, have created beautiful musical pieces in form of devotional lyrics, replete with indications of *ragas*. They are in no way inferior to Kabir, Meera or Surdas.(...) To conclude, the contribution of Jaina culture to Indian art, literature, music etc. is enormous but of which we, the Jainas ourselves, are not fully aware. Let's be conscious of it, and enrich the rich heritage of ours." (From *Gomatavani*, Vol. IV, No. 5, Shravanabelagola, 1989.)

341, 342. Detail of a painted dome in a temple on Shatrunjaya Hill showing in the upper half a figurative dance indicative of the joyous mood associated with the mythical event pictured in the lower half (described above, pages 332/33). The photo **341** (*left*) was taken in the Mirpur Temple in 1992 (*see* pages 172–174). It shows that in Jainism tradition is still very much alive.

*   *   *

Jainism is far from being a cold or bloodless religion and there is a rich literature of praise and devotion to the fordmakers which, in the vernacular literatures of north and west India, reached a particularly impressive extent during the late medieval period.
Dundas, 1992: 181.

243

343 – 345 (*above and opposite*). A Tirthankara is born. The news of it is greeted in the heavens with great joy. God Indra (also known as Shakra), arises from his spendidly jewelled throne and descends to earth accompanied by a retinue of celestial musicians. He, the king of gods, himself dancing to the playing of many instruments, approaches the newborn Tirthankara holding in his lower hands flowers and other offerings, while heavenly nymphs perform a welcoming dance on the palms of his upper hands.

At the sight of Indra and the sound of music, the mother has placed the child on the lap of the king sitting next to her. Before long, both the parents fall into a spellbound sleep, so, without their noticing it, a maidservant takes the child and hands him up to Indra who, now sitting on his many-trunked elephant *Airavata*, rides to the foot of holy Mount Meru on the summit of which the newborn Tirthankara receives his first bath at the hands of the overjoyed gods and goddesses (ill. **343 & 344 >**). This done, the infant Jina is carried back to his parents, again to the sound of music and accompanied by dancing gods and celestial damsels.

These three photos show sequences from the twelve metre long painting on cloth kept in the Sana Gana Mandir at Karanja (*see* page 95). Interestingly, in Jaina pictorial art gods and heavenly musicians can be recognized by their *not* having moustaches.

344, 345.

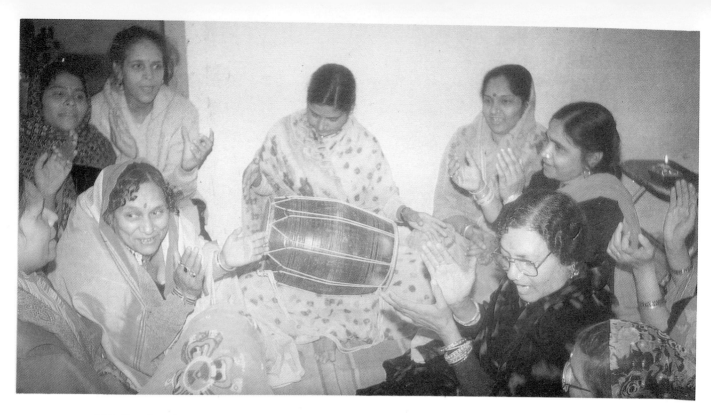

346. Evening time in a *dharmashala* pilgrims' room annexed to the Ramtek Shantinatha Temple. A lady-pilgrim has invited her next-door neighbours into her temporary abode, demonstrating in that way her satisfaction with having had, on this day, the honour of serving food and drink to Acharya Vidhyasagar (*see* ill. **144**). Spontaneous music making and singing, carried on for hours, and saying farewell to each guest by handing her a small present mark the meritorious event.

347. Religious songs, performed by a choir of *samani* nuns, enliven a general meeting of the India-wide Shvetambara Terapanth congregation, held near Ladnun in Rajasthan.

246

348. Two *brahmacharis* of the local *Gurukula* and a group of children have gathered in the court-yard of the Shravanabelagola Mangayi Basti to practise a hymn written and composed by a muni in which the statue of Bahubali is extolled to the skies. The re-occurring and fervently enunciated '*bimba*' – the term for statue – lends the song a passionate flair.*

*   *   *

It was evening, and we went to various bastis *in the town of Shravana Belgola for* darshan. *We lingered long in Mangayi Basti listening to the evening prayers being recited by the children of the Shravana Belgola Jain Gurukula. Seated in neat rows they sang hymns to the various Tirthankaras finishing with Gommateshvara* stutih *– a song in praise of Gommateshvara. (...) From there we went to the* matha *where the evening* arati *was in progress. A special prayer was being said in the honour of Goddess Kushmandini, the patron goddess of Shravana Belgola, who was dressed and decorated in jewels and flowers. The temple musicians played the* shehnai *and the drums to mark the end of another day.*

Saryu Doshi *Homage to Shravana Belgola*, 1981: 32.

* There appeared, too late for being mentioned in this chapter, a new book by Professor M.A. Dhaky entitled *Arhat Parshva and Dharanendra Nexus,* which contains a chapter on Jaina hymnic literature.

349. Interior of the Jaina Temple in Oxford Street, Leicester, UK, the first and so far (1998) the only Jaina Mandir in Europe. The inauguration took place in July 1988. Both Shvetambaras and Digambaras participated in the planning and building of the Centre which is open to all. "It aims to spread knowledge and sympathetic understanding of Jainism, and to promote the non-violent way of life." A study room on the second floor is dedicated to Shrimad Rajachandra, the friend and teacher of Gandhi, *see* page 165. (Courtesy Jain Samaj Europe, Leicester, UK.)

248

JAINA DAWN IN THE WEST

Noel Q. King

The saga of Western humanity's rise and fall and its life beyond the graves of the two world wars has a deep fascination and is of vital significance for the survival of all. If we were historians of plant pathology studying potato famine, we could try to show how the potato disease which caused the great famines of the nineteenth century was killed by the long sailing ship voyage across the equator but steam ships brought it in a virulent form.* We could point to the introduction of another strain and of different storage and transportation facilities as the solution. History of Religions is not as straightforward or as developed a subject but in this essay there is an attempt to set forth an outline history of the knowledge and understanding of and response to Jainism by the peoples of the West from antiquity to the present day. Throughout there is the implication that this religion is an 'exotic' strain which could vivify the incumbent varieties.

Since the days of Alexander, the so-called 'Great', educated Westerners have been fascinated by stories coming in from India about naked mendicants who coveted nothing and were afraid of none. In those stories, with our latter day wisdom, we can hail some of our first news of the Jainas. By the nineteenth century we had learned only a little more. The British officials like H.Th. Colebrooke and missionaries like the Stevenson dynasty and Americans connected with Bombay and Gujerat mission fields begin to tell us more. By the middle of the century, scholars, fascinated by the discovery of the Indo-Germanic theory of languages, were opening up the original texts. German scholars especially made a valuable contribution with their exact and meticulous word studies and their seeking out of scientific etymologies. A *parampara*, a succession of teachers and disciples, has proliferated and continued to the present day. The British and North Americans continued the work, French and Belgians joined in and a number of distinguished Italians.

It is good to expand a little on the work of two people of German origin who gained pre-eminence at a time when the university in the German world had attained its highest distinction. Dr. Georg Buehler (1837–1898) served fifteen years on the staff of Elphinstone College at Bombay. During these years he personally took part in archaeological field work on Jaina remains and travelled extensively, visiting monasteries and manuscript storehouses to search out the most authentic texts. His health broke down, so he continued his activities in Austria and Germany, encouraging Jainology at all levels. He met death by drowning while still actively engaged in research and teaching.

---

* Prof. King is referring to what happened in Ireland in the 19th century, the country where the famine caused by the potato disease was especially severe. *The editor.*

The other notable scholar is Dr. Hermann Jacobi (1850–1937). He visited India in 1873 and 1913–1914. He not only did some of the most fundamental work towards our truer understanding of Jainism but his two volumes in Max Mueller's *Sacred Books of the East,* have for over a century placed soundly and sympathetically written Jaina material before Oxford University Press' world-wide English-reading public. Thanks to him the aphorisms of the Jaina *sutras* have taken a place with the Chinese classics, the Qur'an and the Sanskrit and Buddhist texts. These are but two scholars chosen at random. One could set forward a mighty galaxy of others – German, French, Belgian, Dutch, British, American, Canadian, and Italian – who have done and continue to do distinguished work.

Since our subject is concerned with Western perceptions of 'the Jaina radiance', as J. Stevenson the missionary called it in the 1830's, we have spoken only of Western scholars. Of course the real work all along was utterly dependent on Indian co-operation. All the truly great foreign scholars gratefully acknowledge this and of the very nature of the case it could not be otherwise. Just as inevitably our knowledge of Jainism remained mainly a matter for our scholars and therefore was bound to be eurocentric, lacking popular support and as impersonal and objective as possible. Any deep-going and widespread application of Jaina principles to the people's life in general was not yet imaginable. In a way the use of the swastika is an ironic commentary on this. The Jainas have used this symbol in its good luck iconographical form. We used it in reverse form. After being popular with some for a while, to most of us it has become a sign of ill omen. The Jainas still use it, and in the West, when they do so in public, it can produce consternation.

The first breakthrough on a more widespread level was made by a Mr. Virchand Gandhi. The enterprising conveners of the World's Parliament of Religions, due to meet at Chicago in 1893, had sent an invitation to a Jaina muni. Of course his vows did not allow such a journey. The invitation was passed on to a young Jaina layman from Gujerat who was General Secretary of the Jain Association. He was gaining lawyer's qualifications and eventually attained the bar in both India and Britain. He did brilliantly well in a dignified, rational, and undemagogic fashion. He was very different one might say without invidious comparison on either side, from the charismatic and captivating Swami Vivekananada. In its own way the victory of these men was in the religious sphere as clear a word to those who had ears to hear as the sinking of the Russian fleet by the Japanese in 1905. Mr. Gandhi followed up his success at the Parliament by his teaching and writing in America and Britain and gained a number of faithful Western followers. They went ahead, not making many adherents but preparing the ground for what was to come long after their time. Mr. Gandhi himself unfortunately died at the age of 37 in 1901. The community did not produce another such individual apostle and prophet to the West. But the genius of Jainism is finally a community product, not the achievement of any one person.

Inside India, Jainism itself underwent a revolution which has never been fully written up because as with most things Jaina it emanated from the nature of the body and sought as little publicity as possible. From being a withdrawing and retiring community in the shadows of obscure native states and desert places, the Jainas had set up important centres of power and activity in the great cities and in the progressive elements in Indian life. Known as a group who provided hospitals for birds and rescued sacrificial animals, the Jainas became the financiers who helped to topple British imperialism and provide resettlement and a new prosperity for those driven out of Pakistan, Burma, and Uganda. In the professions they took a leading part. Up till recently they did not set up a private university of their own like the Muslim University at Aligarh or the Hindu University at Vanarasi. But everywhere the Jainas gave university leadership with a certain reserved, quiet, noble dignity which is more their style. They of course went deeper and deeper into Jainology in a way with which outsiders find it difficult to compete, though they receive every encouragement from those within. The academic achievement was signalled by a Jaina winning one of the premier Chairs in 'Indology', as the classicists called it, in the West. In their success and self-confidence the community, still centered in India, is no longer fighting for survival in the face of the outer world. It can perhaps turn more attention to making its teaching known in our world.

The other great new factor has been the establishment of a world-wide Jaina diaspora. In the 1960's economic and legal changes provided a window of opportunity which enabled Jainas to set up communities in Britain, North America, Australia, Malaysia, Thailand, and Hong Kong. Thence perhaps they will spread to Europe, the former Soviet Union, China, and Latin America. Some remain in the earlier Indian diaspora in places like Kenya, Ethiopia and Fiji. The pattern for each settlement seems to be this: Individuals come in, then groups of Jainas gather. Especially as their families arrive, they feel in need of liturgy and teaching as well as social and cultural activity. Lay leaders among them do indeed organize house meetings and conduct services and activities most capably. But still there is a longing for the presence of the monks and nuns. Of course, since most Jainas abroad are professionals or fairly well-to-do business people, air flights home do much to help. But there is need for the presence abroad of Jaina monks and nuns besides Jaina lay men and lay women. Individuals of the mendicant orders are not supposed to travel by any form of mechanical transport. Some of them have dispensed with this provision, justifying their action by the need of the people abroad. Gurudev Chitrabhanu came in 1971 and set up meditation centres over the years. In 1975 Acharya Sushil Kumar (1926–1994), a Sthanakavasi Jaina, came with some monks to the U.S.A. The major *ashram* he founded is at Siddhachalam in Blairstown, New Jersey.

The Western Jaina communities began to organize centres for worship and study and have united in Asscociations and Federations. They hope to set up a World Federation. The centres invite and supervise visits and residence by religious specialists. Acharya Tulsi of Ladnun in Rajasthan authorized selected monks and nuns of his community to travel abroad as *samanas* and *samanis*, and they too are in great demand to visit and live with Jaina groups in various parts of the world.*

The Jainas survived centuries of persecution, genocide, and discrimination perpetrated even by Hindu groups in the days of Shankaracharya and Madhvacharya onwards. Jainas stood in the eye of the storm of the millennial Muslim invasions, yet they survived even in the North West Frontier Province and Sind till 1947. Partly they survived by avoiding publicity, and by seeking to mingle with the others so as to be inconspicuous. We cannot expect them suddenly to open up to an outer world and shout about themselves, even about the glory of the faith they have preserved. Also they tend to prefer to build temples rather than assist publicity through film or publications or patronage of scholars who are on the fringes and could bring knowledge of the Jainas to outsiders. If they turned their mind to it they could do a great deal to rescue a world which seems to be tottering towards self-destruction. They appreciate the remark that they are dragons guarding a great treasure.

In the meantime the shell of self-sufficiency and imagined superiority which had somehow encapsulated the Western mind had cracked and fallen to pieces. Westerners know the fairest flower of Western civilisation had eviscerated itself. They ask whether there is any means of saving a world civilisation to which the West has contributed so much from destroying itself. In the study of the Jaina way there are some clues both to the cause of the destruction and to the hope of survival. We may consider some examples, clothing them in everyday terms. The Jainas teach that depending on various factors, the truth may be represented in different ways. More than one way may be right. Therefore we must respect and learn to live with other points of view. Or again, our universe is interdependent, it is not made more for one member such as the human than it is for others, such as animals. Thus kindness is shown to animals not only out of compassion but because any kind of injustice or violence is destructive to the whole and obviously of oneself. Everything is mutually interdependent and co-exists in the whole. Therefore a total and universal sense of responsibility is required of us not only in regard to replacing warfare and violence with fullness of life for all but with regard to proper behavior towards the environment. Humans have to learn to see themselves in their proper and due place, prepared to use only what is necessary and to give up with grace and appropriateness. For some this can include a process of euthanasia which is not suicide, but that is a matter not easy to explain in anything short of a few volumes.

* See chapter LADNUN, page 144. *The editor.*

To sum up and conclude. The Jainas are poised at a place in history where their teachings are vitally necessary to world civilization. If they are willing to propagate them world-wide (in the best and early sense in the word), and we are willing to receive and make them our own, there will be a new dawn of purpose for us all, including the insects and bacteria, viruses, and disease syndromes.*

It is said the story of King Arthur or of Abelard and Heloise are a paradigm of the European Middle Ages or Dr. Faustus of the Renaissance and Enlightenment. The Jainas have an endless stock of stories with which they have enriched the vernacular literatures of the cultures they have entered. We can await the appearance in Western garb of for instance the following gem as recreated by a Jaina producer at Hollywood. A King and Queen had a lovely daughter. With joy and anticipation they made ready for her marriage to the most perfect prince and world conqueror. Immediately after the betrothal and all the ceremonies were over, the Prince went off into the wilderness, threw aside his regalia, plucked out his hair and renounced the world.** The Princess followed and did the same and as he found his way into perfection, she too entered thereinto.

* Bacteria, for instance, are indipensable when it comes to heal injuries done to earth and water.

** The prince in this story is Neminatha, the 22nd Tirthankara, also named Aristanemi. It was the sight of the fenced-in animals meant to be slaughtered and served to the wedding-guests that made him act in this way. Scenes of this legendary story are depicted in the ceiling relief-plaque in front of cell 11 in the Luna-Vasahi shrine at Dilwara on Mount Abu. The Luna-Vasahi is dedicated to Neminatha. *The Editor.*

'The West has great need for Jainism'

On this occasion I recall my first invitation by a Jaina community, years ago, in Matunga to a religious service held by Sadhvishri Goranji, which impressed me deeply. I was sitting among the shravakas *and* shravikas *and heard the Sadhvi elucidate explanations of the scriptures and her preaching against pride, greed,* himsa *and deceit, and against falsehood, theft, egoism and materialism. It appealed very much to me that she called 'ahimsa' the 'parama dharma', the first of the commandments and the highest virtue. Never shall I forget the sublime, spiritual and peaceful appearance of the Sadhvi. At this particular opportunity it originated in me an admiring, deep and lasting impression of Jainism and its principles (...).*

Helmuth Dietmar
Formerly Commercial Attaché of Germany in India

I myself am a Christian, and I see clearly, that the Jain philosophy embraces all faiths and all believes. (...) The obvious happiness of the Jains, in spite of all renunciation of material things, is so evident. Perhaps I should not say 'in spite of' but because of this renunciation. I should like to see Jainism, and that for which it stands, expand to each country. It can be nothing but a blessing. The West has great need for Jainism.(...)

Baron von Blomberg, Boston, U.S.A.

Source of these two quotations: *ACHARYA TULSI - Fifty Years of Selfless Dedication,* Jaipur, 1985.

350. Deogarh, seated Jina. End of ninth century. During recent restoration work this impressive image was chosen to represent Mahavira and accordingly marked by carving his emblem, a lion, into the blanket of his throne (*see* page 112).

APPENDIX

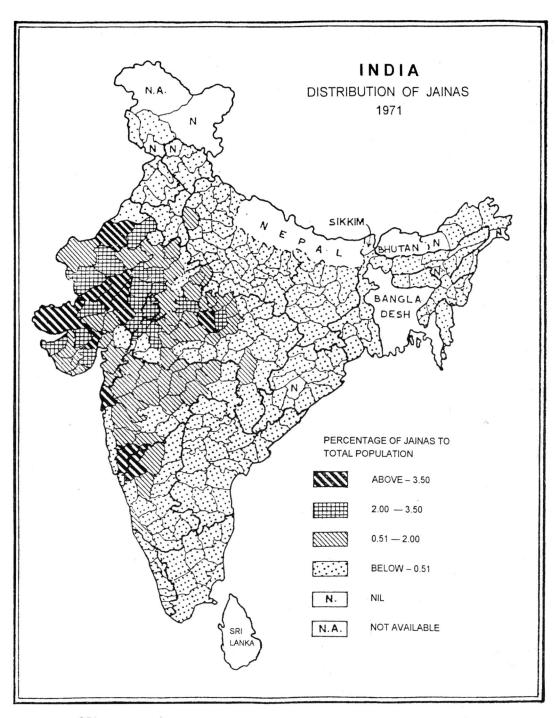

351. Courtesy Vilas A. Sangave. *Jaina Community – A Social Survey,* Bombay, 1980.

Table showing distribution of the Jaina Population (statewise in descending order)

Total Population of India (1991): 846,300,000

State / Union Territory	Total Jaina Population 1981 Census	Total Jaina Population 1991 Census
I n d i a	**3,206,038**	**3,352,706***
1. Maharashtra	939,392	965,840
2. Rajasthan	624,317	562,806
3. Gujarat	467,768	491,331
4. Madhya Pradesh	444,960	490,324
5. Karnataka	297,974	326,114
6. Uttar Pradesh	141,549	176,259
7. Delhi	73,917	94,672
8. Tamilnadu	49,564	66,900
9. West Bengal	38,663	34,355
10. Haryana	35,482	35,296
11. Bihar	27,613	23,049
12. Punjab	27,049	20,763
13. Assam	–	20,645
14. Andhra Pradesh	18,642	26,564
15. Orissa	6,642	6,302
16. Kerala	3,605	3,641
17. Chandigarh	1,889	1,531
18. Jammu & Kashmir	1,576	–
19. Nagaland	1,153	1202
20. Himachal Pradesh	1,046	1206
21. Manipur	975	1337
22. Goa, Daman & Diu	602	699
23. Meghalaya	542	445
24. Dadra & Nagar Haveli	372	529
25. Tripura	297	–
26. Pondicherry	277	470
27. Sikkim	108	40
28. Arunachala Pradesh	42	64
29. Andaman & Nicobar Island	11	17
30. Mizoram	11	4

* Paul Dundas (1992: 232) writes of seventy to eighty thousand Jainas now living outside India, other sources speak of about hundred thousand. As many Indians tend to think of themselves of firstly belonging to a particular caste, which in some cases can be either Jaina or Hindu, the total number of Jainas is generally estimated of being considerably higher than the above stated figure of 3,352,706.

BIBLIOGRAPHY (A SELECTION FOR THE GENERAL READER)

Comprehensive Studies of Jainism

DUNDAS, Paul, *The Jains*. London and New York: Routledge, 1992.

GLASENAPP, Helmuth von, *Jainism: An Indian Religion of Salvation* (Berlin 1925). English translation: Shridhar B. Shrotri. Delhi: Motilal Banarsidass, 1998.

JAINI, Padmanabh S., *The Jaina Path of Purification*. Delhi: Motilal Banarsidass and Berkeley University Press (U.S.A.), 1979.

SCHUBRING, Walther, *The Doctrine of the Jainas*. Translated from the revised German edition by Wolfgang Beurlen. Delhi: Motilal Banarsidass, 1978. (For advanced students.)

Canonical Works in Translation

JACOBI, Hermann, *Jaina Sutras*. Sacred Books of the East, Volumes 22 and 45; Oxford University Press, 1884, 1895. Reprinted by Motilal Banarsidass, Delhi, 1964, 1968, 1973, 1980, 1989.

JOHNSON, W. J., *Harmless Souls – Karmic Bondage and Religious Change in Early Jainism with special Reference to Umasvati and Kundakunda*. Delhi: Motilal Banarsidass, 1995.

LAWANI, K. C.,*Uttaradhyayana The Last Testament of Bhagavan Mahavira* (Prakrit text with English rendering in verse form). Calcutta: Prajnanam (12 Duff Street, Calcutta 6) 1977

—: *Kalpa Sutra of Bhadrabahu Svami*. Delhi: Motilal Banarsidass, 1979.

Art, Architecture and Places of Pilgrimage

BRUHN, Klaus, *The Jina-Images of Deogarh*. Leiden (Netherlands): E. J. Brill, 1979.

DHAKY, M. A. and U. P. SHAH (eds.), *Aspects of Jaina Art and Architecture*. Ahmedabad, 1975.

DOSHI, Saryu, (ed.), *Homage to Shravana Belgola*. Bombay: Marg Publication, 1981.

—: *Masterpieces of Jain Painting*. Bombay: Marg Publication, 1985.

DOSHI, Saryu (text) and Thomas DIX, (photographs), *Dharna Vihara, Ranakpur*. Stuttgart (Germany): Edition Axel Menges, 1995.

FISCHER, Klaus, *Caves and Temples of the Jains*. Aliganj (India), 1956.

GOSH, A., (ed.), *Jaina Art and Architecture*, 3 Volumes. New Delhi: Bharatiya Jnanpith, 1974–1976.

JAYANTAVIJAYAJI MUNI, *Holy Abu,* (translated by U. P. Shah). Bhavnagar (India), 1987.

METHA, Jodh Singh, *Abu to Udaipur*. Delhi: Motilal Banarsidass, 1970.

PAL, Pratapaditya, *The Peaceful Liberators – Jain Art from India*. Copublished by Los Angeles County Museum of Art and Thames and Hudson, New York and London, 1995.

PEREIRA, José, *Monolithic Jinas – The Iconography of the Jain Temples of Ellora*. Delhi: Motilal Banarsidass, 1977.

SANGAVE, Vilas A., *The Sacred Shravanabelagola - A Socio-Religious Study*. New Delhi: Bharatiya Jnanpith, 1981.

SETTAR, S., *Sravana Belgola – An Illustrated Study*. Dharwad: Ruvari, 1981.

SINGH, Harihar, *Jaina Temples of Western India*. Varanasi, 1982.

SIVARAMAMURTI, C., *Panorama of Jain Art*. New Dehli: The Times of India, 1983.

VYAS, R.T. (ed.), *Studies in Jaina Art and Iconography*. New Delhi: Abhinav Publication, 1995.

Cosmology and Cosmography

CAILLAT, Collette and Ravi KUMAR, *The Jain Cosmology*. Basel, Paris, New Delhi, 1981: Kumar Gallery, 11 Sunder Nagar Market, New Delhi - 110 003.

Religion and Culture

AMAR, Upadhyaya Muni, *Amar Vani* (translated by Dr. B.B. Jain). Agra: 3rd edition, 1988.

CORT, J. E.,*Liberation and Wellbeing: A Study of the* Shvetambar *Murtipujak Jains of North Gujarat*. Ph. D. Dissertation, Harvard University, 1989.

FOLKERT, Kendall W. (revised and enlarged by John E. Cort), "Jainism." *A New Handbook of Living Religions*, second revised edition, 340–68. Ed. John R. Hinnels. Oxford: Blackwell, 1996.

JAIN, Jyoti Prasad, *Religion and Culture of the Jains.* New Delhi: Bharatiya Jnanpith, 1983.

JAIN, Surendra K. (ed.), *Glimpses of Jainism.* Delhi: Motilal Banarsidass, 1997.

PARMAJ, D. S., *Light of Jain Teaching*, 2nd. edition. Bahubali (Kolhapur): Sanmati Prakashan Publishers, 1981.

RAJACHANDRA, Shrimad, *Atma Siddhi* (*Self-Realisation*), trans. D.C. Metha. Bombay, 1976.

SANGAVE, Vilas A., *Aspects of Jaina Religion.* New Delhi: Bharatiya Jnanpith, 1990.

—: *The Jaina Path of Ahimsa.* Sholarpur (Maharashtra): Mahavir Research Centre, Padmashri Sumatibai Vidyapith Trust, 1991.

SHAH, Nagin J., *Jaina Philosophy and Religion.* Delhi, 1998.

SHANTA, N., *The Unknown Pilgrims: History, Spirituality, Life of the Jaina Women Ascetics.* Shri Staguru Publications (a Division of Indian Books Centre 40/5 Shakti Nagar, Delhi - 110 007), 1997.

TOBIAS, Michael, *Life Force – The World of Jainism.* Asian Humanities Press (U.S.A.), 1991.

TULSI, Acharya, *On Contemporary Problems.* Ladnun (Rajasthan): Jain Vishva Bharati, 1993.

WILLIAMS, R., *Jaina Yoga.* Delhi: Motilal Banarsidass, 1983.

ZIMMER, Heinrich, *Philosophies of India* (Jainism: 181–279), ed. Joseph Cambell (first printing 1951). Delhi: Motilal Banarsidass, 1990.

Social and Historical Studies

CARRITHERS, M. and C. HUMPHREY (eds.), *The Assembly of Listeners: Jains in Society.* Cambridge University Press, 1991.

FILLIOZAT, Vasundhara (ed.), *The Vijayanagar Empire.* National Booktrust New Delhi, Reprint 1980. Contains Fernao Nuniz's observations he made in Hampi early in the 16th century.

FLÜGEL, Peter, "The ritual circle of the Terapanth Shvetambar Jains". In Bulletin D' Etudes Indiennes N°ˢ 13–14 (1995–96).

JAIN, Kailash Chand, *Lord Mahavira and his Times.* Delhi: Motilal Banarsidass, 1974.

SANGAVE, Vilas A., *Jaina Community - A social Survey* (second revised edition). Bombay: Popular Prakashan, 1980.

—: *Jaina Society Through the Ages.* New Delhi: Shri Raj Krishen Jain Charitable Trust (Ahimsa Mandir, Daryaganj), 1992.

TUKOL, T. K., *Sallekhana is Not Suicide.* Ahmedabad (Lalbhai Dalpatbhai Series), 1976.

Literature

GRANOFF, Phyllis, *The Clever Adulteress (and otherStories).* First published: Ontario, 1990. Delhi: Motilal Banarsidass, 1993.

MAHENDRA KUMAR, Muni Shri, *Jaina Stories As gleaned from canonical texts.* English translation: K.C. Lalwani. (3 Volumes bound in one). Delhi: Motilal Banarsidass, 1984.

Worship and Rituals

ACHARYA SUSHIL KUMAR, *Song of the Soul - An Introduction to the Namokar Mantra and the Science of Sound.* Blairstown, New Jersey, U.S.A.: Siddhachalam Publishers, 1987.

BHADRABAHUVIJAY MUNI, *Guidelines of Jainism.* Mehsana (Gujarat): Sri Vishwa Kalyan Trust, 1986.

CORT, J. E., "Following the Jina, Worshipping the Jina. An Essay on Jain Rituals." In *The Peaceful Conquerors* (*see* PAL, Pratapaditya). Also by J.E. Cort: "Murtipuja in Svetambar Jain Temples", in *Religion in India*, 212–23. Ed. T. N. Madan. Delhi: Oxford University Press, 1991.

FISCHER E. and J. JAIN, *Art and Rituals, 2500 Years of Jainism..* New Delhi: Sterling Publishers, 1977.

TUKUL, T. K., *Yoga, Meditation & Mysticism in Jainism.* New Delhi: Raj Krishen JainTrust, 1978.

GLOSSARY

acharya: head of a mendicant group, preceptor.

agama: scripture; canonical literature.

ahimsa: non-harming, non-violence.

ailaka: probationary monk, also the highest state of a Digambara layman, wherein he retains only one piece of clothing.

anekantavada: the doctrine of manifold aspects (in the philosophical sense).

aparigrahavrata: the fifth vow, meaning voluntarily setting a limit to one's possesions and spending any income above the set limit on matters of religion and charity.

arati and *mangaldeep*: lamp-waving and camphor-burning rite in front of the Jina image, usually performed after sunset.

arhat: Thirthankara or Jina.

aryika: Digambara nun.

atman: soul; self.

avasarpini: regressive half-cycle of time.

basti and *basadi*: other words for temple in South India.

bhattaraka: a class of Digambara pontiffs.

bhojan-shala: kitchen and eating hall.

brahmachari: celibate male student.

brahmacharini: celibate female student.

chaturmukha or *chaumukha*: shrine with openings on all four sides.

chaturvidha-sangha: term describing the Jaina community consisting of monks, nuns, laymen and laywomen.

chauri: fly-whisk.

dana: a charitable gift.

dharma-chakra: 'wheel of the law'.

dharmashala: inn for pilgrims.

devakulika: small shrine facing the main temple.

diksha: formal initiation into ascetic order.

doli: palanquin for carrying pilgrims.

gandharva: celestial musician.

gurukula: traditional Jaina school guided by a spiritual teacher.

jambu-dvipa: 'Continent of the Rose-apple Tree'.

jinalaya(m): shrine housing a Jina image.

jirnodhar: reconstruction.

Kali Yuga: the present 'Corrupt Age', *see avarsarpini*.

karma: according to Jaina philosophy, is not 'deeds' but matter consisting of fine imperceptible particles which form a vail around the soul, that in turn hampers the progress towards self-realization and salvation (Saryu Doshi).

kesh lonch: pulling out one's hair.

kevalajnana: infinite knowledge; omniscience.

kshetra: sanctified place of pilgrimage.

kshetrapala: 'guardian of the region', e.g., of a temple complex.

kshullaka: junior monk who wears three pieces of clothing.

lechya: karmic stain, the colour of which indicates a soul's degree of purity.

manastambha: a pillar in front of a Jaina temple.

mandapa: temple hall.

mandir: temple (common term in North India).

mastakabisheka: head-anointing ceremony, also *mahamastakabisheka* (*maha* = great).

matha: residence of a Digambara Battaraka.

mithuna: amorous couple.

moksha: salvation; emancipation from the cycle of births and deaths.

muhpatti: piece of cloth worn over the mouth by Sthanakavasi monks and nuns.

nandishvara-dvipa: the island-continent of the Jaina cosmos where the gods meet to celebrate the birth of a Tirthankara.

nandyavarta: a diagram.

nirvana: release from karmic bondage; liberation of the soul; death.

nirvana-bhumi: place of death.

nishidhi: death by the rite of *sallekhana*.

nityavada: eternalism.

paduka: footprint.

pancha-kalyanaka: the five auspicious events in the life of a Tirthankara.

panjarapolas: shelters for abandoned and sick animals.

parabadis: pigeon houses.

paramatman: the highest (the liberated) soul.

prayashitta: rite for atonement of sins.

pujari: temple attendant responsible for attending to the daily rites of ablution and authorized to conduct *puja*.

sadhus, sadhvis: monks, nuns.

sallekhana: ritual death by fasting.

samadhi: meditative process towards attaining salvation of the soul.

samavasarana: mythical assembly arena with a Tirthankara in the centre.

sangha: community; ascetic order.

shikhara: temple tower.

shramana: a non-Vedic mendicant, usually a Jaina or Buddhist.

shravaka, shravika: layman, laywoman.

siddha: a liberated soul.

siddha-chakra: 'saint wheel'.

siddha-loka: the permanent abode of the soul

sutras: the canonical scriptures

tri-murtika: panel of three Jina images

tirtha: sacred site of pilgrimage, literally a ford.

torana: ornamental entrance.

upashrayas: rooms for religious teaching and for providing shelter to monks and nuns.

vidyadharas: minor mythological figurs.

vihara: another word for temple.

vimanas: miraculous chariots used by the gods.

yaksha, yakshi: demigod, demigoddess (in Jaina art each Tirthankara has his particular *yaksha* and *yakshi*).

ADDRESSES AND MISCELLANEOUS NOTES IN ALPHABETICAL ORDER

AHMEDABAD. Dipak Sutaria, Jaina Guide and Tour Escort. 38, Jain Society, Ahmedabad - 380 006, Gujarat, India. Fax: 0091–272–468542.

ARRAH. Jain Oriental Library (and other facilities). Write to the Honorary Director of Shri Jain Siddhant Bhawan, Devashram-Mahadeva Road, Arrah - 802 301, Bihar, India.

BAHUBALI (Kolhapur). Also known as Kumbhojagiri. For information or booking a room in the guest-house write to: The Principal, Bahubali High School, Bahubali (Kolhapur) - 416 008, Karnataka, India. Nandani, a large village and seat of a Digambara Bhattaraka (residing in a tenth century temple compound), is within easy reach from Bahubali. The hospitable inhabitants of Nandani belie the often made assertion that Jainas cannot be farmers.It is a recommendable area for students of sociology.

BIKANER. Hotel Bhanwar Niwas (*see* page 149); Rampuria Street, Bikaner - 334 005, India.

BOMBAY (MUMBAI). Bharatvarshiya Digamber Jain Tirth-Kshetra Committee. Provides information about Digambara sacred places. Office: Hirabaug, C.P. Tank Road, Bombay - 400 004.

DHARMASTHALA. The Secretary to Shri Veerendra Heggade, Dharmasthala - 574 216, Karnataka, India. A unique place of Jaina/Hindu pilgrimage; hosts an annual conference of all religions.

DELHI. Atma Vallabh Sanskriti Jaina Mandir (*see* p. 136). 20th km., G.T. Karanal Road, P.O. Alipur, Delhi - 110 036. The *Bhogilal Leherchand Institute of Indology* is situated in the basement of the Mandir. A guest-house provides board and lodging to scholars from within India and overseas.

NEW DELHI. Ahimsa International, Secretary General Satish Kumar Jain, 53 Rishabh Vihar, Vikas Marg Extension, Delhi - 110 092. / Adhyatma Sadhana Kendra. A Terapanth Jaina Centre of Preksha Meditation and Yoga, Shri Dharmanada, Director. Fax: 6803678. Located at Chhattarpur Road, Mehrouli, New Delhi - 110 030. Open to all. / Mahavir International. Regd. Office: 21/85, Lodhi Colony, New Delhi - 110 003.

GERMANY. Jain Association International (Germany). Ajit Benadi, Schweriner Str. 5, D-24558 Henstedt-Ulzburg, Germany. Fax: 04193 – 968361.

GINGEE. Hotel Shivasand, Mahatma Gandhi Road, Gingee - 604 202, Tamilnadu, India. Ask the manager for a guide to the '24 Tirthankaras' (*see* page 62).

GREAT BRITAIN. Institute of Jainology, Nemu Chandaria (Co-ordinator), Unit 18, Silicon Business Centre, 26/28 Wadsworth Road, Greenford Middlesex UB6 7JZ, Great Britain.

HUMCHA. H. H. Devendrakeerti Bhattaraka Swami, Shri Hombuja Jain Matha, P.O. Humcha - 577 436, Karnataka, India. Guest rooms. Ideal place for study and meditation.

JAIPUR. Anuvrat Global Organization (A Transnational Centre for Peace and Non-violent Action). Conference Secretariat: Dr. S. L. Gandhi, B-94, Saraswati Marg, Bajaj, Jaipur - 302 015, India. Organizes conferences, foreigners are welcome. Publisher of *ANUVIBHA,* a quarterly journal./ About 15 km south of Jaipur lies Podampuri, a new Digambara *samavasarana* temple.

KHAJURAHO. Hotel Surya; well suited for individul travellers and small groups; the owner, Mr. Jain, is a Jaina who speaks German. Moderate rates. Jain Temple Road, Khajuraho- 471 606, India.

LADNUN. Jain Vishva Bharati Institute, Ladnun - 341 306, District Nagaur, Rajasthan. *See* page 144.

MOODABIDRI. H. H. Charukeerthi Bhattaraka Swamiji, Sri Jain Matha, P.O. Moodabidri - 574 227, Karnataka. Information office and guest-houses.

RAJGIR. Veerayatan Jaina Ashram and Eye Hospital, Rajgir - 803 116, Bihar, India. Board & lodging. A guide to Rajgir and photographs of the monuments and antiquities can be obtained from the Superintending Archaeologist, Archaeological Survey of India, Patna Circle, Patna.

SHRAVANABELAGOLA. H.H. Karmayogi Charukeerthi Swami, Shri Jain Matha, Shravanabelagola - 573 135, Karnataka. Guest-houses. Frequent buses available to and from Bangalore, Mysore, Hassan, Moodabidri and Dharmasthala. Every ten to fifteen years thousands of pilgrims throng at this holy site for the traditional *mahamastakabisheka* (head anointing ceremony); a feast, lasting for two weeks and longer during which the famous statue of Bahubali is re-consecrated.

SHOLAPUR. Jaina Women's Ashram: Padmashri Sumatibai Vidyapitha, Shravika Sanatha Nagar Trust, Budhawar Peth, Sholapur - 413002 (Maharashtra) India.

U.S.A. Federation of Jain Associations in North America. Headquarters: Morningside Dr., Grand Island, New York 14072, U.S.A. / Jain Academic Foundation of North America, Premchand Gada (Vice-president), 4410, 50th Street, Lubbock TX 79414, U.S.A.

VARANASI. American Institute of Indian Studies, Centre for Art and Archaeology. Chief Court House, Ramnagar, Varanasi - 221 008, India.

BOOKS ON JAINISM – where to buy them:

BHARATIYA JNANPITH, 18, Institutional Area, Lodi Road, New Delhi - 110 003. Publishers of *JAINA ART AND ARCHITECTURE* in three Volumes, and other titles.

JAIN LAL MANDIR (Bookstall), Chandni Chowk, Delhi - 110 006. *See* page 134.

MARG PUBLICATIONS, Army & Navy Building, Mahatma Gandhi Road, Mumbai - 400 023.

MOTILAL BANARSIDASS, 41 U.A., Bungalow Road, Jawahar Nagar, Delhi - 110 007. Branches: Chowk, Varanasi - 210 001 / Ashok Rajpath, Patna - 800 004 / 8, Camac Street, Calcutta - 700 017 / 16, St. Mark's Road, Bangalore - 560 001 / Sanas Plaza, Shop 11-13, 1302 Baji Rao Road, Pune - 411 002 / 120, Royapeettah High Road, Mylapore, Madras - 600 004 / 8, Mahalaxmi Chambers, 22 Warden Road, Mumbai (Bombay) - 400 026. / Overseas Distributors: Motilal Books, 73 Lime Walk, Headington, Oxford OX3 7AD (U.K) / South Asia Books, P.O. Box 502, Columbia, MO 65205 (U.S.A.).

INDIAN BOOKS CENTRE, 40/5 Shakti Nagar, Delhi -110 007.

JAIN ORIENTAL LIBRARY, Siddhant Bhavan, Devashram, Mahadeva Rd., Arrah - 802 231, Bihar.

JAIN VISHVA BHARATI INSTITUTE, Ladnun - 341 306, Rajasthan.

PARSHWANATH VIDYASHRAM RESEARCH INSTITUTE, I.T.I. Road, Varanasi - 221 005.

DHARMASHALAS (also *dharamshalas*). Though not specifically mentioned, at almost all pilgrimage sites featured in this book lodging for pilgrims is available. The main rules to be observed while staying in a Jaina *dharmashala* are: no drinking of alcoholic liquids, no drugs, no smoking, no meat, no eggs, no honey, no eating of roots, and no radio and recorder music. When staying in a *Dharmashala* that offers its services free of charge, the giving of a donation is a customary gesture of thanks.

DO'S AND DON'TS. Articles made of leather, animal skin or fur should not be taken inside a temple, nor carried up to such holy places as Shatrunjaya and Sammeta Shikhara. To keep animals as pets is not approved of by Jainas. When asking for or making an appointment, one should not suggest or choose a time around sunset. Many Jainas observe the rule not to eat anything after sunset. Thus it is advisable, when with a Jaina, to take one's leave well before sunset. Fruits are a suitable present when visiting a Jaina family (fruits with many seeds, like figs, should not be chosen) In company with Jainas, never kill a fly, spider or mosquito. A Jaina will never try to sever you from your religion; but if you are not a vegetarian, you would give him or her the greatest satisfaction if you would let him or her convert you to a diet devoid of meat, fish, eggs and honey. *See* also 'Meeting Jaina monks and nuns' page 20.

LETTERS. Letters to the author should be addressed to: c/o The Director, Motilal Banarsidass, 41, U.A. Bungalow Road, Jawahar Nagar, Delhi - 110 007, India. To readers in German, Kurt Titze's book *Keine Gewalt gegen Mensch, Tier, Pflanze • Worte des Furtbereiters Mahaviras* may be of interest. ISBN 3 88468 054 - 4 (a paperback) Published 1993, Zerling Verlag, Berlin, Germany.

MANTRAS. For Jaina *mantras*, in addition to the Namokar Mantra (page 241), *see* Padmanabh Jaini's *The Jaina Path of Purification*, 162–166.

MEDITATION (*dhyana*). For meditation in Jainism, *see* Paul Dundas 1992: 143–146. In practice there is no 'school of meditation' applicable to all Jaina sects. The temple-going Jainas – and they are in the majority – seem to be content with their meditative form of worship (*puja*) in which the Jina image is seen and worshipped as the representation of the enlightened, perfect human being. Of late, the Shvetambara Terapanthi and Sthanakavasi, who have done away with temple *puja*, have – influenced perhaps by the world-wide trend – developed new forms of meditation. In the case of the Terapanth it was Yuvacharya Mahaprajna, now Acharya Mahaprajna, who envisaged a new philosophy and technique of meditation which he called *Preksha Dhyana* (*see* page 146) whereas the late Acharya Sushil Kumar based his technique of meditation on the 'science of sound'. *See* page 241: *Namokar Mantra and Song of the Soul. See* also under New Delhi.

PHOTOGRAPHING. The taking of photographs inside a Jaina temple usually requires permission, which, with some exceptions, is easily obtainable in Karnataka, Tamilnadu and Maharashtra. It is not so – again with notable exceptions (*see* Khumbaria page 160) – in the northern States. The problem is that the person who has the authority to give permission is usually not present. The *pujaris*, who in the Shvetambara temples are no Jainas, can in many cases be bribed, yet doing this tends to spoil the expectation with which one enters such a hallowed place as a temple. Some years ago, at Palitana in Gujarat, I met a young Englishman who was furiously coming down the holy hill with the vow never to return. He had arrived the night before and early that morning climbed the sacred mountain full of expectations; back home he would tell his family and friends what he had seen in so short a time and show them the photographs he had taken. But these photographs he was not allowed to take. He had no permit. This meant that he had to leave his camera at the entry office. All his begging and pleading was in vain. The man in charge would not give him a permit, and that in spite of the fact that no one is ever refused a permit, providing he asks for it in the temple office down in Palitana town. But this office is not open early in the morning. Thus, to comply with the rule would have meant for our traveller – if he had known of it, which he had not – wasting valuable daylight hours in order to get a piece of paper instead of leisurely walking about the famous 'temple-city' and taking a photograph here and there, which was what he had dreamt of doing when he was planning his first visit to India. By now this unreasonable regulation may have been discontinued.

PERIODICALS. *AHIMSA,* a quarterly magazine of The Institute of Jainology, Greenford, UK.

AHIMSA VOICE, Satish K. Jain (ed.), 53 Rishabh Vihar, Delhi - 110 092, India.

ARHAT VACANA, a quarterly research journal in Hindi with an English section. Dr. Anupam Jain, (ed.), Kundakunda Jnanapitha, 584, M.G. Road, Tukogunj, Indore - 452 001, India.

ANUVIBHA Reporter (quarterly). Dr. S L. Gandhi (ed.).Vishwa Shanti Nilayam, P.O Box 28, Rajasmand - 313 326, Rajasthan, India.

JAIN ANTIQUARY, published by Jain Oriental Research Institute, Arrah - 802 301, Bihar, India.

JAIN DIGEST, Dr. S. K. Jain (ed.), R Ransom Road, Athens, OH 45701, U.S.A.

JAIN JOURNAL, published by Jain Bhavan, P-25, Kalakar Street, Calcutta - 700 007, India.

JAIN STUDY CIRCULAR, Jain Study Circle, 99-1160 Avenue, 3D, Flushing, N.Y. 11368, U.S. A.

JINAMANJARI, a bi-annual Jaina magazine in English. Published by the Bramhi Society, 4665 Moccasin Trail, Mississauga, Ontario LAZ ZW5, Canada.

SHODHADARSHA, a journal in Hindi with reviews and comments in English, Dr. Shashi Kant (ed.), Jyoti Nikunj, Charbagh (Behind Roadways Bus Station), Lucknow -226 004, India.

TIRTHANKAR VANI, Dr. Shekhar Chandra Jain (ed.), 6 Umiyadevi Society No. 2, Amaravadi, Ahmedabad - 380 026, Gujarat.

TULSI PRAJNA, published by Jain Vishva Bharati, Ladnun - 341 306, Rajasthan, India.

YOUNG JAINS, a quarterly *International Newsletter.* Dr. Atul Shah (ed.), 160 Squires Lane, Finchley, London, N3 2QT, UK. Invites contributions (also photos) from any country.

SPELLING. Among Indians there is the tendency of dropping the 'a', especially in names: Mahavir instead of Mahavira; Jain(a); Shravana Bel(a)gola; Karkal(a); Hastinapur(a), raj(a), etc. The 'i' pronounced as the *e* in *be* may be spelled 'i' or 'ee', thus Mahavira is sometimes spelled Mahaveer. To facilitate pronunciation, 'c' and 's' are habitually, but not in all cases, spelled 'ch' and 'sh'. The Gujarat district of Kutch is also known under the name of Kachchh. These are just a few examples. To learn the proper use of the many diacritic marks used by scholars of Indology requires a fair knowledge of Sanskrit.

PLACE INDEX

NAME INDEX

SUBJECT INDEX

<<<<<◇>>>>>